THE FUGITIVE RACE

THE FUGITIVE RACE

Minority Writers Resisting Whiteness

Stephen P. Knadler

University Press of Mississippi / *Jackson*

www.upress.state.ms.us

Copyright © 2002 by University Press of Mississippi
All rights reserved
Manufactured in the United States of America

10 09 08 07 06 05 04 03 02   4 3 2 1
⊗

Library of Congress Cataloging-in-Publication Data

Knadler, Stephen P., 1963–
   The fugitive race : minority writers resisting whiteness / Stephen P. Knadler.
      p.   cm.
Includes bibliographical references and index.
   ISBN 1-57806-506-2 (alk. paper)
      1. American literature—Minority authors—History and criticism.   2. Human
skin color—Psychological aspects.   3. Identity (Psychology) in literature.   4. Group
identity in literature.   5. Ethnic groups in literature.   6. Minorities in literature.
7. Ethnicity in literature.   8. Whites in literature.   9. Race in literature.   I. Title.

   PS153.M56 K59   2002
   810.9′920693—dc21   2002003008

British Library Cataloging-in-Publication Data available

CONTENTS

v

INTRODUCTION
"Fugitive Race" Culture

In 1853 Frederick Douglass published a fictional account of Madison Washington's 1841 slave mutiny in his novella, "A Heroic Slave." While this use of fiction to respond to the fugitive slave crisis signaled Douglass's increasing belief in the legitimacy of violent protest as opposed to Garrisonian tactics of moral suasion to end slavery, Douglass's "heroic slave" is, as William Andrews notes, a "liberator through language" (Introduction 131).[1] But just what is the power of this fugitive slave, especially since this text that celebrates the "black voice" relates the rebellion aboard the *Creole* only secondhand through the embedded narration of a chorus of working-class whites? Published in the year after the popular success of Harriet Beecher Stowe's *Uncle Tom's Cabin* (1852), Douglass's "A Heroic Slave" has one of its famous predecessor's central plot devices: the conversion of the "patriarch" to abolitionist sentiment when confronted by the fugitive slave.[2] However, whereas Stowe's Senator Bird alters his conscience out of pity for the helpless, feminized, and female victim of slavery, Eliza, Douglass's Ohio representative, Mr. Listwell, extends his sympathies in admiration of the manly "wordsmith." In the concluding scene, Douglass describes Listwell's encounter with the fugitive slave five years after first overhearing the slave's dramatic soliloquy during his travels through Virginia. When Listwell informs Madison Washington that he still recalls the memory of the "life-changing" night when he had heard this black man's words, this disclosure sheds light on the repressed scene within antebellum public discourses on "whiteness":

Mr. Listwell at once frankly disclosed the secret; describing the place where he first saw him; rehearsing the language which he [Madison] had used; referring to the effect which his manner and speech had made upon him; declaring the resolution he there formed to be an abolitionist; telling how often he had spoken of the circumstance, and the deep concern he had ever since felt to know what had become of him. . . .

"Ever since that morning," said Listwell, "you have seldom been absent from my mind, and though now I did not dare to hope that I should ever see you again, I have often wished that such might be my fortune; for, from that hour, your face seemed to be daguerreotyped on my memory. (138)

Although Listwell's praise of the black orator is itself an important counter to arguments insisting on black inferiority, his comment that Madison's words had "seldom been absent from my mind," were indeed "daguerreotyped on my memory," suggests that his identity as a white man has been susceptible to what David Theo Goldberg has called "transformative incorporations" (220). In this repressed scene, Douglass does not validate the subjectivity of the black male through the authority of the white man's gaze; rather, it is the patriarch Listwell who incorporates this imprint of the fugitive slave's spoken word into his interiority and is thus physically transformed by the voice of the black man. In his historical fiction, Douglass does more than employ sentimentality to energize an abolitionist protest. He makes white male embodiment the visceral site of revision. In so reforming the body of the white abolitionist as the location of the black male's political intervention, Douglass suggests that there are two fugitive races within antebellum society: the fugitive slave who must elude capture within the literal and the representational bonds of Anglo-Saxon supremacism and those of the white race who equally enact their own fugitive flight from the influence of the black man in the formation of white identity. By conceding that the black man's words were "imprinted" within the "private" inner mind, Listwell names an abject specter within antebellum culture, the psychological complement to the dread of slave revolt, the specter of reverse acculturation: the recognition that white identity might evolve through the introjection of tabooed identifications with the black other. In Douglass's "A Heroic Slave," white identity is inherently amalgamated. As the novella's opening invocation implies, nineteenth-century Americans were instructed to emulate the Revolutionary War heroes' actions, but in telling the story of Madison Washington, Douglass not only renders the pantheon of representative American men more inclusive (Sale 174), he also seeks to make another Washington a "Founding Father" in a color-blind nation's ego ideals. In this scene, Douglass at once both prescribes an American future and describes a foundational repression within white identity: the possibility that the white reformer may already be a fugitive "rehearsing" the language of the colored races.

The Fugitive Race: Minority Writers Resisting Whiteness has been written to map a literary and historical tradition tracing minority writer's interventions into the production and circulation of white racialized identities.[3] Although this book discusses a number of works from the antebellum period to the post–Civil Rights era, my project does not intend to suggest a single, coherent meaning for whiteness or a unifying tactic of minority, or what will be referred to as "coracial," intervention.[4] This study approaches each fictional work as a cultural product whose formal and discursive structures have inscribed within themselves the social, political, and economic conditions of the historical moments in which they were produced, and indeed, it is important to note, there can be no single antiwhite tradition with a common interventionist strategy. As Ruth Frankenberg argues in *White Women, Race Matters*, whiteness consists of a set of socially constructed locations that include one's identity, worldview, and unconscious desires, and thus white women and men do not occupy the same positions at all times toward all the different people of color (209). Since whites employ many different and often competing strategies to maintain the territorial and psychic boundaries of whiteness, this volume has been written to recover the varying practices that writers have used within their own historical context to unmask the "lies of whiteness." Hence the term "fugitive" to designate the counter-hegemonic cultural work of influential people of color who, like Frederick Douglass in his own fugitive slave narrative, sought to intervene in whiteness's multiple racial formations by revealing its heterogeneous meanings. However, since white people perceive their possessive racial investments as biological and cultural property that they themselves own, manage, and take profit from, they have buried and repressed these interventions into whiteness.[5] Insisting that so-called white people are equally fugitives who do not in fact control the terrain of white racial discourse, this study charts a long history of minority interventions, articulating and shaping the performance of whiteness within nineteenth-century and early-twentieth-century narrative fiction.

Although it has become fashionable to speak about whiteness as "unmarked," "transparent," and the "unexamined norm," citing "the privilege of not having to think about race," there is a disturbing insularity and ahistoricism in such remarks.[6] Only in recent times, as Matthew Frye Jacobson has demonstrated in *Whiteness of a Different Color*, has whiteness been defined oppositionally along a single axis as "not black, or colored" and been viewed within this biracial paradigm as not needing conscious racialization or naming (106). Particularly in the nineteenth century, as Reginald Horsman, Thomas Gossett, and Ronald Takaki have documented, racial discourse about Anglo-Saxonism pervaded American society and provided a convenient language for discussing a number of controversial issues not, at first glance at least, having anything to do specifically with "race." In such a historical context, people of various regions, ethnic origins, or classes were highly self-conscious of what they understand as a "white" racial difference.[7] If we are not to project onto the past the conventions of our own possessive investment in whiteness, we must remain attentive to the mutability of racial definitions at various times in U.S. history.

To say that whiteness is transparent also conflates whiteness as a universalized and unexamined cultural norm or ideology, with whiteness as a racial position. Too often "whiteness studies" is stretched as a loose and baggy term to cover any of a number of different meditations on antiracism, eliding distinctions among whiteness's different systems of meaning. At the risk of oversimplifying for a moment, I would point out that investigators of whiteness have tended to perceive it in one of two broad ways: either as a "racialized" ethnic positionality or as a universal entity or norm enacted through exclusionary practices. By suggesting that whiteness is seen as either an "identity" or an "ideology," I do not mean to suggest that these two forms of whiteness are not interrelated. While whiteness as an ethnic identity may have no timeless content, it generates ways of understanding history, the self, and the world or, to state the obvious, is tied to cultural norms. Nevertheless, it is necessary to keep these two approaches to whiteness differentiated because the predominance of one or the other meaning tends to affect the history that is told of whiteness and the understanding of the reparative work that must be done. To keep in play the particularity of whiteness in different locations, this work encompasses a range of racial self-definitions, from the deliberate and very examined self-naming of antebellum New Englanders as geniuses of an "Anglo-American" race to whiteness as an unconscious disciplinary practice within immigrant writings designed to promote unity through "Negrophobia" and "disaffiliation" with other coracial groups. If the ultimate goal of whiteness studies is to "abolish" or recode this race meaning, we need a more precise, and less theatrical, mapping of what it means and how it is used.

To contend that whiteness is "unmarked" is not only to be guilty of presentism and imprecision; this widely held belief in the transparency of whiteness reinscribes the very dissent built into the structuring of white subjectivity. The now familiar deconstruction of whiteness begins from a white perspective and reproduces one of the central narratives shaping white identity: the urgent spatial segregation and psychic insulation from the black gaze that might force uncomfortable, at times even traumatic, self-alienating moments.[8] In "Representations of Whiteness in the Black Imagination," bell hooks has spoken of white people's amazement, one that acts as a form of racism, that "black people watch white people with a critical 'ethnographic gaze'" (hooks 167). Yet theories of whiteness have tended to be guilty of just such a disregard. While whites are also constantly defining their identity against the spectatorship of others, they deny that such an observation takes place. Whiteness is not just "racial discourse" disseminated to maintain economic or social hierarchies, or even more benignly a subject position that provides a sense of belonging as well as privileges. The originating premise of this book is that white identities have always been dialogical struggles in which the imagining of whiteness involves the prior primary repression of other racial namings. In using the term "dialogical," I want to invoke the Bakhtinian idea that the meaning of a word, or a historical idea such as "whiteness," is the result of give and take, the interaction and interplay between speakers. While Bakhtin concludes that "the word in language is half someone else's" (293–94), the possessive investment that people of European and other descent take in "whiteness" adheres to an unshakeable belief that whiteness's meaning is never "half someone else's." Such a denial of the possible role people of color might play in the meaning of whiteness is suggested in Judith Butler's observations about the different levels on which constraint takes place in her discussions on free speech and censorship. Although tolerance as a principle might suggest an openness to the other, such a willingness to allow the person of color to enter, after the fact, the white Union often rests on the prior and founding assumption that the other played no part in the formation of U.S. national identity. The acceptance of multiculturalism as the emergent U.S. cultural identity denies a knowledge of the other as already having been a constitutive partner in U.S. white and national identity formations (Butler, *Excitable Speech* 155). Simply to tolerate or respect the humanity of the other may serve to naturalize the normative idea that whiteness is performed within its own insulated space, without the agency (indirect or otherwise) of other racial interlocutors. In fact, whiteness studies has already been a quite well established academic discipline, one that has been practiced by feminist and minority scholars for decades but has only gained recognition as a movement as it has become practiced by white males who have fallen from their naturally accepted state of privilege that allowed them simply to admit dissenting opinions or marginal voices to a white center.

Focusing on a number of writers' tactics of intervention, the analysis that follows draws heavily upon the notions of performativity associated with postcolonial, feminist, cultural studies, and queer theorists such as Homi Bhabha, Judith Butler, Ann Pellegrini, bell hooks, Diana Fuss, and Kobena Mercer.[9] As Ann Stoler points out, race is used both as a category to organize group self-awareness and as a concept organizing individual subjectivities (50). While in recent years a number of books in the social sciences, law, history, and communications have investigated how whiteness operated as a constitutive marker of working-class culture, national formations, conservative politics, or legal decisions, this investigation emphasizes how whiteness functions in the work of "biopolitics."[10] Starting from the premise of performance theorists that identities are always partial and subject to failure, this project highlights the need to see how white racial identities are thus formed through a process of reiteration, the repetition of racial norms and disciplinary practices, a process always open to the possibility of interference or the failure of white people to repeat their racial identity correctly. While coracial writers marginalized within U.S. culture used fiction as a vehicle for authorizing alternative voices of blackness, of femaleness, or gayness, their work also intervened in the narrative process of making whiteness. African American writers from William Wells Brown to James Baldwin, for example, have not just struggled to force whites toward a conscious recognition of racial injustice or even the fictions of their own superior identities, but these writers have attempted to create in their texts moments that threaten the white identity with dismemberment and desubjectification. Indeed, there is a genealogy of texts that are dialogic struggles in which the self-definition of both players is at stake.

Attempting to move beyond the rhetorical or discursive analysis that has predominated in whiteness studies (Nakayama and Martin 7), this project questions as well those assumptions that read race, or white racial identifications and group categories, as only part of the public domain. While discursive analysis uncovers important truths, racial identities, like sexual identities, as Christopher Lane argues, have a public and private component (3–20). Not merely a linguistic construct, whiteness, as Franz Fanon insists in his important analysis of the postcolonial experience, *Black Skins, White Masks*, involves unconscious and phantasmic identifications (156). An understanding of whiteness, especially in looking at the cultural work performed by "imaginative" literature, must "add" psychoanalysis to other critical approaches, while remaining cautious of the universalism within psychological paradigms. As my study of works by writers such as William Wells Brown, Younghill Kang, Arturo Islas, Pauline Hopkins, and Richard Wright shows, whiteness is as much about unconscious anxieties and fantasies as it is about discourse.

There is a third standpoint of intervention that is often overlooked in current literary histories organized around racial, ethnic, or gender affiliations. While most literary genealogies tend to define "intervention" in terms of representing a new subjectivity of color through the return to native cultural, religious, or national roots or in terms of trying to resignify the oppressive mainstream white tradition, there is an understudied literary history of the "white problem," a tradition that, as James Baldwin · argues, tries to unsettle the narrative foundation of whiteness ("On Being White" 80–84). Rather than investigating this third tradition by tracing out a coherent or linear genealogy of historical interventions by coracial writers into the performance of whiteness, this study examines a diverse grouping of texts by asking a particular set of questions: How did these texts position themselves in relation to the shifting social dialogue on "race" and "whiteness" at that particular historical period? What work did these texts do in trying to interrupt and re-mediate the narratives of whiteness? How do these texts restore a sense of interventionist agency to the "whiteness" debate? In insisting on the idea of "intervention," I am deliberately avoiding the often widely used terms within critical race theory of "resistance" or "subversion" because these conceptualizations fail to note how fiction by women and men of color might be a constitutive part of the dynamic process of whiteness's formation. Too often black or colored agency tends to be addressed only after the fact, as a complicity with or reappropriation of a white practice that is represented as a coherent whole already in place. But such readings, even those that are subtle and nuanced, tend to reduce the coracial writers' work as reactive. Despite a new vocabulary of "resignifying," "reappropriating," and "revisioning," postmodern critics can still conceive the time of the writer's interventions as secondary: to be resistant is to be responsive to a culture that is already dominant and, to overstate for the moment, purely constructed, and thus it resecures whiteness's racial priority in time. This book has been driven by the urgent need to better understand the ways that the reciprocated gaze of the other has acted upon the various articulations of whiteness from the beginning.

Extended Play: Theorizing Black Agency in Whiteness Studies

The publication of Toni Morrison's series of lectures at Harvard University as *Playing in the Dark: Whiteness and the Literary Imagination* (1992) is a defining moment that remapped race criticism for "American" studies. By examining how American literature and culture imagined itself against the "overwhelming presence of black people" (5), Morrison opened up a space for questioning "whiteness" as an imaginative, social, and literary construction, and she furthered the investigation of embedded assumptions of racial, and not just racist, language within American culture. Yet Morrison's critical unmasking of the "lie of whiteness" gains part of its power by speaking within a long African American tradition of strategic interventions into the "ways of white folks." In her analysis, Morrison points the way toward more complicated questions about "black agency" that haunt the cultural imagining of whiteness. By suggesting that we need an "extended play," Morrison opens the space for a more complete set of questions, articulating agendas for a research that has become collectively named "whiteness studies." Discussing Hemingway's *To Have and to Have Not*, Morrison recovers what she calls the "serviceability of the Africanist presence" (76). To prop up his own troubled masculinity, Hemingway needed to belittle the manhood of black men while degrading and dehumanizing black women as erotic subordinates. Black characters are present within Hemingway's representative American imagination not as human beings but as figures for psychological and often literal service. To reverse the "critical gaze," Morrison argues, critics need to challenge a whiteness that has defined its "autonomy, authority, newness and difference" (90) against black others.

Yet while critics of whiteness have looked at how the encounter with the African enabled whites to think about themselves in "ego-reinforcing" and "economically advantageous" ways (Morrison 45), African Americans in whiteness studies, as they were in Hemingway's fiction, have remained largely passive, "serviceable" presences. Although most critics have noticed that whites used the black presence, their framing of the central questions structuring whiteness studies has denied African Americans a complicated agency arising from the oppositional gaze Morrison identified. Even David Roediger in *Black on White* (1998), while aware of the omission of the black perspective on the white problem, finally offers only one more version of the politics of inclusion that leaves blacks and whites in their, albeit various, segregated spaces. While Roediger gives us the reverse of Morrison's study, the overwhelming presence of whiteness in the black imagination, this effort takes these writings out of their dialogic context. Placing these views in a separate anthology, Roediger asks us to read these resistant texts as self-contained works and not against the social and literary discourse of white society. Through this division we are not invited to consider how these African American texts might have challenged, interfered with, and threatened the formation and spread of various articulations of white identity. Indirectly, Roediger's efforts, although offering an important body of primary sources for whiteness studies, have defined an antirace movement that has reproduced the color line, one in which black agency is always something separate or secondary to a self-perpetuating and insulated whiteness.

In her sociological study based on actual interviews, *White Women, Race Matters*, Ruth Frankenberg includes a chapter entitled "Growing Up White," which reports the stories of several women who grew up in apparently all-white communities. Although they often had black maids or other domestic help, these women were not really conscious of the presence of these other people in their lives. This invisibility that strips black people of their subjectivity has been frequently referred to in the conversation on race in the U.S., but this invisibility is rarely examined as more than a complaint about discrimination. Yet this segregationist habit of mind functions as an essential tactic within a white consciousness based on what Chela Sandoval has called inoculation (88). Extrapolating from the comments of one of her interviewees who had a white suburban childhood, Frankenberg writes, "it is primarily through employer-employee, class-imbalanced relationships that women from apparently all-white homes encountered women of color. If not themselves in a position of clear authority, these white middle-class women must have seen their parents in such position, able to summon and dismiss the racially different Other at will" (*White Women* 51). Frankenberg's final phrase, "to summon and dismiss the racially different Other at will," comments on the practice of current whiteness studies. By "summon" and "dismiss," Frankenberg, of course, suggests literally here the orders given to domestic help. Yet the process of summoning and dismissing at will can be taken, metaphorically, as mental strategies when theorizing white consciousness. It has become commonplace to talk about how white people project and displace onto others what they fear or secretly long for in their own identity. This habit of defining the racial self through systems of difference, however, may obscure the more complex way this habit of "othering" involves both summoning and dismissing. Although white identity needs to summon the other as the binary opposite against which to define itself, it also retains the privilege to dismiss at will the "others," to deny a consciousness of them and thus to render them invisible.

In her autobiographical stories for *Killers of the Dream*, Lillian Smith includes a personal memory that is symptomatic of the summoning and dismissing that allows white people to never have to occupy a border or in-between space where their subjectivity evolves out of a dialogical relation with multicentric communities of color. Whiteness, as Smith's story discloses, insists on being a standpoint that never has to endure boundary moments when it must see itself from the outside in as well as from the inside out. Beginning with the statement that "the white man's burden is his own childhood" (17), Smith's *Killers of the Dream* recalls the Smith family's temporary "adoption" of the pale-skinned "colored girl," Janie, whom they presumed to be "white." Although Smith's Freudian-based analysis of the home as a primary site for producing white identities seems privatized and schematic at times, her argument about the childhood "trauma" involved in the learning of racism still has much to say about the dynamics of white identity formation in adults as well as children. When a group of white clubwomen discover what they assume to be a white girl living in the "colored" section of town, they appealed to the town marshal to take the child away from the "dirt" and "ignorance" of the shantytown. Out of tenderness and pity for the little girl, Smith's mother brings her into the family home, clothing and teaching her as if she were her own daughter. After three weeks during which time Lillian and Janie developed a "deeply felt bond" (27), Smith's mother learns, after inquiries at the orphanage, that Janie is a "colored child" and hence must return to the segregated town on the other side of the tracks. Janie, trying to understand why she must leave, asks Lillian, "Are you white?" to which Smith responds, "I'm white . . . and my sister is white. And you're colored. And white and colored can't live together because my mother says so." Although she sensed something was not right, Smith recalls that she felt a slow poison begin "to seep through me: I was white. She was colored. We must not be together" (29). While there are certainly many ways of unpacking the resonances of this story in regard to questions of "race"—the arbitrariness of race classifications, the role parents play in teaching whiteness—the cross-racial encounter appears here as a starkly framed boundary moment. Smith first asserts that she is white when she is "hailed" by the other. Although one acquires one's white sense of self, as Smith understands, in the school, in church, at home, her whiteness also evolves out of seeing herself in the mirror of the other. By "boundary event" I mean those moments of disruption when people become conscious of their membership in a (racial or ethnic) group because of their experience of rejection or counteridentification by a member of another group.[11] African American writers from Harriet Jacobs to Zora Neale Hurston repeatedly describe characters who experience moments of initial forced acknowledgment of racial identity because of how they are perceived as different by whites. Whiteness is not just "transparent," "normative," "unmarked"; it might more correctly be described, once decentered, as "insulated." A white consciousness depends on the privilege of dismissing the other's gaze, literally here by sending the threatening Janie of Smith's memoir back to colored town but, more important, repressing a consciousness of black people's surveillance.

Later in *Killers of the Dream*, Smith again reverts to autobiographical anecdotes to map out one of what she calls the three ghost relationships in childhood memory: "white man and colored woman, white father and colored children, white child and his beloved colored nurse." Smith's reflections on her relationship with her childhood caretaker, Aunt Chloe, like her childhood encounter with Janie, equally complicate our understanding of racial treason. Now Smith's account of Chloe is not without its residual racism: too often Chloe is sentimentalized, and hence depersonalized, as the all-giving, all-enduring, long-suffering, stereotypical "mammy." As Grace Elizabeth Hale argues, in the New South of middle-class suburban whites, childhood recollections of one's mammy served as sign of status-conferring ties to the old aristocratic order (87). Yet Smith complicates her contemporaries' middle-class reinscription of the plantation myth by attempting to psychoanalyze the sentimental family romance. "This dual relationship," Smith writes, "which so many white southerners have had with two mothers, one white and one colored and each of a different culture that centered in different human values, makes the Oedipus complex seem by comparison almost a simple adjustment" (127). After introducing the concept of a dual maternity, Smith describes the southern male's tendency to perceive women as either the virgin or the whore that arises out of this "crack that extends deep into his personality" (128). While Smith's description of the southern white male's Oedipus complex reveals her attempt to distance herself from the past by reverting to a generic male child after prefacing the essay with her own memories of Aunt Chloe, Smith's southern white child with two mothers, as importantly, points out the shaping power of the "other" as fundamental to the constitution of the self and to racial as well as sexual identity. While Smith pictures the sexual character of whiteness as male, possibly to disguise her own lesbian identity, she remains significantly reticent in her autobiographical essay about the connection between race relations and the engendering of the white daughter of the South who had a second black mother, either a literal servant in the house or a black presence in the community.

While Smith's psychoanalytic model of the development of racial identity may seem limited, it nevertheless helps to interpret the intersubjective historical formation of whiteness. As Jacques Lacan has argued, a child takes on a stable, preordained subjectivity when he/she sees himself/herself in the symbolic language of patriarchy, which may be embodied in the literal father or, more generally, one's culture. Therefore, subjectivities are formed out of a "troubled, never-completed, unconscious dialogue with—this internalization of—the 'other'" (Hall, *Representations* 238). Prior to the mirror stage, the child has an incoherent and undifferentiated self. However, when the child views herself/himself in the language and law of the external or patriarchal world (the father) during the mirror stage, she/he accepts this identification as her/his unified self. As this sense of self forms in relation to the significant other of the father, the child splits off his/her unconscious identification with the mother. The child experiences, as a result, a sense of lack because his/her identity formed in relation to the symbolic of the father can never complete him/her. Although postcolonial theorists have studied how the "white" other of the father refuses to give recognition to people of color (Bhabha, *Location of Culture* 158), we must consider how the white person also needs recognition from the black gaze. At first glance it would seen obvious that, given the segregation of U.S. society, the white child is simply insulated from the mirror of black others, who are rendered as peripheral or invisible. But as Lillian Smith's narrative concludes, the black (m)other may already be a constitutive, if repressed, part of a white subjectivity. Certainly not every child has had a black primary caretaker as Lillian Smith did, but in the formation of white identities, there are boundary moments when children first encounter how they are perceived as different from the other. This other's gaze becomes threatening, a site of danger, a reminder of the splitting within the self. For children to maintain their identification with the white image ideals of the father and not the other, they must, as Smith notes, "dismiss" at will and render invisible the black other. But in Smith's "dismissal," we see the institutionalizing of a primordial repression as well as symbolic violence. This dismissal erases retroactively the prior encounters with the other as influential, insisting on the core integrity of the white self prior to its chosen admission of an integrated other. To integrate the other is to repress the iterability of such an act and to deny that introjection might be part of an ongoing and open-ended action within whiteness's becoming.

A Space for Whiteness Studies

In his essay "Toward a Proletarian Art," which appeared in the socialist *Liberator* in 1921, Michael Gold with Whitmanesque anti-elitist élan boasted that "I was born in a tenement. That tall, sombre mass, holding its freight of obscure human destinies, is the pattern in which my being was cast. . . . The tenement is in my blood. When I think it is the tenement thinking" (64–65). While Gold was "hellbent on casting himself as a child of the ghetto" (Folsom 247), his autobiographical *Jews without Money* (1930) did not take an orthodox or sentimental view of the tenement that would homogenize the diverse ensemble of peoples and collectivities into a singular organic community. Despite his insistence in his 1921 essay on the artistic nurturance of the Jewish tenement that thinks through and constitutes his identity, Gold later acknowledged that this ghetto is a "profane" site of hybridity, or as he says in *Jews without Money*, "what a crazy mingling of races and religions on my street. I heard most of the languages when I was a child. Germans, Poles, Russians, Armenians, Irish, Chinese; these were always a few of those aliens living among our Jews. Once my father fetched a Negro to supper" (174). In his second-generation immigrant text, Gold writes back into representation of the ghetto space all the alien multiethnic and racial conflicts that earlier stories of Americanization had ghosted out of the immigrant's struggle to assimilate into a simply identified Anglo-European or white culture.

While this study reconceptualizes the question of race in U.S. literature as a "white problem" to better understand how coracial texts worked to interfere in the reproduction of white bodies, it also struggles to reimagine the space in which cultural practices of whiteness were developed, practiced, and resisted. As Edward Soja has argued, historical approaches must also include a politics of space that recognizes the social relations within mixed cultural worlds. Built into critical studies of minority texts has been, however, a certain bifocalization, one that affords only a crude picture of most individuals' social existence, which frequently involved an unruly, disorderly, unfixed, and ever evolving relation not just with a dominant culture but with other minority groups in complicated borderland spaces. The critical work of mapping coracial texts must start, therefore, from a "trialectical" understanding of the history of whiteness, a "trialectical" understanding that complicates our search for a simple emancipatory rhetoric to "denaturalize" or "abolish" race thinking (Soja 70–73). Particularly, since German-born Jewish sociologist Louis Wirth's famous 1938 essay, "Urbanism as a Way of Life," the psychological boundaries of the ethnic community, or for Wirth the Jewish ghettoes of Chicago, have been seen within familiar structuring binaries: *gemeinschaft* versus *gesellschaft*, rural versus urban, past versus present, tradition versus modernism, and most important for this study, parochialism versus the integration of a larger U.S. culture. But such a mapping of the space of U.S. ethnic relations ignores, as Edward Corsi wrote in his 1925 essay for *Outlook* magazine entitled "My Neighborhood," that even the ghetto of the Lower East Side in Manhattan was a "polyglot boarding house" (92). To resist the overdetermined binary logic of a U.S. nationalism that represses in ethnic and racial studies the multiple axes along which identities in the U.S. have been and continue to be formed, this study emphasizes the formative influences of interethnic and interracial relations on writers within third multicultural spaces, whether those spaces were the amalgamated hovels on the "commons" of nineteenth-century New England communities or the heterogeneous tenement houses of most Lower East Side districts. In his discussion of the "black and tan" borderland districts around the Bowery, Jacob Riis in *How the Other Half Lives* discloses how such "third spaces" loomed as sites of disturbing racial and ethnic miscegenation as well as sexual and moral promiscuity: "the aptly named black and tan saloon, has never been debatable ground from a moral standpoint. It has always been the worst of the desperately bad. [Greater] than this commingling of the utterly depraved of both sexes, white and black on such common ground, there can be no greater abomination" (153). As Lillian Smith in *Killers of the Dream* repressed those boundary moments that would cause an encounter with the black look, immigrant texts would similarly struggle to erase from the narrative consciousness images of promiscuous borderland interethnic contacts that would disrupt the self-contained story of being caught between two worlds.

In the call for an abolition of whiteness, however, whiteness studies has tended to ignore or alarmingly mystify these third spaces of interethnic and racial contact. In the inaugural editorial for the journal *Race Traitor*, Noel Ignatiev announced a paradigm shift in the way we think about the work for social justice in the U.S. Yet Ignatiev's abolitionism or treason to a "denaturalized" whiteness raises troubling questions about the specific racializing of control within this social transformation and offers a spatial conceptualization of racial communities that evacuates them of their complex interrelations. By definition, there is something ungenerously self-focused, if not deliberately arrogant, about a movement based on a voluntary self-displacement by whites from the center as an answer to the challenges from those at the margin. But the problem lies not only in thinking too much that the abolition of whiteness is a question of white self-activity to prove Anglo-Europeans can be authentic antiracists but also in the spatial conceptualization of embracing marginality that has emerged as a familiar way of imagining resistance to a dominant society. In his editorials for *Race Traitor*, Ignatiev frames the actions of the white abolitionists repeatedly through an analogy to the "club." "The abolitionists are traitors to the white race; by acting boldly they jeopardize their membership in the white club and their ability to draw upon its privileges" (Ignatiev and Garvey 36). Yet this metaphoric presumption that "whiteness" is a country club, a property that was always owned and fenced off from other ethnic and racial minorities, must be seen as a dangerously misleading and obfuscatory mapping of the long historical formation of whiteness.

At the crux of Ignatiev's appeal for the abolition of whiteness are naive assumptions about "relocation." By moving out of the white country club into another more integrated or black neighborhood, according to the race traitor, one can stop being white or betray his/her race. But it is ludicrous to think that one stops being white by renting an apartment in Harlem, in Chicago's South Side, or on Atlanta's Auburn Avenue. Hardly is one ever more "white" in these black worlds. Such integrated borderlands, moreover, are also sites of their own interethnic tensions that cause more recently arrived immigrant groups to ally themselves with whites or invest themselves in "whiteness." In place of a white-controlled and -controlling abdication of privileges, whiteness studies may more forcefully be relocated, as Michael Gold demonstrated, by insisting on the liminality that has always been at the core of whiteness. By placing it back within the productive and reproductive space of the polyglot boardinghouse and tenement, we thus expose the inner divisions that already exist within whiteness because it is formed through an intersubjective relationship with others.

Whiteness and Postidentity (and Queer) Politics

If a cultural history of coracial interventions into whiteness points out the limitations of a naive faith in racial treason, such a genealogy also exposes the white perspective and privilege behind some late-twentieth-century postidentity thinking, particularly within queer theory. In his May 1961 *Esquire Magazine* essay on the White Negro Norman Mailer, "The Black Boy Looks at the White Boy," James Baldwin identified that even the countercultural hipster shares a dependence on foundational and embedded narratives behind white identity, however different his/her professed views might seem from mainstream racism. The hipster, like "the man in the gray flannel suit," perceives his/her identity as earned property, a property that is self-made without the presence, either contributory or disruptive, of others. His/her romanticization of "going with the flow," of open-endedness or a queering of identities, is therefore a nostalgia for a privileged white adolescence in which one can role-play, even play at being "bad," without fear of losing the ground of white privilege. As Baldwin's essay suggests, the challenge to whiteness has to extend its play to the innocence of this countercultural rebel:

> "Man," said a Negro musician to me once, talking about Norman [Mailer], "the only trouble with that cat is that he's white." This does not mean exactly what it says—or, rather, it does mean exactly what it says, and not what it might be taken to mean—it is a very shrewd observation. What my friend meant was that to become a Negro man, let alone a Negro artist, one had to make oneself up as one went along. This had to be done in the not-at-all-metaphorical teeth of the world's determination to destroy you. . . . This is not the way this truth presents itself to white men, who believe the world is theirs and who, albeit unconsciously, expect the world to help them in the achievement of their identity. But the world does not do this—for anyone; the world is not interested in anyone's identity. And, therefore, the anguish which can overtake a white man comes in the middle of his life, when he must make the almost inconceivable effort to divest himself of everything he has ever expected or believed, when he must take himself apart and put himself together again, walking out of the world, into limbo, or into what certainly looks like limbo. (232)

Much has been made of Mailer's repetition of primitivist myths of black male hypersexuality and spontaneity in his construction of the White Negro. But Baldwin calls attention less to Mailer's demeaning reduction of African Americans than the White Negro's preservation of "white privilege" even as the hipster allegedly renounces allegiance and entitlement to mainstream middle-class Euro-American culture. Mailer's countercultural politics in practice functions as an oppositional stance built into the racial structures of normative society and specifically works to co-opt a real dissent to the lure of a possessive investment in whiteness.

Baldwin's "The Black Boy Looks at the White Boy" talks back to a countercultural whiteness that assumed its foundational logic from the "identity society" emerging in post–World War II America (to borrow the language of Erik Erikson's psychosocial study of American culture). In contrast to Freudian-based psychoanalysis, Erikson's ego psychology, which became the basis of the new "identity society," arose out of the intersection of classical liberalism with the consumerism of third-stage capitalism. To the liberal democratic society of the 1950s, the rebellion of the primitive id against the patriarchal superego was too anarchic, unconscious, and rigid. Classical liberalism had always emphasized the notion of an inner-directed rational self capable of standing apart from society and making voluntary choices about the direction of one's life. Thus in the consumer-oriented culture of the mid-twentieth century, as democratic freedom was slowly being limited and privatized into a matter of free choices about material goods and lifestyle decisions, Erikson reenvisioned psychological development as a process of testing, selecting, and integrating identifications and images into a coherent personality (see also Welchman 118). According to this developmental identity psychology, the end of adolescent role-playing is a stable, unitarian identity, one that also signals the success of socialization, the proving of one's "adaptiveness" to society by finding a role that fits within a range of choices.

In the White Negro's repudiation of any normative identity for an adolescent innocence of countercultural role-playing, Baldwin writes, hipsters may think they have refused to play the game, but they are going along with the flow of whiteness, assuming its privilege of youthful performativity while assured that they will only be seen as "acting out" or being "rebellious," the very words assuring all that they are not "naughty by nature" or "degenerate." As Baldwin indicates in "Black Boy Looks at the White Boy," this refusal of any identity (and, it might also be argued, the right to be "queer") while posited as a liberation from all norms or conformist roles represents the white male insistence on his historical privilege of innocence, that he is free from any social positioning, that he is unmarked and undetermined by any racial, gender, or social practice that he cannot "destabilize" and "denaturalize" through his own sheer anarchic and theatrical gesture. The male white countercultural hipster believes in his own voluntary exemption and defection, that even if he cannot always take himself out of determinate social and discursive categories, he can reacquire the innocent and pure expressive role-playing of the Eriksonian adolescent before socialization. But as Baldwin notes, not all performances are judged equally. Nor do all races have equal access to the play at identity. As the African American musician reminds us, the African American has to make herself/himself up as she/he goes along against "the not-at-all metaphorical teeth of the world's determination to destroy" them.

The brilliance of Baldwin's "The Black Boy Looks at the White Boy" lies in his attempt to create a boundary moment when even the White Negro hipsters who have abandoned their membership in the club must encounter the black look and, in doing so, must face, possibly for the first time, the determination of the world to destroy their innocence. While the hipster likes to celebrate a queering of identities—a fantasy of open-ended, nonnormative performativity—Baldwin reminds this white other that identitarian performances are "dialogical" or "contested." While the white hipster male might accept that he makes himself up as he goes along, he cannot accept being in limbo, that he has lost both his innocence and his control over the racial masquerade. He cannot accept that this fabrication is implicated within a complicated social reality involving a dialogue with others. In his essay, Baldwin restores a dialogue that bursts the adolescent innocence of the White Negro but also, through implication, of some contemporary critics who would "abolish" whiteness, or even more largely identities, only to maintain a false faith in the white privilege of self-transformed, if not always self-owned, identities.

In the chapters that follow, I pick up the various themes that I have argued need to be a part of a revisionary whiteness studies: the extended black agency of reverse acculturation, the role of women in the formation of white identities, the third mixed space of white racial formation along multiple axes of difference, and the preservation of whiteness within queer and other countercultural postidentity thinking. The first chapter, "Narrative Interruptions of Panic: Reverse Acculturation in the Early African-American Literature of William Wells Brown and Harriet Wilson," thus recovers the particular traumatic unconsciousness or panic that arose within antebellum ideas of the capital or property in "white" character to be developed in the middle-class home. The white woman's legitimacy as the "Republican Mother" depended on her ability to "pass" her "maternal influence" as homogeneous and uncontaminated, to repress and police against any possible reverse acculturations that might come in the contact between her children and "colored" others. In their "sentimental" fiction in the decade before the Civil War, William Wells Brown, and Harriet Wilson attempted to disrupt this racializing project of "whiteness" by invoking the panic on the home front about reverse colonization or the permeability of the white self to "others."

In the following two chapters on the work of Rebecca Harding Davis and Pauline Hopkins, my study addresses more directly the question of "female racism." While much revisionary work has been done on nineteenth-century women's sentimental fiction and how it reenforced racial ideologies, critics often ignore the alternative possibility that white women might have engaged in their own "gendered" forms of racial activity, ones that did not correspond to or act in complicity with a racism that is by default seen as public and masculine. By looking at Rebecca Harding Davis's relation to the "civil-izing" war discourse in the *Atlantic Monthly* circle, chapter 2 contends that her novel *Waiting for the Verdict* works to oppose and overturn a particular regional and gender-based inscription of whiteness and thereby to create a particular "feminine" and "liminal" version of white racial power, what I call "miscegenated whiteness." The next chapter, "'Corporeal Suspicion': The Missing Crimes of Neoabolitionist Rape Culture in Pauline Hopkins's Detective Histories," investigates Hopkins's resignifying of the conventions of detective fiction to challenge and disturb a rape culture that sanctions the "everyday" crimes of whiteness against black women. Talking back to a "neoabolitionist" whiteness among Garrison's New England heirs whose antiracist strategies failed to move beyond individual apology or the persecution of "abnormal" criminals, Hopkins's work shows how antiracists need to look at the larger structural forms of race thinking within a rape culture that preserves a white privilege intertwined with misogyny.

In the fourth chapter on the Korean American writer Younghill Kang and the fifth chapter on Jewish immigrant writers Mary Antin and Abraham Cahan, I investigate specifically the "trialectics" of whiteness. Attempting to create a refurbished cosmopolitanism, Kang reveals that the minority writer's relation to or renegotiation of white imperial power can repeat in an alarmingly analogous way the subsuming or erasing of African Americans in the dominant fiction of a reputedly white American culture. Chapter 5, "Dis-integrating Third Spaces: The Unrepresented in Mary Antin's and Abraham Cahan's Narratives of Americanization," attempts specifically to problematize the binary logic of the immigrant text between what Werner Sollors has outlined as the conflict between the New World of consent (America) and the Old World of dissent/ descent (the homeland). This abstracted conflict between two worlds represses those third public spaces where different ethnic and racial groups mixed in a dynamic interaction. In their own evasive or elided description of "multicultural" public spaces, Jewish immigrant writers such as Mary Antin and Abraham Cahan revealed an ambivalence about boundary loss: at once a simultaneous dread of catastrophic loss of borders and impotence in multicultural contact zones and also a fantasy of pleasurable liberation from and transgression of ghetto boundaries. By identifying with "whiteness," these writers were repressing an "unsayable" fear about identitarian "dis-integration" in "third spaces."

In the last two chapters, my study builds on the work of Kobena Mercer, who has argued that queer studies needs to begin to theorize the way that race is sexed and sex is raced. Looking at "white life" novels by African Americans during the "era of integration," chapter 6 "White Dissolution: Homosexualization and Racial Masculinity in White Life Novels," identifies a preoccupation among African American writers with the Cold War–era "homosexual menace" as one of the obvious sites of the split within white male subjectivity. These white life novels have numerous references to homosexual characters and invoke the rhetoric of homosexual panic. But while for writers such as Richard Wright and William Demby the discourse of the homosexual menace was a way to "reembody" the white male's "savage state," the figuring of the homosexual dissolute, as Zora Neale Hurston's *Seraph on the Suwanee* reveals, was also a vehicle for preventing narrative failure precisely at those moments in which homoeroticism would erupt as constitutive of black male homosociality. In the final chapter, "Queering Aztlan, Mestizing 'White' Queer Theory: Arturo Islas's *The Rain God*," I look at the way that Islas, like Chicana feminists such as Gloria Anzaldua, reappropriates the archetypal figure of Tlaloc (the rain god), who is the deity of fertility and the embodiment of the land, to locate a space for a queer gay male identity within the Chicano history of Aztlan. But in using the ideas of queer theory to explicate Islas's *The Rain God*, I also use Islas's novel to "brown" or "mestize" queer theory. Islas's *The Rain God* exposes the white racial ideologies that often underlie contemporary queer conceptualizations of identity and community.

In tracing these modes and methods of coracial and ethnic agency in the historical formations of white subjectivities in the more than hundred-year period from antebellum New England to the post–Civil Rights era of "multiculturalism," this book continues the work of retrieving the white perspective still submerged in academic discourse while reaffirming the complexity and the agency of early African, Korean, Chicano/a, and

Jewish American art. Whiteness is a fugitive race in that it insulates itself from the dialogical struggle over the meaning of its identity in a way that other racial and ethnic groups do not have the privilege to do, and it hides and buries the heterogeneity that is already at its core through its formation in miscegenated third spaces. Only by beginning to retrieve these ignored voices on whiteness (and whiteness's forms) can we really start the work of displacing this racial identification from the implied core and center of "race" studies. Yet in trying to push whiteness into limbo, as James Baldwin has written, my study finally challenges the adolescent "innocence" within a whiteness studies movement that believes it can move itself beyond identity, that it can even abolish or queer identities, without acknowledging that this postmodern play itself can continue to summon, but in fear dismiss, the not at all metaphorical teeth and not at all metaphorical glance back of the "other."

THE FUGITIVE RACE

1. NARRATIVE INTERRUPTIONS OF PANIC

Reverse Acculturation in the Early African American Fiction of William Wells Brown and Harriet Wilson

What would it mean for an early African American writer to be "impudent"? In Harriet Wilson's 1859 novel, *Our Nig*, the title character, Frado, is scolded by her cruel mistress for her "impudence," and on several occasions Mrs. Bellmont threatens in response to "cut her tongue out" (72), thus forever silencing the black woman's ability to talk back to white authority. But through these scenes of seemingly self-evident racist cruelty and muted resistance, Wilson enacts a particular kind of "impudence," an affective racial intervention expressed in narrative eruptions of a white panic about what could be called "reverse acculturation." In one key scene in Wilson's novel that is symptomatic of a traumatic interruption of racial panic, the elder son James returns home and insists that Frado dine with them. At the conclusion of the dinner, Frado, known as "Our Nig," sits in Mrs. Bellmont's chair to take her meal. When Mrs. Bellmont orders her servant to eat off her dirty plate, Frado, in defiance, has the family dog, and her sole "faithful" companion, Fido, lick the plate clean before she dries it for use on the table cloth. Frado's impudence here is less this insult to her mistress's spiteful arrogance than the effect her behavior has on Mrs. Bellmont's son, who conspires with Frado in a derisive "subversion" of his mother's authority. James rebukes his mother, insisting that "Nig" is only responding to Mrs. Bellmont's failed maternal influence: "You have not treated her mother, so as to gain her love; she is only exhibiting your remissness in this matter" (72). In this domestic scene, Wilson makes it clear, Frado and Mrs. Bellmont are not just rivals for a place at the table; they are in competition for "influence" over the nation's patriotic sons. After James leaves Frado alone with his mother, Mrs. Bellmont immediately beats her, demanding that she never "expose[] her to James" again or she would "cut her tongue out." Frado oversteps her subordinate place less in usurping Mrs. Bellmont's chair than by intruding upon the white woman's property in what Ann Douglas has described as a feminine "influence" on the home front (45–48).

In her discussion of the link between the bourgeois cultivation of self and nineteenth-century racial projects of empire building, Ann Laurie Stoler argues that the increasing attention to questions of character and moral upbringing disclosed the fear that the domestic domain, not the public sphere, was where the nation's masculine and racial identity might be undone. Colonialists, Stoler points out, had to keep a close vigilance over their children's character lest their children's moral disposition, sentiments, or sexual purity be contaminated by the nonwhite household members who loomed as an enemy within (95–135). While writing sketches of New England life rather than the empire abroad, Harriet Wilson in *Our Nig* taps into this tension between a formation of whiteness defined through a segregation from the other and domestic arrangements that were often more hybrid than pure blood. Although the middle-class home was figured as a clean white haven in the heartless world away from the competitiveness and self-interest of the commercial world, as Wilson's description makes clear, this sentimentalized domesticity with its often colored servant class might as accurately be seen as a "contact zone" that aroused a simultaneous dread about a possible catastrophic boundary loss. To advice-manual writers such as Mrs. A. J. Graves in *Woman in America*, domesticity entrusted women with the sacred duty to rear the moral character of the nation's leaders, but the upbringing of this future Washington or Franklin required a maternal management that guarded against polluting influences: "It seems now to be conceded," Graves enjoined, "that the vital interests of our country may be aided by the zeal of our mothers. A barrier to the torrent of corruption, and a guard over the strongholds of knowledge and virtue may be placed by the mother as she watches over her cradled sons" (68). In her language of warding off the dangers to the "stronghold" and to the "barrier" of the cradle, Graves compares the home front to an outpost on the empire, and it is the mother's influence that secures individual bodily boundaries within the imagined national community from incursions of alien others. Although as Ann McClintock has argued, the Victorian middle-class home served as a "space for the display of imperial spectacle and the re-invention of race" (34), the home front was the space where race, and particularly whiteness, might be destabilized. Whiteness's clear boundaries always stood in danger of being literally unsettled by transgressive emotional and sexual encounters and its fixed "character" blurred by reciprocal exchanges that only a rigorous "maternal management," as Mrs. Bellmont tries to implement, might prevent.

To say that the bourgeois home was often endangered by an alien presence from within that might unsettle female power and influence raises questions about the current critical understanding of what Linda Kerber called the "Republican Mother" (111). Although the ideology of the Republican Mother outlined within nineteenth-century guidance manuals emphasized that a woman's power and duties resided in her role as the character builder preparing the nation's citizenry for the public work of empire building, these Republican Mothers helped to instill and institutionalize a particular "private" and unconscious emotional style of racism. This domestic racism acted to complement more public narratives of race centered on images of manifest destiny, violence, and national conquest.[1] In her study of the role white women played as authorizing figures of nineteenth-century political and social identities, Karen Sanchez-Eppler has asserted that the identifications within sentimental fiction often obliterated the alterity of the marginalized figures of sympathy or, in other words, that the largely female readers could only feel the suffering of the other when that person had become the same (31). But such an astute reading of the epistemological violence within the antislavery depiction of the African American finally tells only a partial truth, a truth that can doubly erase the voice of the other. This guilt-ridden confession over the illegibility of the other preserves the purity and the priority of whiteness and obfuscates the fact that, although white women might have had a national mission to rear proper "American" subjects, very few of them were so innocent of the "contagion" or formative influence of the "other." In Fanny Kemble's *Journals*, Catharine Sedgwick's *The Linwoods*, and Lydia Sigourney's *Letters to Mothers*, this "feminine" domestic version of racism would focus on the purification of the family romance

or on forming and educating a private body free from reverse acculturation.

It is covertly to such a "panic" about reverse acculturation that Wilson's early African American novel speaks. The current attention to white
discourse and its circulation within a specific historical context at times
flattens and obscures whiteness's performative power because this criticism fails to tie specific rhetorics of whiteness to their "affectivity."[2] In
Colonial Desire: Hybridity in Theory, Culture and Race, Robert Young has
called for a postcolonial analysis of discourse that probes how imperialism worked on "two conflictual levels," the manifest and the latent or
unconscious. In addition to a discursive analysis of racial domination and
colonial expansionism, Young contends, we need to investigate "the
ambivalent protocols of fantasy and desire"(168). Whether invented to
divide and conquer possible working-class alliances across "color" lines
or to rationalize territorial expansion as manifest destiny, whiteness as a
means of mass regulation and demographic classifying is complemented
by a second level of technological power centered on the disciplining of
individual bodies. This imbrication of race and bodily discipline within
antebellum America expressed itself in a particular psychosis of panic, a
panic first about the indeterminacy of whiteness but equally about the
aggressive constitutive power of the black other.

Although David Roediger writing about race in antebellum working-
class culture starts with W. E. B. DuBois's often cited remark about the
"wages of whiteness," we might as accurately speak, especially in reference to middle-class Northerners before the Civil War, about the "property" or "capital" of the "white" character. Within an emergent middle-
class U.S. culture that was defined less by economic status than by its "distinctive family organization and accompanying domestic strategies"
(Blumin 11), whiteness assumed a slightly different meaning and form. In
manuals such as Joel Hawes's *Lectures to Young Men, On the Formation of
the Character* (1832), antebellum religious and civic leaders developed an
ideological narrative in which the cultivation and formation of character
issued in commercial profit as well as self-improvement. As Hawes states
with a booster's lack of equivocation: "If a young man completes the time
of his apprenticeship, or clerkship, with good principles and a fair character, he is made for life. His reputation is better to him than the richest
capital" (111). While Cheryl Harris has argued that the legal system turned
white identity into a property to be owned and invested in because this

identification granted access, opportunity, and privilege (103), antebellum conduct books increasingly in the 1840s and 1850s began to speak about the capital of a white character to an audience securely settled in the private middle-class home, isolated from the wider commercial and urban world (Ryan 98). While this middle-class culture insisted on a list of traits for the "sincere" character, the psychological validation and marketplace value of this property depended on the fantasy of its "insularity": its spatialized privacy and freedom from reverse acculturation with its alien influences. While black abolitionists such as Henry Highland Garnet played upon the dread of slave revolt among white slave holders, early African American writers of domestic fiction such as William Wells Brown and Harriet Wilson invoked this complementary panic about reverse colonization on the "home front," a dread that circulated as a traumatic unconsciousness even within seemingly antiracist, antislavery texts. By including narrative interruptions of panic, these early African American writers created a subtext restoring to the national imaginary the "unsayable" within a sentimental discourse about the molding of the capital of character, a buried story of the reciprocal, constitutive black gaze.

The Character of Middle-Class White Panic

In 1862, when the North was losing the Civil War, British-born actress Fanny Kemble published her *Journal of a Residence on a Georgian Plantation*, a book that began as a series of letters written to her friend Elizabeth Dwight Sedgwick during her year-long visit in 1838–39 to her husband Pierce Butler's Southern property near Saint Simons Island, Georgia. To stunt growing British sympathies for the Confederate cause, Kemble revised and expanded her diary to provide an insider's view of slavery's atrocities (Rushmore 102). While Kemble discloses the horrors of slavery particularly as they assault black women, her diary reveals a remarkable candor about the fears and anxieties of white women, even those involved in the antislavery cause. In order to better theorize the particular sentimental design of antebellum racism, I want to look at several key scenes that are emblematic of the particular panic that lay as an organizing structure of feeling behind even these antislavery fictions on race. Throughout Kemble's journal, there is an insistent emphasis on the role white women ought to play in purifying the home of "alien," mostly racial, influences. Yet at the same time, these narrative moments of anxi-ety-ridden disclosure reveal Kemble confronting the fact of "impurities" already within the supposedly domestic character of whiteness.

To understand the work of sentimental fiction, we need to reimagine its space of labor as not the kitchen or the lecture hall, that is the private hearth or the public arena, but something similar to the border space that Roger Abraham in his study of the development of African American cul-ture in the plantation South has called the "Yard," a contested area between the Big House and the slave quarters where the black and white worlds met and where white and black cultural meanings and practices were inevitably open to transformation and reinvention (xxiii). As wit-nessed in Kemble's private reflections on the "exploration" of Georgia plantation life, sentimental fiction had, in order to open up a space from which it could speak, to enact a racially purifying evacuation of the dia-logue within domestic life. By using the word "dialogue," I want to recall the Bakhtinian idea that meaning is never fixed but contested, that this meaning always takes shape only in the struggle between different speak-ers, and that meaning is constantly being modified and transformed by the interaction and interplay of this other (293–96). Although Kemble would try to omit this dialogue, seeing black agency as only a passive invading "dirt" or "pollution" that comes from outside and can be "washed off," in several telling moments we see the suppressed anxiety behind this representation of the "blackened" other.

Throughout her *Journal*, Kemble works to establish empathy between black and white women by commenting on their shared oppression. But even though Kemble appeals to her readers on behalf of the abused slave woman, her identification with the slave's plight depends on her simulta-neous denial of their domestic power and influence. Describing the return of her daughter after an afternoon with the slave children, for example, Kemble writes,

I am amused, but by no means pleased, at an entirely new mode of pronouncing which Sally has adopted. Apparently the Negro jargon has commended itself as euphonious to her infantile ears, and she is now treating me to the most ludicrous and accurate imitations of it every time she opens her mouth. Of course, I shall not allow this comical as it is, to become a habit. This is the way Southern ladies acquire the thick and inelegant pronunciation which distinguish [*sic*] their utter-ances from the Northern snuffle, and I have no desire that Sally should adorn her mother tongue with either peculiarity. (281)[3]

Although Kemble defied Southern prohibitions to teach her husband's slaves how to read, she did not allow for a reciprocal instruction of her children in "black language or culture." As a British-born woman who took on the responsibilities of a Republican Mother who would teach her children a purer English than even the common "Northern snuffle," Kemble felt it her duty to keep the "mother tongue" "unadorned" by the alien "peculiarities" of slave speech. While the characterization of blacks as "imitative" by nature recurred as a common argument in the slave debate to justify European cultural hegemony, we see from Kemble's comments that such an insistence on black mimicry hid a more primordial fear about white "imitation." In the borderland space that often was the antebellum domestic Yard, a "dialogue" took place between blacks and whites, a dialogue that sentimental women novelists usually suppressed lest "Negro jargon" commend itself as "euphonious" to our ears. The everyday or domestic practice of racism within antebellum fiction by women writers consisted of just such a denial of the dialogue within white identity formations. In contrast, whiteness had to become a privatized family romance, a purified encounter only with one's "mother tongue."

In another episode from her journal, Kemble recalls the instruction she was forced to give her African American servant Molly because she was contaminating her daughter Sally's speech. Reassuring Molly that it was only "her want of training and not any absolute original impotence" that caused her to disfigure the "white words," Kemble proceeded to correct her jangled pronunciation. Reflecting upon this incident afterward, Kemble writes that

the utterance of many of them [the slaves] is more like what Prospero describes Caliban's to have been than the speech of men and women in a Christian and civilized land: the children of their owners, brought up among them, acquire their Negro mode of talking—slavish speech surely it is—and it is distinctly perceptible in the utterances of all Southerners, particularly the women, whose avocations, taking them less from home, are less favorable to their throwing off this ignoble trick of pronunciation than the more varied occupation and the more extended promiscuous business relations of men. (252)

In her reference to herself as a modern-day Prospero civilizing the savage Caliban of Shakespeare's *The Tempest*, Kemble calls attention to the "colonial" language informing her perception of the slaves. Yet while Kemble expresses cultural racism, she also discloses her anxiety about the purity of the woman's sphere of the home. Because of their circumscription within the domestic life, women, especially Southern women, are susceptible to linguistic miscegenation, although Kemble by setting up a difference that associated promiscuity with men, tries to bury any suggestion of actual sexual intermixing. Since the women's sphere is racially and culturally diverse (Kemble's nurse for own her child is Irish), this domesticity conferred on her both the moral authority of maternal influence and simultaneously a particular anxiety about purity and about whiteness. As Kemble notes, the fear is that the "mother tongue," as a result of sympathetic contact or aberrant desires, might depreciate into a "slavish speech." While antebellum women attempted to figure "otherness" as outside the middle-class home and the corresponding property of the "white" self, Kemble's observation that "slavish" speech is "distinctly perceptible" in Southerners shows her idea of them not as "degenerates" but always already hybrid bastards and hence not true whites.

This is the paradox that recent reevaluations of nineteenth-century middle-class sentimental fiction has elided and which we need to make visible if we are to understand fully the narrative strategies within early African American fiction. The white female writer of domestic fiction could not simply leave the privacy of her home for the public sphere because her home was not "private." She could not simply obfuscate the identity of the other because she herself already contained multitudes of others. To theorize the cultural work of domestic fiction, we need to reclaim the racial dividedness within the historically constituted idea of "true womanhood" and to trace its subsequent paranoiac denial. This British-born "American" mother's task involved not only forming the national character but also perpetuating a historical silence about the multiethnic relational nature of her and her readers' own identity. In the antislavery sentimental text, such as Kemble's, therefore, there are two narrative trajectories: first, to arouse sympathies on behalf of the oppressed slaves, and second, to ensure, at the same time, the white woman's own emancipation from the multivocal domestic space through her entrance into (and identification with) a particular female style of white racism based on the purity of the "mother tongue."

We can see the particular gendered form of women's racial activity as it was disseminated within antebellum guidance manuals by looking at Lydia Sigourney's *Letters to Mothers* (1838). In the decades before the Civil War, Sigourney loomed as one of the most important public poets in the nation, and her collected poems appeared as the fourth volume—after those by Bryant, Longfellow, and N. P. Willis—in the Cary and Hart series (1848) on the great works by American poets. Although Sigourney often showed great sympathy for Native Americans whose treatment she saw as an offense against Christian principles and tutored African Americans in her Hartford school for impoverished children, she shared her New England contemporaries' investment in a racialized nationalism. In her opening chapters on "The Privileges of the Mother," Sigourney borrows the language of imperialism to elevate the importance of a mother's influence: the mother is described as the "universal agent of civilization," and "in proportion as it prevails, national enmities will disappear, prejudices become extinguished, civilization spread itself far and wide" (12–13). Yet while Sigourney ties the mother's domestic management to the fate of the Republic and its expanding empire, she also taps into familiar republican rhetoric about contamination within the "body politic." If civic leaders are now calling for female education, Sigourney writes, such an appeal to the duties of the mother "by legislation and sages" shows that they are alarmed by an alien presence in the national body: "It has been discovered that there are signs of disease in the body politick which can be best allayed, by the subordination taught in families, and through her agency to whom is committed the molding of the whole mass of mind in its first formation" (12–13). In her discussion of the national mission of women on the home front, Sigourney invokes the tradition of the Republican Mother who was to shape the national character, and she thus attributes to women a powerful agency within this limited sphere of influence. But while Sigourney prophesies a maternal revolution, one similar to that seen within a number of midcentury sentimental "women's" novels from Stowe to Harriet Wilson, she draws upon a language of bodily invasion that adds a racialized dimension to this narrative of female empowerment. In subsequent pages, Sigourney makes clear what she sees as the dangerous "disease" or contaminant of American society.

It seems now to be conceded, that the vital interests of our country, may be aided by the zeal of mothers. Exposed as it is, to the influx of untutored foreigners, often unfit for its institutions, or adverse to their spirit, it seems to have been made a repository for the waste and refuse of other nations. To neutralize this mass, to rule its fermentations, to prevent it from becoming a lava-stream in the garden of liberty, and to purify it for those channels where the life blood of the nation circulates, is a work of power and peril. The force of public opinion, or the terror of the law, must hold in check these elements of danger, until Education can restore them to order and beauty. (14)

Now it is hardly a novel revelation to suggest that Sigourney, like many women of her age, was not free of race thinking. But Sigourney's comments suggest that a panic about the incorporation of the foreign and the alien within the individual and national body circulated as a structural form within nineteenth-century discussions of character. Since the advice manuals saw children as impressionable (literally in a "waxen state"), the preservation of the "whiteness" of their character (their capital of opportunity) emerged as the primary duty charged to women.

We need then to broaden our understanding of the link between domesticity and race, between mothering and whiteness. While recent theorists have argued that the home was tied discursively to manifest destiny, another racial narrative, that of segregation, emerged within domestic literature. While the middle-class home as the site of early education was to stand apart from the competitive commercial world or the ethnic and racial "ghetto," the segregation guarded over by the Republican Mother's influence involved the preservation of the individual white character, as well as physical body, from outside influences. We can clearly see the connection between the racial language of segregation and character in the following admonition from the anonymous pamphlet *Woman's Influence and Woman's Mission* (1854):

A man may even wander for a time from the path of rectitude, and even by adverse circumstances become desperate, but never lost if his early training and home influences were good; that mother's or father's voice will come to him; it may be at midnight, the silent watches of the night, after a day spent in wickedness, or on the bed of sickness and of anguish; and even amidst the orgies of a lawless band, will that voice be heard above the Baccahanalian [*sic*] shouts, and that man arrested in his course, and saved by the home monitor. (6)

Although behind the instruction within *Woman's Influence* lies the image of westward expansion and of empire, we should not fail to note the different inflection. The pamphlet invokes not a rhetoric of manifest destiny but more of surrender and invasion, of a possible reverse colonization. Mobility here does not mean conquest but susceptibility to foreign influence. Within its image of "orgies of a lawless band," the writer appeals to a fear of the savage other and to a fear of the influence of this "other," whether racially or morally dark, upon the white character. In speaking of the "home monitor," the treatise invokes the whole racialized language of the home as a space where there should be no alien impressions, and this internalized domesticity of the "home monitor" ensures that the value of one's capital, one's property in white character, will not depreciate, in the marketplace of exchange, no matter where one may travel. The "home monitor" assures that there will be no loss of racial difference, that whiteness is a space that, like the middle-class home, can never itself be conquered or even enlightened from outside.

The connection between female empowerment within the domestic sphere and a panic about a black presence within the home can be seen more clearly in the plotting of Catharine Sedgwick's 1835 novel, *The Linwoods*. Like her friend and correspondent Fanny Kemble, Catharine Sedgwick grew up in a family with a long history of antislavery sentiments. Her father, Theodore Sedgwick, made an important contribution to the abolition of slavery in Massachusetts when he defended the slave Elizabeth Freeman using the Declaration of Rights and Grievances (October 19, 1765), which, in response to the Stamp Act, declared that all colonial residents had the same rights and liberties as the citizens of England. Later, in speaking of her own recollections of childhood, Sedgwick would even refer to the freed slave Elizabeth, or Mumbet, as the family called her, as one who had "more to do with the formation of our characters than all our didactic and perceptive education" (qtd. in M. Kelley 378). Despite her own personal and familial history of respect for African Americans, however, Sedgwick would use her fiction to rework her own private past and the nation's to remove this slavish acculturation that might debase the character of her white readerly daughters. Possibly aware of the affective underlife of this widely popular antebellum sentimental novel, William Wells Brown in his 1864 revision of *Clotel* renames Horatio Green, the husband of Clotel in the 1853 original edition, Herbert Linwood after the scion in Sedgwick's novel. While the reasons why Brown invokes Sedgwick's earlier novel remain undocumented, in Sedgwick's novel he would have found a model of the sentimental author as creator of a racialized national identity. He also would have found in *The Linwoods* a novel particularly troubled by the presence of the black male within the contact zone of domestic space.

Set during the time of Sedgwick's father and of the "Founding Fathers" associated with the Revolutionary War, *The Linwoods* recounts the divisions that the rebellion caused in the eponymous Tory family. At the end of the novel, the marriage of the novel's heroine, Isabella Linwood, to the war hero Eliot Lee, the self-made son of humble Yankee Bostonians, implies that the new Jacksonian man is a hybrid or offspring of the marriage of the Republic's aristocratic (Federalist) ancestors and the "portionless son of a New England farmer" (274). By showing the private lives of the novel's young men and women, Sedgwick attempts to disclose, moreover, that a woman's "voluntary service of the heart" (261) has played a prominent role in the war equal to the battlefield bravery of great men such as Washington and Lafayette. Sedgwick's *The Linwoods* is finally, that is to say, about the Republican Mother as the defender of the property of the "white" national character against its corresponding invasions from abroad and from within the domestic space.

In her figuring of the role of the "true woman" within the new national community, Sedgwick discursively links the empowerment of white women to the effacement of the black man from domestic space as well as history. In her opening chapter, Sedgwick depicts Isabella Linwood as a "woman made for empire," but while Sedgwick shows this innate royalty of moral character that qualifies her protagonist to be among America's new cultural elite, Isabella feels constrained by the black male servant Jupe, the "tiresome old fool," who guards over her. Against the wishes of her mother, Isabella decides to enter the public square to visit the fortuneteller Effie, but for this symbolic assertion of independence to occur, her heroine must cast off the intrusive supervision of her black attendant. Once in the public square, as a consequence, Isabella attempts to belittle and scare Jupe with the ghosts of the "Negro plot" said to still haunt the pillory (16). In 1742 a group of slaves led, as William Wells Brown wrote in *The Rising Son* (1874), a "formidable insurrection" before they were captured and hung (278).[4] By making Jupe fearful of the specters of the "Negro plot" and a superstitious coward who certainly could not stand up to these forbearers' example, Sedgwick counterposes in schematic opposition Isabella's "love of freedom and independence of control" and the black male domestic servant's subordination. Yet Isabella in this scene does not just prove the feeble manhood of her slave (a familiar stereotype); she, more significantly, discredits black male protest and the black voice in order to establish her influence within the "empire of the home." Connecting domesticity with a fear of a rival black agency, *The Linwoods* suggests that within antebellum society antagonisms did not just coalesce around a single axis of difference (gender) but that other sets of opposition (race) come into play as well. In defying the patriarchal authority of the fathers, Sedgwick displaces this antipathy into virulent disdain for other possible male authority in the home. In the opening scene of *The Linwoods*, Sedgwick reproduces in miniature the racial dynamics that governs sentimental antislavery fiction. The white woman's power as the moral guardian who has the duty like Isabella to enter the public sphere depended on the silencing of the "Negro plot," a "Negro plot" that is not just the tradition of self-authorized black protest in the public square but a plot that might arise from within the "dialogic" nature of the middle-class home.

This fear of the hidden presence of black agency within the middle-class home, and particularly black male agency that works too much on behalf of patriarchy, erupts in one of the unmotivated plot twists in Sedgwick's novel. At the key moment in the novel when Isabella begins to work secretly on behalf of her American brother, Isabella feels she must remove the interference of Jupe, or allegorically, the destabilizing presence of the black man from the matriarchal kitchen. To aid the American cause and to subvert the Tory authority of her father from within the home, by acting as the true Republican Mother of influence, Isabella must dismiss Jupe (although not the less threatening mammy figure, Rose) from the house. To justify this unmotivated plot development, Sedgwick writes that "Isabella congratulated herself that she had long before this persuaded her father to dismiss Jupiter (an irreclaimable gossip), on the ground that he was a useless piece of lumber; but really, because Rose had declared that it exceeded the ability of her commissary department to supply his rations" (102). Now the representation of the black man as lazy and prodigal in this remark needs little explication, but its function within the larger narrative strategies of Sedgwick's novel demands careful reconsideration. In a novel about the infusion of different characters into a new, coherent, stable "American" identity, Sedgwick's satire of Jupe's worth is not just a predictable denigration; it possesses an important tactical value. Within traditional republican discourse, it is effeminacy and luxury that weaken the characters of a people and precipitates the nation's decline (Bercovitch 180). By displacing these traditionally "feminine" defects of character onto the black man, Sedgwick persuades her readers of the white woman's fitness for service in the formation of the national character. In her rewriting of history as a defense of a new middle-class matriarchal culture, Sedgwick continues to pay homage to the martial character of typical male icons such as Washington and Lafayette, but what she refuses to make known is the valor of black men. Although George Bancroft in his history of the revolution (volume 7) exclaims that "nor should history forget to record, that, as in the army of Cambridge, so also in this gallant band, they [free blacks of the colony] had their representatives," in Sedgwick's novel there is a deliberate silence about the black man's honor (421), for honor must be reserved as a property of the white middle-class hero. Like her heroine, Sedgwick needed to scoff at the "Negro plot," since the return of its ghostly presence would overturn her sentimental authority in the newly segregated empire of the national "white" home. Whiteness depended, as Sedgwick shows, on the refusal to acknowledge its irreconcilable relation with the black other, and it is precisely these equivocations and contradictions within whiteness's sentimentality that William Wells Brown and Harriet Wilson mirror for their readers in their own counterfictions for genteel middle-class readers.

"Taking On" Whiteness, or Whose Assimilative Panic

In his "Memoir of an Author," which he inserted at the beginning of his survey of representative black men in U.S. history, *The Black Man: His Antecedents, His Genius, and His Achievements* (1863), William Wells Brown recalls how he was mistaken for "a white boy" by strangers who visited the Young household, and on one occasion a major visiting Dr. Young presumed that Brown was his master's son. As a result of this incident, Brown avers he was flogged by his mistress (19). In her biography of her father's life, Josephine Brown retells the same story but slightly alters the details. In her account, Brown was specifically mistaken for Dr. Young's nephew, who shared the name William, and as a consequence of this proximity in complexion and character, his mistress changed his name from William to Sanford (41). Whether Brown's story of being misidentified as the doctor's son or nephew is apocryphal or not (and Brown was prone to alter the facts of his own life to suit the political needs of the occasion) is less important than its recurring theme of the instability of whiteness. Although in neither scenario is the young mixed-raced William Wells Brown allowed to speak, his presence reminds Mrs. Young of the miscegenation within her own household. What is particularly striking in his daughter's version is the emphasis placed on the power of language to set up, and undermine, racial differences and boundaries. By naming him as the other, "Sanford," Mrs. Young tries to deny "impurities" on the domestic front. By contrast, throughout his writing career, it might be argued, Brown speaks back specifically to a white femininity that would try to erase blackness's constitutive presence within the domestic family. Not only does Brown write about other "tragic mulattoes" disowned by their "white" families, he employs as a recurrent strategy within his fiction the denaturalization of whiteness.[5] As Brown further remarks in this same memoir about his youth in the Young plantation household, he would amuse other slaves with his "representations of what was going on in the great house" (17). He had learned to "take on" the injustices of antebellum American's racial order through a subversive and satiric representation (taking on) of whiteness that restores black agency.

In taking on whiteness, Brown was building on tactics of resistance that William Pierson has studied. In his examination of slave cultures, *Black Legacy: America's Hidden Legacy*, Pierson investigates the widespread practice of sarcastic mimicry, one that can be traced back to the Ashanti tribe's traditional ceremonies allowing for the ridicule of authority as a tactic of protest (60). Although histories of African American culture have tended to value more the seemingly "manly" forms of protest, violent rebellion or collective action, traditional African cultures placed a high value on the satiric parody of white authority. While we have in the past, as William Andrews notes, been prone to evaluate nineteenth-century slave narratives and early African American fiction according to the writer's evolution toward self-consciousness and a black voice (*To Tell a Free Story* 145), such a criterion for assessment may overlook, in the light of present values, alternative forms of resistance in antebellum American culture. Although Brown was certainly aware that, when addressing a white audience, he bore the burden of speaking for his race, he sketches out his life with dizzying inconsistency in his writing, creating his "authorial identity" often less as an individual voice per se than as a positional effect within a dialogical encounter with others. At the end of his own personal memoir for *The Black Man, His Antecedents, His Genius*, Brown recounts how, while working for the Underground Railroad in Cleveland, he helped a fugitive cross Lake Erie by disguising him as a "white woman": "In an hour, by my directions, the black man was as white, and with as rosy cheeks, as any of the Anglo-Saxon race, and disguised in the dress of a woman, with a thick veil over her face" (25). It would not be too great a stretch to see this implausible incident, with its boundary crossing of racial and gender differences, as Brown's statement about his own poetics in *Clotel*, one in which freedom is linked with the impersonation, or taking on, of styles of white female performance.

Throughout his life, Brown was a "liminal figure," one who straddled, as a mulatto, black and white worlds. As a house slave, he lived largely in the feminine world of the Big House rather than in the masculine world of the fields. It was not simply a matter of literary accommodationism that would cause him to tell the story of his life within the "feminine" genre of sentimentalism or to respond to Harriet Beecher Stowe's *Uncle Tom's Cabin* with his own *Clotelle*. Brown's use of domesticity as the space in which to reimagine U.S. race culture is one that would have recommended itself because of his own past experiences. As someone excluded from the parlor and limited to speaking through his satiric mimicries of whites for the other household servants in the kitchen, Brown knew that whiteness feared the black look, this return look that might challenge whiteness's own self-conceptions and expose the gaps in its identity formation. Thus in his portrait of the house servant Sam in *Clotel*, Brown offers a metacommentary on his own narrative strategies. Although at first Sam seems a comforting and familiar type within plantation fiction, the clownish and sycophantic Sambo whose comic airs provide grinning relief to reassure whites of their innate superiority, Sam's buffoonish imitation of whiteness uses laughter to hide the ridicule in his gaze back across the color line. Sam's tomfoolery, seen as a slavish imitation of his white master's notions, permits a subversive masquerade, and in many ways, Sam, though at first a stereotype, stands in for Brown himself, who as an author first deceives us with his deference to literary conventions. However, after the master Mr. Peck's death, his daughter, Georgiana, while walking past the slave cabins with her fiancée, the Northerner Carlton, overhears the more honest sentiments of her house servant. Rather than acting as the presumed faithful darkie mourning over the lost of his master, Sam sings, "I laughed myself when I heard/That the old man's spirit had fled" (155). Overturning expectations he had established earlier about Sam's character, Brown shocks his white readers into a recognition of the black look that they have tried to exclude from their domestic space. Liberated from the need for imposture, Sam indeed proves not a clown but a man devoted to his people who shares their laughter, tears, and songs and who, as the next overseer, instructs them out of love and not through the use of force and punishment (167). In *Clotel*, Brown implicates his white readers in their own investment in categories of race and gender. While at first seeming to share their beliefs in whiteness's difference, he evacuates these identities to expose their ideological usefulness.

After Stowe's celebrated success with the publication of the bound versions of *Uncle Tom's Cabin*, Brown at first eagerly heralded the novel as he declaimed in an open letter published in the *Frederick Douglass Papers* on December 10, 1852, as a powerful piece of antislavery propaganda, but like many others in the black abolitionist movement, he grew increasingly ambivalent about its perpetuating of images of black inferiority (Banks 214). But Brown's relation to Stowe and white women is more complicated than a quarrel over representation. As the British journalist William Farmer wrote in a letter to William Lloyd Garrison, the publication of *Uncle Tom's Cabin* arrived as a needed boost to Brown and the abolitionists in England, for "Uncle Tom's Cabin had created a deep interest in American Slavery in this county," and as a result Brown's lectures during his 1853 tour of England would be "well attended and his sketches now more widely read" (qtd. in Farrison 209). Brown's fictional voice, and not just his style of writing, depended largely on the success of the white woman's slave tale for its hearing. Such a consciousness of dependency could only have stung Brown, who liked to boast of his self-sufficient manhood that never went a "begging."[6] In his revisions of *Clotel*, as a consequence, Brown not only seeks to challenge the little-lady-who-started-the-big-war's disparaging images of African Americans; he also sought to depict, particularly in his alterations for the 1864 editions of *Clotelle*, a black and white domestic interdependency. Overturning the "sentimental design" of a female racism that we have seen in the antislavery writing of women such as Fanny Kemble and Catharine Sedgwick, the 1864 version of *Clotelle* challenges the "unamalgamated" whiteness of the mother tongue. Amid the 1864 story of the mulatto Clotelle (renamed with the added French feminine ending), the mulatto former houseboy Brown restores to the white American sentimental narrative the interstitial world of the Yard, a place where white and black identities were always dialogically formed and already miscegenated.

While Brown in *Clotel* appeals to the familiar pathos of the destruction of families, the separation of mothers and their children, and the loss of feminine purity to elicit sympathy, he also invokes his readers' emotional insecurity about the value, security, and purity of the property of white character. As Brown remarks through the voice of the good white republican Henry Morton, nineteenth-century Americans continually linked national prosperity to moral character and feared the decline of the Republic with the "degradation" of this national character: "Our nation is losing its character" (184). To assuage these fears about the segregated property of the nation's character, Brown in his initial version of *Clotel* emphasizes the true woman's domestic influence, offering readers the reassuring story of Georgiana Peck, whose power of moral persuasion and matriarchal influence alters the nation's conscience. True to the narrative codes of the white Republican Mother, Brown's 1853 version of *Clotel* depicts Georgiana Peck as the heroic white woman whose influence converts the "atheist" George Carlton. When Georgiana brings to Carlton the true spirit of the Gospels, Brown writes that "Georgiana had succeeded in riveting the attention of Carlton during her conversation, and as she was finishing her last sentence, she observed the silent tear stealing down the cheek of the newly born child of God" (121). Not only is Georgiana the white savior who has all the "plans for bettering the conditions of [her] slaves" (163) so that they have no self-authorized agency, but she, in directing the national character, assures its racial purity. In contrast, Clotel, despite all the repeated celebrations of her heart as "true to woman's nature," is not allowed the power to transform and convert others. Although she can manage, while dressed in male clothes, to bring about her own and Williams's escape, she cannot mold, fashion, or significantly influence the predetermined characters of the novel's white cast.

In Brown's changes from the 1853 version of *Clotel* to the 1864 edition, *Clotelle*, we see, however, his attempt to rewrite the racial purity of sentimental fiction's domestic ideology. One of the major changes between the first and second editions is the rescripting of the story of Georgiana Peck (or Wilson, as she is called in the later edition). While in the original version of *Clotel* Brown casts Georgiana Peck as a Stowe-like heroine, he greatly alters the representative white woman abolitionist in his 1864 revision. It is significant, too, that Clotel's daughter, Mary, in the 1853 edition is now renamed as the title character, Clotelle. By changing the titular focus from the mother to the daughter, Brown places emphasis not on the victimized slave mistress and tragic mulatto but on the "pure" daughter who achieves the ideals of marriage and domesticity. Such a resignification of the plot, however, does not suppress the gender questioning of the original version; instead, it allows Brown during these Civil War years to reenvision his novel from a story of slave flight and suicidal escape to a political allegory about the nation's future, one in which interracial domesticity will serve as a trope for an acculturation that exceeds the sentimental design of female racialism. Thus unlike in the earlier edition, Clotelle now finds in Georgiana "more a sister than a mistress, who unknown to her father, taught the slave girl how to read, and did much toward improving and refining Clotelle's manners" (288), and Georgiana finds in Clotelle more a "companion than a menial" (291). More important, in the novel's most significant reverse operation, it is Clotelle who converts the white woman in the novel. When Clotelle heroically changes places in prison so that her lover, Jerome, can escape to freedom disguised in her clothes, it is Georgiana who is altered. In fact, in a melodramatically implausible but thematically telling scene, Brown writes that with the imprisonment of Clotelle, Georgiana fell "in decline, and any little trouble would lay her on a sick bed for days. She was therefore, poorly able to bear the loss of this companion whom she so dearly loved" (301). Georgiana's sudden "Eva-like" death, with the "sons and daughters of Africa" around her, affects no one's change of heart in the 1864 novel. Rather, Brown rewrites this conventional death-bed scene to return the repressed narrative of the "Negro plot" to sentimental fiction. Georgiana's sudden passing away signals the inefficacy of the white woman's moral suasion; her death at the loss of her sister, Clotelle, the dependency of the white woman on her colored sisters for her own multiracial relational identity; and, as important, because the self-sacrificial act of Clotelle that breaks the heart of her mistress also frees Jerome, the man who prophecies that he will work to see the day "that the negro will learn that he can get his freedom by fighting for it" (294), Brown structurally links the two figures that always lay in tension within the antebellum sentimental novel: the white woman's moral suasion and the black man's activist protest. In place of Georgiana's inability to secure clemency for Clotelle, we hear Jerome's impassioned speech.

As if to link his revised sentimental design with the nationalistic formations imposed through the fiction of white women reformers, Brown also appends new chapters to the conclusion of the 1864 *Clotelle*. In these new scenes, after the original romantic closure of Clotelle and Jerome's marriage, Brown describes their honeymoon grand tour to Europe's romantic landmarks. Jerome and Clotelle visit the originary sites of romantic nationalism, traveling "under the shadow of Mont Blanc" (338) and "at the birthplace of Rousseau and the former abodes of Byron, Gibbon, Voltaire" (339). Here the former escaped slaves are reunited with Clotelle's estranged father, Herbert Linwood, but he is a changed man from the earlier slave master in the novel, and, as significantly, he is different from Sedgwick's founding father. Herbert Linwood has learned that he can no longer define himself apart from his multiracial family. In the novel's concluding depiction of the conversion of Linwood, Brown releases into the main storyline of the novel the panicked reverse influence that lay buried within the national unconscious: "every day Mr. Linwood became more and more familiar with Jerome, and eventually they were on the most intimate of terms" (338). No longer will the national "race" engendered by this founding father, as in Sedgwick's novel, be merely the confluence of Federalist elites and Jacksonian democrats but a national admixture that recognizes its incorporation of and family resemblance to the African other. At the end of *Clotelle*, Herbert Linwood embraces his "rising son" as an equal agent in creating the national character.

The guarded fugitive narrative in the insistent thematizing of slavery's horror was a panicky dread of whiteness's vulnerability to the allure and the transformative power of blackness. Disguised behind the public (masculinized) bombast of manifest destiny was the more troubling private fright of the "Negro plot," which would corrupt the innocence of the American character from within its very domestic spaces. Brown's 1864 revision of the ending of *Clotelle* represents an important intervention into the circulation of antislavery fiction's sentimental design. In contrast to the "female white racialism" in sentimental fiction, Brown brings the black family into the white home. And not only is this family integrated, but their inclusion causes a moral change in the character and in the very identity of whiteness. While white women assumed the right of influencing the national character and identity, in Brown's revised *Clotelle* it is Clotelle and Jerome who uplift the whites and help them to reach a moral, if not ontological, purity. At the center of William Well Brown's *Clotelle* are narrative moments that bring to light the dark unconsciousness of the white racial identifications pictured within sentimental fiction. As a good mimic, Brown enacts a form of ironic negation, playfully repeating a feminine style of whiteness so as to unsettle its apparent naturalness. In short, he tapped into the abject horror within the racial unconsciousness: an abject horror that the borders of whiteness were unstable and irrelevant since the African American was already at home and already a coauthor of whiteness.

Never Come into the House Again

In looking at the panic about reverse acculturation in antebellum domestic literature, we as critics must supply the missing words and affect that the dominant discourse forbids. To encounter black female agency in Harriet Wilson's *Our Nig*, we need similarly to recover the transcriptive subtext that allows an inscription of the traumatic underlife of antebellum whiteness. While critics have frequently defined *Our Nig* as an admixture of the conventions of antislavery and sentimental fiction (Gates, Introduction to *Our Nig* xl–lv; Stern 441), Wilson's novel does not just "signify" on the conventions of domestic fiction to locate a space for an alternative black female identity; it discloses, though white Northern petit bourgeois women such as Mrs. Bellmont might try to deny it, that the middle-class home is already a "contact zone," where the voice of "others" might be essential to its meaning and competing for its formative "agency" and influence. In her preface, Wilson calls attention to the narrative lacunae required so as not to offend a potential audience of sympathetic Northern white women readers: "I do not pretend to divulge every transaction in my own life, which the unprejudiced would declare unfavorable in comparison with treatment of legal bondmen; I have purposely omitted what would most provoke shame in our good anti-slavery friends at home" (3). Yet in announcing her textual inhibitions for fear of reprisal, and announcing them more heinous than the enormities of slavery, Wilson invites the reader (and calculatedly so) to imagine what has been elided and to read for the interstices of the text. This coded subtext is one that would bring "shame" to antislavery friends at home, metaphorically in New England but literally so as well, in the home of sentimental domesticity.

The buried referent within Wilson's domestic fiction can be unearthed by looking at the dominant trope of space that recurs, often indirectly, in the language of the narrator and the characters. While Wilson's autobiographically based plot of *Our Nig* proceeds in a simple linear order with the history of Frado's mother, Mag, and then Frado's abandonment at the

Bellmonts, the initial story of Mag serves to juxtapose two different "domestic" spaces. What Wilson underscores in her account of Mag's social degradation is her residence in the "hovel" (7, 8), her choice to dwell in an "unclean" place out of a desire to escape a "sneering world." Once there, Mag further underscores the "connotation" this "home" has for the town's more respectable residents by confiding to Jim that "folks seem as afraid to come here as if they expected to get some awful disease" (9). Although this "hovel" is a space of "disease" and "uncleanliness" because of the literal dirt and poverty there, Wilson indicates that it is taboo because it is also a place of "amalgamation," both in terms of inter-racial sexual unions and in the disruption of racial difference: In her initial story of the dark-skinned Frado's white mother, Mag, Wilson begins with a Gothic inversion of domestic fiction, one in which black men have the "white heart" (12) and white womanhood lives neither in piety nor purity, those vestiges of true womanhood, but infamy.

Yet in setting up Mrs. Bellmont's home against Mag's hovel (and Mag's quarters are never blessed with the designation of "home"), Wilson gives her readers less a contrast than a thematic counterpoint. Mrs. Bellmont's domestic space is haunted by the shadow of this earlier amalgamation, for it is a space where the "other," here the mixed-blood girl-child, might have a voice to rival the white woman's influence as part of her home management and to mold and build the "white" character. It is not surprising then that Mrs. Bellmont's punishment of Frado almost consistently involves an attempt to silence her and to alienate the Belmont family's affection for their servant. While certainly *Our Nig* enumerates the cruelties of Northern middle-class whites toward freed blacks, Wilson identifies the intention of this catalog of corporeal punishment as the silencing of Frado. When Frado, "indisposed" by illness, defies her mistress's command to work, Mrs. Bellmont not only inflicts a "blow which lay the girl prostrate on the floor," but she "stuffed the mouth of the sufferer [with a towel]" (82). In muffling Frado's voice, Mrs. Bellmont dreads less that Frado will testify publicly against her, since she is inured to such accusations, but that Frado will win the support of her sons. On another occasion, this time when Mrs. Bellmont whips Frado for informing her son James that his mother had forbidden the visits of his aunt, the mistress similarly seeks to mute the voice of her ward and "cure her of tale bearing" by "placing a wedge of wood between her teeth" (93). If this scene is horrifying, yet a seemingly familiar atrocity within antislavery tales, it elides what is the subtext in domestic fiction: Mrs. Bellmont does not want her son to hear her abuses. More important, she does not want Frado to "influence" her son to challenge her authority in the home and her maternal influence over him.

In the conflict that Mrs. Bellmont has with Frado's Christian education as it has been directed by her sister-in-law and son, Wilson points out this incompleteness in the middle-class woman's domestic supervision. After Mrs. Bellmont refuses to let Frado read her Bible, Wilson writes that "there was one little spot seldom penetrated by her mistress' watchful eye: this was her room, uninviting and comfortless; but to herself a safe retreat" (87). This space of Frado's room, where Frado develops her own thoughts, is what lies outside the reach of the public discourse on domestic ideology. Mrs. Bellmont's ownership over the domestic scene as the privilege afforded by her possessive investment in the white female character is not omniscient, and in these disconnected scenes that do not always make "narrative sense," Wilson seeks to give "free associative range and symbolic play," as Ed Guerrero has argued about the horror genre, to the pent-up panic of society's repressed racial discourse (35). In the middle-class home, there never was complete privacy or a lack of interference from the outside world, and as *Our Nig* reveals, there were spaces that were outside the white woman's domestic management.

I want to turn for a moment to a scene in the antislavery travelogue written by C. G. Parsons, *An Inside View of Slavery* (1855), a tract that Harriet Beecher Stowe cites in her *Notes to Uncle Tom's Cabin* and for which she wrote the introduction. Like Fanny Kemble, Parsons describes his encounters with the slavery South, and among his anecdotes is his story of his visit to the plantation of Mr. A. By telling the story of Mr. A, Parsons wants to show the familiar antislavery theme of how "slavery hardens the heart." Yet even as Parsons repeats the injurious effects of slavery on the white slaveholder, as did Douglass in his story of Sophia Auld, he extends his concern more generally to the absence of civilizing influences on the Southern character. Appealing to a discourse of racial degeneracy, Parsons notes that the rural plantation slaveholder "has no Northern men about him to influence his conduct, to check the full indulgence of his appetites or to restrain his passions" (6). In reporting the contradiction within Mr. A's character, that he is both affectionate to his mammy and yet still cruelly whips his slaves, Parsons thus invokes and then placates the unconscious panic about reverse colonization that might form the white male character.

Parsons's story of Mr. A begins with his shock at witnessing while out riding in the coach with Mr. A that the slaveholder stops to kiss a slave woman: "When they met, he threw his arms around her neck, and kissed her—and she locked her arms about his neck, and kissed him!" (158). Only after first arousing his reader's interest in the sexual miscegenation between slave owners and their women does Parsons reassure us, as Mr. A. appeased him, that this woman was the "slave mother [who] nursed me when I was an infant; and whenever she saw my own mother abuse me, she would take me up in her arms and carry me away to her little hut, to soothe me, and caress me" (159). Yet while Parsons out of reticence or naivety accepts Mr. A's story, the disruptive transgressive sexuality of plantation life that the text opens up cannot be so easily contained within the reassuring stereotype of the self-abnegating and enduring mammy. While Parsons attributes the "trouble" this scene gave him to the hypocrisy of the slave master who could abuse the race of the surrogate mother who loved him, he experiences a more disturbing crisis within his cultural categories as he sees slip and blur the boundary separating the Southern mammy from the black Jezebel and between white and black maternal influence. Parsons's story reveals a disruptive admixture of displaced sexual desire and maternal gratitude. But it also sets the black mother's "influence" against the white woman's "abuse" in ways that imply that the domestic domain harbored its own potential threats.

What frightens Parsons, as his immediate need to question Mrs. A to discover what she knows about this other woman, is the overlap of the black passive (m)other and the black woman as erotic object choice. Mr. A's tryst with his former mammy implies not so much adultery as a perversion between black slave women and their charges, a perversion that is at once sexual and educational. In Mr. A's knotted desire and appreciation for the woman who "caressed" him arises the specter of the power of the black woman over the moral disposition and emotional/sexual character of her white charges. To deny this image of the domestic Jezebel directing the dispositions and libidos of her white children, Parsons reroutes his anxiety from the power of the black woman to seduce or form moral character to the harmful influence of an abstract and depersonalized slavery. In bemoaning "slavery's corruption" rather than confronting the complex relations with the black (m)other, Parsons can eliminate, or at least minimize, the constitutive role of black women in the creation of white identities. Parsons's concluding horrific image of cruelty, moreover, underscores his need to deny that black women, too, might act as bearers of a phallic power that would replace the white master's language. Before Parsons leaves, Mrs. A forces her house servant Sylvia to show Parsons how Mr. A cut off "her four toes on one foot, and two on the other" (160). Through this punitive dismemberment, Mr. A precludes Sylvia's ability to "run," but he also "neuters" these displacements of a possibly competitive phallic agency. At the end of Parsons's story, the reader is left to occupy in fantasy two contradictory positions at once: that of the voyeur titillated and appalled by the violence of plantation life but also that of the nervous white traveler who has not quite been reassured of his invulnerability to the signifying power of the black slave woman.

Parsons's account of Mr. A and his mammy reveals the psychodynamics of a reverse acculturation that Wilson would incorporate into *Our Nig*. In his introduction to Wilson's novel, Henry Louis Gates Jr. notes the "complex relationship" between the son James and Frado, a complex relation that has been frequently interpreted as Wilson's coding of white male sexual violence against black women (Johnson 97). But the "oddity" and the "violence" in this relation must be understood as giving narrative shape to the traumatic unconsciousness that Parsons's story divulges in the white imagination. This narrative cannot be divorced from the larger discourse about the enemy within the white middle-class domestic space. In contrast to Parsons's retreat into the abstraction of slavery's cruelty, Wilson writes the repressed scene of New England antiracism back into her "domestic" fiction. She writes a counterfactual history not just of racial discrimination in the North but of the everyday tactics by which the middle-class white body was being produced, and in turn seduced and recolonized, by the unacknowledged presence of figures such as Frado on the home front.

While at first it may seen that Wilson figures James as the great white "protector" who converts the docile and adoring slave to Christianity, Wilson complicates the putative surface meaning of the text by insisting on this man's invalidism. Almost all the Bellmont children—with the exception of the cruel daughter Mary, who serves as a mother surrogate—are plagued by debilitating yet unnamed illnesses that leave them bedridden and defenseless against Mrs. Bellmont's tyranny. The connection between invalidism and subjugation to the mother can be seen in Wilson's description of the Bellmont daughter Jane, whom Frado, at first, before the return of James, would have turned to for succor: "The invalid, Jane, would gladly befriend her; but she had not the strength to brave the iron will of her mother. Kind words and affectionate glances were the only expressions of sympathy she could safely indulge in" (37). In the symbolic dreamscape of Wilson's novel, the association of this invalidism with the powerlessness of the children to help Frado and of their infantile submission to the mother is obvious, with the Bellmont children's morbidity acting more as a psychological displacement of a crippling maternal conscience than the manifestation of a physical disease. This associative web among invalidism, maternal submission, and white passivity to racism comes into play in Frado's relation to James. Frado's relation to James is indeed an odd mixture of dependency and control, of erotic desire and maternal care, a pattern of conflicted interaction that we saw in Parsons's story of Mr. A. While ostensibly James is "to her a shelter" (67) and is a "dear, kind friend to her" (85) whom Frado wants to follow to the heavenly "home" (95), James is as much converted by Nig as she is brought to Christian enlightenment by him. The attraction, both brotherly and erotic, that James feels for this caretaker, the dark and kind (m)other in the home, causes him to rebel against and to find consolation from his own mother's abuses. Underneath the familiar story of the "slave's conversion" through the tutelage and finally death of the white savior, Wilson spins a story in which this very white savior must face the dividedness within his own "white identity" and defy the mother. Unlike his father, who insists that "his word became law" (31) but cannot "rule my own house" because "women rule the earth, and all in it" (44), James does intervene to help "our Nig."

While critics have frequently read Wilson's *Our Nig* according to the paradigm of slave narratives and have identified the novel's climax as Frado's defiance of Mrs. Bellmont's physical abuse, Frado's freedom and power arise not through her "escape" but through her remaining inside the home to challenge Mrs. Bellmont's influence over the domestic property of the white character. Although at the beginning of the novel Frado had hoped to find a "wild" space outside the home by running away and hiding in the swamp, she discovers that this segregation only fulfills the desire of Mr. Bellmont and white patriarchy. When Mrs. Bellmont strikes Frado once too often, Mr. Bellmont declares as the solution that Frado "would never come into the house again" (44). The arrival of James, however, marks a shift in Frado's response to Mrs. Bellmont's racist authority from self-segregation to subversion within the home. With the arrival of James, Frado discovers her own possible role as the molder and builder of the nation's character. In telling him of his mother's abuses, Frado does not mainly look to him for aid; she appeals to the suppressed nightmare within the antebellum middle-class imagination. Although James works to educate and to evangelize Frado and thus repeats a history of white patronage, Frado in turn wins the son's affection away from the mother and becomes the "home monitor" of his white character.

Throughout the novel, Wilson emphasizes the acceptance her heroine has won through her "prattle." While Wilson may seem to depict Frado as the comic pickaninny or the Topsy figure who wins white indulgence because she amuses her master's children with her mirth and mimicry, Frado's prattle acts as more than comic relief. It directly defies Mrs. Bellmont's authority and influences the men. "The men employed on the farm were always glad to hear her prattle; she was a great favorite with them" (37). Frado's stories tell a different truth from the white mother's, and this "prattle" wins the loyalty of the son. "Occasionally she would utter some funny thing for Jack's benefit, while she was waiting on the table, provoking a sharp look from his mother, or expulsion from the room" (53). When Frado finally exposes the fact that Mrs. Bellmont has prevented James from seeing his aunt, she replaces Mrs. Bellmont as the source of care, trust, and truth in her son's life. Although still seemingly the object of James's Christian pity, Frado becomes the black (m)other who wins James over to "slave speech," to a speech that speaks a different vernacular and also tells a different story from the mother's official narrative. "But after much entreaty, she told him all, much which had escaped his watchful ear. Poor James shut his eyes in silence, as if pained to forgetfulness by the recital" (84). In her description of James's response, Wilson pinpoints the panic that always lay as the affective underlife of maternal management. Bringing a different kind of witness that reveals what "escaped his watchful ear," Frado nudges him to "forgetfulness," a forgetfulness of maternal association. Such forgetfulness invokes the fear within antebellum maternal discourse that the child would lose remembrance of the maternal associations that were to constitute an organic part of his/her character. By overlaying the feared tale of the black domestic servant as possible seductress with one of maternal influence, Wilson underscores the complex panic about miscegenation on the home front, a miscegenation that would not just blur racial categories but would seduce the nation's leaders to "forget" the mother's influence.

Henry Louis Gates Jr. has accredited Wilson with bringing a new form to black literature. Yet she brings as well a new form to black female subjectivity. While the white children of Mrs. Bellmont can find freedom by lighting out for the territories and escaping west, such a narrative of flight into freedom is not applicable for the freed black woman. This freed black woman must find her space within the domestic scene, for flight would only be disempowerment and would not redistribute the property women own in whiteness, a domestic squatter's right in the molding and building of an American identity. Seeking an inclusion that is not pluralist but transformative, Wilson's heroine turns her everyday duties into a subversive opportunity to remake the national character and culture. In coding the panicked possibility of the black woman's formative influence in the story of James's invalidism and "forgetting" of maternal authority, Wilson, like William Wells Brown, restores the unconscious fears of antebellum culture. While antebellum conduct books and antislavery fiction both assumed that a man remains white at least as long as he remains in the home and under the watchful gaze of the "mother," Wilson divulges that the character of this place supposedly controlled by the white mother might in the next generation be "unmanned," reduced to invalidism, and seduced by the (m)other and her reverse acculturation.

2. MISCEGENATED WHITENESS

Rebecca Harding Davis, the "Civil-izing War," and "Female Racism"

In Rebecca Harding Davis's 1868 Civil War novel *Waiting for the Verdict*, the heroine, Rosalyn (Ross) Burley, tells her aristocratic Southern suitor, Garrick Randolph, that "I not only belonged by birth to the class which you place on par with your slaves, but I worked with them. I was one of them. I believe in my soul I am one of them now" (230). By having Ross Burley identify with the slaves, or claim to be "one of them," Davis names her protagonist's outcast status as a poor working-class heroine of illegitimate birth. But Rosalyn's statement that she is in her very soul the same suggests more than a commonality based on economic exploitation, oppression under patriarchy, or even existential isolation.[1] Davis's novel is organized around an extended comparison between the tragic mulatto John Broderip and the domestic angel Ross Burley. Through this equation of a revised "true womanhood" with the tragic mulatto, Davis relocates the traits of the tragic mulatto in the "white" heroine, thereby comprising an alternative cultural fantasy to the panic about reverse acculturation with its relation among women, race, and national identity. In making her protagonist "one of them," Davis enacts a telling metaphoric transference, one that amalgamates the body of the Reconstruction-era Republican Mother. This tactical reversal, this reenvisioning of the domestic heroine as a tragic mulatto of whiteness, suggests that Davis did not simply take the middle-class home or the marriage of the Northern Ross Burley with the Southern Garrick Randolph as a fictional

31

model for a reconstructed nation (Pfaelzer 159; S. Harris 135–36); rather, she sought to embody a dissenting representation to the nationalized and racialized Anglo-American identity which she saw unfolding within the pages of James T. Fields's *Atlantic Monthly*, in which Davis's two previous novels, *Life in the Iron Mills* and *Margaret Howth*, as well as fifteen short stories had been published.[2] In *Waiting for the Verdict*, Davis creates in Rosalyn Burley a liminal figure of whiteness, a figure who would function to renegotiate and "recivilize" the national body reconstructed within the Northern discourse on the War of Rebellion.

Although in the last chapter I argued that "mothering" is what helped sustain the racial cultivation of the bourgeois self linking capital and character, Davis's description of the Republican Mother's "racechange" (Gubar 11) between white and black complicates our understanding of the cultural work of nineteenth-century women's fiction as it has been described within recent revisionist literary and cultural histories. While literary historians such as Daniel Aaron have maintained that the Civil War remains unwritten by nineteenth-century American authors, such a generalization of the war's unrepresented history has recently been challenged as omitting the significant number of professional and amateur women writers who wrote about the conflict. As Elizabeth Young argues in *Disarming the Nation: Women's Writing and the American Civil War*, it was "[t]hrough the language of civil war, that 19th-century [women] writers thematize[d] new forms of individual and national identity," which allowed for possibilities of gender and sexual expression challenging received norms (20). In *Waiting for the Verdict*, Davis reveals that femininity and masculinity are unstable and mobile constructs during a civil war that blurred the boundaries between the battleground and the home front. But Davis also opens up the meaning of race and particularly whiteness in her fiction. While critics have tended to look for images of intermarriage or miscegenation between black and white men and women as a sign of a "redemptive transracial consciousness," these critics often focus too literally on actual mixed race unions or bodies rather than at the way race operated as a specific discursive strategy within a particular historical moment (Devere Brody 745). Davis's *Waiting for the Verdict* uses this discourse of amalgamation not just to promote interracial relations per se but also to refigure the national body of whiteness. In *Conjugal Union: The Body, the House, and the Black American*, Robert Reid Pharr elucidates how early African American writers sought to invent self-evident racial bodies, often within the prominent discourse of nineteenth-century domesticity, in order to legitimate a distinct literary and nationalist tradition (64). Davis's *Waiting for the Verdict* is less a novel awaiting the Reconstruction-era verdict on the "Negro question" than the literary reimagining of a different kind of self-evident white national body, a national body that did not rest on the same dissociative logic demanded by Davis's largely male New England counterparts.

This connection between women's fiction and historically produced performances of whiteness has often been omitted in revisionist histories of the "sentimental design." Critics of nineteenth-century women's fiction have left in place the "transparency" and "normality" of whiteness even as they have struggled to disclose how the ideology of domesticity often reinforced racial and class hierarchies while inviting readers to extend their sympathies across social divides. In "Manifest Domesticity," Amy Kaplan has shown the "shared racial underpinnings of domestic and imperialist discourse," as men and women were allies against foreign or racial others even as they were confined to separate public and private spheres of influence (584). Yet this explication of race neglects to examine how the meaning of "whiteness" or "Anglo-Saxonism" was itself contested. Even astute critical readings such as Kaplan's tend to begin with the assumption of a singular white racialized nationalism or imperialism, and sentimental authors are evaluated according to the extent to which they cooperated with or tapped into this stable and preexisting field of white racial discourse. But this moral and political argument "by complicity" ignores that, as Ruth Frankenberg has noted in *Displacing Whiteness*, whiteness is really a set of socially constructed locations that include one's identity, worldview, and unconscious desires, and all white women and men do not/did not occupy the same positions at all times toward all the different people of color (20). Recent revisionist histories tend to render whiteness, and its reputed manifest destiny, as a monolithic racial imagining rather than as a conflicted series of different positionalities. Thus the current interest in showing the link between domesticity and nation building, by the very way it poses the problem as a deconstruction of the separate spheres, trivializes the work of women, even as it attempts to claim a public role for a domestic or matriarchal influence. Again, the misleading question often asked is whether white women participated in the public arena of race, but that very initial framing of the investigation denies the alternative possibility that white women might have engaged in their own gendered forms of racial activity that did not correspond to or act in complicity with, as Vron Ware has argued, a racism that is by default seen as always public and masculine (289). In *Waiting for the Verdict*, Davis simultaneously works to oppose and overturn a particular regional and gender-based inscription of whiteness and to create a particular "feminized" and "amalgamated" version of white racial power that allows for an indeterminate white body.

In her study of the early years of the Boston-based *Atlantic Monthly*, Nancy Glazener contends that its contributors promoted a "philanthropic literary nationalism" that shaped the rise of realism. By teaching the higher form of realism, the *Atlantic* group sought to provide a cultural "reconstruction" for the South and West, not simply by imposing their own "high culture" on the nation but by providing bourgeois groups across the country a literary strategy for cultural hegemony that they could adapt to reflect their own interests. Through this tendency to equate their sectional identity and tastes with the national character, the Boston Brahmins thus were legitimating their own class-specific cultural authority (37–43). But to Glazener's reading of the emergence of realism within the *Atlantic*'s ambivalent project of stewardship and national self-imagining should be added the question of how much this attempt to elevate a sectional identity as a national identity depended on prevalent theories of race and on the construction of a stable white New England body that involved no borderland genealogies or indeterminate, deviant identifications.

In contrast to the *Atlantic Monthly*'s attempt to create a preexisting, stable, white New England body that could become the character of the reconstructed nation, Davis restores the complications of the border, allowing for whiteness to be a hybrid formation that both challenged the *Atlantic Monthly*'s race thinking yet also revealed itself as a construct that implemented its own set of repressions and exclusions. Popularizers of nineteenth-century Anglo-Saxonism tended to see "whiteness" as itself variegated, or fragmented, according to a hierarchically arranged set of distinct white races that corresponded to regional, national, and class distinctions. As a consequence, to the members of New England's intellectual elite, the individual could be both white and not white, a Southerner, for example, of Anglo-Saxon descent but also a barbarian "other" in need of civilization. Given such a genealogy of white racial variations, an Anglo-Saxon American could then also be a hybrid, one who amalgamated different class, regional, and national blood types (Jacobson 41–52). Within this hierarchy of variegated whiteness, Davis positioned herself as one who, as she repeatedly remarks in her retrospective memoir, *Bits of Gossip* (1904), lived on the "border." Most studies of whiteness within nineteenth-century American culture, from Toni Morrison's ground-breaking observations in *Playing in the Dark* to the seminal studies of David Roediger and Noel Ignatiev on working-class and immigrant cultures, have started with the assumption that "otherness," especially blackness, is necessary to the production and strategic practice of whiteness. Nineteenth-century U.S. citizens of European descent transferred the unwanted parts of themselves onto African Americans or recovered those lost parts of a fuller humanity under the new capitalist system by marking difference through a "black" presence. But patterns of othering were rarely so singular or so straightforward. What is striking in Davis's *Waiting for the Verdict* is her refusal to make a white identity visible for her readers by always distinguishing it from a primitive or preindustrial black "other." Ross Burley, a woman from the North with a Southern father, both is and is not "one of them." This is not to say that Davis's novel by any means allows for a true ethical engagement with the different types of identity performed by her black characters or to cover over the fact that she resorts at times to common racial stereotypes. But Davis's substitution of Ross Burley's bastard femininity and its hybrid domestic whiteness for the emergent New England nationalized character brings back into the frame of Davis's "realist" fiction a crossing of class, regional, and race borders, a crossing that was usually denied within the pages of the *Atlantic Monthly*'s commentary on the Civil War.

Davis's emphasis on questions of "race" and "blood" in her Civil War novel did not pass unnoticed by contemporary readers. In his scathing review in the *Nation*, Henry James called Davis's "clear-eyed realism" "distasteful" ("Waiting" 410), suggesting the uncomfortable sympathies and identifications into which she forced particularly her elite Northern white readership. In her critique of the novel for the *Standard*, the abolitionist Charlotte Forten more specifically pointed to the novel's obsession with the "body" of its main characters, seeing this concern for heredity as evidence of a lingering racism: "I would not do the author injustice," Forten wrote, "but it seems hardly possible to overstate her belief in the importance of 'blood,' 'Anglo-Saxon blood,' 'Negro blood,' 'the Burley blood,' 'the Randolph blood'" (qtd. in Pfaelzer 161). Although

Forten's observation that Davis's novel frequently addresses character as instinctive and natural to different races ignores the way that Davis invokes this ethnographic typology only in order to call it into question, her review highlights the centrality of the white question in Davis's novel, a question that most contemporary critics of the novel have overlooked in their focus on her representations of blackness or some ahistorical miscegenation.

During her correspondence with the New York–based *Galaxy*'s editors, F. P. and William Church, about serializing her novel *Waiting for the Verdict*, Davis urged them to create a "national magazine in which the current of thought in every section could find expression as thoroughly as that of New England does in the *Atlantic*" (qtd. in Ellery Sedgwick 77). While Davis sent her stories to the *Galaxy* in part to take advantage of their higher fees for contributors, as her letter indicates, she also viewed her association with the *Galaxy* as a step toward creating a "hybrid voice" representative of "every section" and speaking back to the hegemony of New England nationalism. Rebecca Harding Davis's relation with James Fields and the editors of the *Atlantic Monthly* has often been a matter of investigation among scholars of her work. Although Davis had a deep friendship with Annie and James Fields (whom she saw as her champions), as Jean Fagan Yellin documents in her study of Davis's *Margaret Howth; A Story of Today*, James Fields pushed Davis to curtail her social protest within sentimental optimism and to limit her character and themes along the conventional lines of "women's fiction" (203–19). That Davis's social outlook differed notably from her *Atlantic* publishers has been the starting point from which the work of recovering the implicit messages of her fiction has begun. But not only did Davis reveal in her writing an unsentimental portrayal of industrialization or female entrapment, she also disclosed an awareness of how the *Atlantic Monthly*'s reporting of the Civil War functioned in complex ways to implement nineteenth-century ideologies of race. Changing publishers permitted Davis to resist more readily the racial ideology tied to the romantic egotism of Boston's literary establishment. In her "civil-izing" war novel, *Waiting for the Verdict*, Davis transcodes the *Atlantic*'s "white racial" discourse, specifically writing back into the historical narrative what is left out of the monthly's interpretation of the war and interrupting her reader's self-imagining in terms of difference from the "black presence." As Davis later wrote about her life during the Civil War: "I lived, during three years of the war, on the border of West Virginia. Sectional pride or feeling never was so distinct or strong there as in New England or the lower Southern States. We occupied the place of Hawthorne's unfortunate man who saw both sides" (*Gossip* 109). It is from this borderland of a "white mulatto" who saw both sides—North and South, cultural elite and working class, and black and white—that Davis imagines a different American national identity, one based on a miscegenated whiteness. But it is a racial fantasy that, in the novel's moments of narrative crises about Margaret's longing for the sexual other, cannot finally countenance a crossing of racial borders that would compromise the white woman's sexual purity.

Speaking from the Border, Speaking Back to the *Atlantic Monthly*

Rebecca Harding Davis's disillusionment with the Concord Circle and its literary mouthpiece, the *Atlantic Monthly*, forms a large part of *Bits of Gossip*, published in 1904 during the last decade of her life. In her chapter "Boston in the 60s," Davis begins to explain her skepticism by noting the Brahmin leadership's geographical distance and egotistical disengagement from the wider affairs of the world: "That was the first peculiarity which struck an outsider in Emerson, Hawthorne, and the other members of the '*Atlantic*' coterie; that while they thought they were guiding the real world, they stood quite outside it, and never would see it as it was" (32–33). In part, Davis's critique is that of the realist chiding the impracticality of the transcendentalist or the romantic. But Davis's quarrel with the New England leadership, and more specifically the cultural elite associated with the *Atlantic Monthly*, was more than a matter of aesthetics. As Ellery Sedgwick notes in his study of the *Atlantic Monthly*'s first half century, this magazine founded by Francis Underwood in 1857 along with some of New England's most noted writers (Emerson, Holmes, Lowell, Stowe) believed that it ought to be the agent for propagating the moral and cultural values for the nation (6). Davis's criticism of the *Atlantic Monthly* circle is intimately linked with her own self-imagining as an outsider both drawn toward and resistant to the social and political values of this "new Athens." Indeed, throughout *Bits of Gossip*, Davis repeatedly emphasizes her particular ambivalence about a New England–authored American culture, an ambivalence expressed in her desire for a "border" or "amalgamated" consciousness set against the nationalized civilization of New England's "finest."[3]

Raised in Wheeling, West Virginia, after the age of six, having spent the first years of her life in Big Spring, Alabama, Davis was indeed, in terms of geography, an outsider to the *Atlantic Monthly*'s New England coterie. Yet Davis's persistence, even fifty years later, in naming herself as the woman from the backwoods, from the margins, or from the border, speaks of the significance of this location for her self-imagining. At the time of Davis's childhood, Wheeling was still part of Virginia and had only recently been chartered as a steel-manufacturing town standing along one of the leading thoroughfares for westward migration (Rose 2). Growing up in Wheeling, Davis would thus have seen herself as someone living within a borderland between East and West, North and South, between the old world of agriculture and the march of industrialism, between, as well, lawlessness and civility. Now Davis's self-fashioning of her world as "hybrid," as a space in-between, did not mean that she had freed herself from sectarian self-interest. By attempting personally to embrace a borderland consciousness, Davis works both to disrupt and destabilize various regional, class, and gender boundaries, while in the end conserving her position in a female-authored color line. As Samira Kawash has noted, the "real challenge" of hybridity needs to be to the category of subjectivity itself (50), but Davis does not want to make racial identities so much ethically untenable as to create a different kind of white subjectivity, one that would be more inclusive of outsiders but not one that would finally challenge the distinct sexual purity and racial difference of white women.

In Davis's *Bits of Gossip*, what we see is a recurrent pattern of imaginatively trespassing across racial categories so as to overturn New England's dominant performances of whiteness as "non-Southern," "non–middle class," or "nonblack," yet in the end a retreat toward reified racial boundaries when the slippage between civility and commonality threatens to reach the point of the white woman's corporal move toward actual miscegenation. We can see this pattern acted out in Davis's description of her first encounter with Ralph Waldo Emerson and in her later repudiation of the Concord sage's "romanticizing" of the Civil War. As is typical of Davis's memoir, she begins her story by emphasizing her marginality from the cultural center of New England: "I went to Concord a young woman from the backwoods, firm in the belief in Emerson" (42). Yet her illusions and her deference to this cultural authority soon disintegrate as she observes the intellectual remoteness and egotism of New England's cultural elite more closely. To connote her perception of sympathetic abandonment by the Brahmins, Davis resorts in a way parallel to her heroine Ross Burley in *Waiting for the Verdict* to racial tropes, specifically comparing herself to the fugitive slaves whom the New England leadership betrayed in the 1850 Great Compromise: "If Edison had been there, he [Emerson] would have been just as eager to wrench out of him the secret of electricity, or if it had been a freed slave, he would have compelled him to show the scars on his back and lay bare his rejoicing, ignorant, half-animal soul, and an hour later he would have forgotten that Edison or the negro or I were in the world" (42). The extreme antithesis of Davis's comparative self-imagining in this passage is significant: she is both allied with the epitome of nineteenth-century (white, male) genius, Edison, and the uncivilized, even savage, "half animal," fugitive slave, as if to suggest her own contradictory and divided identifications. In the sudden shift from metaphorical displacement to first person, Davis underscores that she sees herself as on par with the "slave." While certainly Davis's figuring of her situation as similar to the escaped slave trivializes differences and draws upon a nineteenth-century feminist rhetoric that equates racial and gender oppression, it is significant in terms of her own white and female identifications that she sees herself as so amalgamated between "white genius" and "black simplicity." This wedding of images finally complicates the minstrelsy of her black face, for it allows her to identify with both and yet neither, finally enunciating her position only as different from the representative New England man.

Similarly, in explaining her different views on the Civil War from those of her senior New England literary statesmen, Davis claims an outsider status that is then elaborated upon through her relation to racial and ethnic others. Once again Davis remarks, "I had just come up from the border where I had seen the actual war," but while the Bostonian establishment assumed the "War may be an armed angel with a mission," she realized that "the chances in it, well improved on both sides, for brutish men to grow more brutish, and for honorable gentlemen to degenerate into thieves and sots. . . . she [the war] has the personal habits of the slums" (34). By embodying war in the debasing and depraved habits of the fallen woman of the tenements, with her intrinsically soiled body, Davis brings into discussions of the war the questions of gender, class, nationality, and race that were all too often ignored in the *Atlantic Monthly*'s abstract moral pronouncements about national uplift. On the one hand, her metaphor is more than figurative, for it was the buying of German and Irish substitutes that allowed many of the New England elite to avoid the draft, and even Davis's own husband, Clarke, avoided service by paying for a foreign replacement. On the other hand, even as war causes the moral and cultural chaos associated by the New England elite with the "degenerate" life in the "slums," Davis feminizes the war itself, specifically substituting (in an analogous way to the draft dodgers) the dissolute ethnic or colored woman of the slums for a white lady liberty. While Davis could imagine herself as one with the slave, she could not, for fear of losing the authority of her maternal influence, occupy the same common space as the fallen or degenerate women of color.

To elaborate on Davis's negotiation of a subject position from which to speak as a white woman back to the white male establishment of Boston, I want to look more closely at one of the stories that Davis tells about her childhood in Wheeling. Among the town's residents that Davis writes about was an old impoverished woman, Knocky Luft, who waited as patiently as Penelope for the return of her son who lit out to the western territories to seek his fortune. It is this story of Knocky Luft that Davis later used as the germ of her short story "Out of the Sea," which appeared in the May 1865 edition of the *Atlantic Monthly*. As a preface to the "true" history of Knocky Luft in *Bits of Gossips*, Davis pictures the "Commons" where the widowed mother is forced to live, a filthy and poverty-stricken place that exists on the fringes of respectable society and of racial and ethnic boundaries: "The Commons was the plague spot of the village, a collection of wretched cabins tenanted by drunken free Negroes and Irish. Among its other horrors were goats and jimson weeds and a foul pond covered with yellow slime" (22). In contrast to Emerson's Boston Common that one can transcend to become a transparent eyeball, Davis's Commons is a space of disorder, depravity, filth, and, by implication, the "yellow slime" of mixing and miscegenation. Although Davis reveals some residual racism and xenophobia in this passage, its importance lies in her discursive linking of the "plague spot" as the opposite of domesticity. Knocky Luft must go to live in the Commons with Widdy Kate (and be so degraded) because she does not have a home and will not or cannot have such a home until her son, Jim, returns in "his charyut an' six" to deliver her. Although Davis's recollection is a trite sentimental tale of a mother's separation from her child, within this sentimental formula she displaces anxieties about the loss of identity and racial integrity. What prevents women (and here women in particular are the focus of Davis's ruminations) from degenerating into brutishness, into a world of possible racial amalgamation, is the home life. Knocky Luft is in many ways the repressed specter of the older woman—unwanted, homeless, infertile— that haunts and motivates many of Davis's fictional narratives. Although Davis sought to challenge the New England establishment's possessive investment in a particular formation of racial Anglo-Saxonism, or whiteness, she equally feared that this alternative site of resistance might itself become "common(s)," a miscegenated space blurring all distinctions between civility and commonality. In her reimagining of this childhood story for "Out of the Sea," Davis significantly omits any reference to interracial habitation. In fact, Davis emphasizes that the seaside town in which Old Phebe dwells is a "queer lonesome country . . . shut out from the world," and when an emigrant ship tries to land there, all "seven hundred and thirty souls" are lost in a seemingly preemptive shipwreck (140–41). If "Out of the Sea" omits the "plague spot of the village Commons," this absence was a concession to the sunny disposition of the *Atlantic Monthly*'s literary mandates but also an effacement within Davis's fiction of the panicked possibility that the unmarried or single woman, whether by choice or by the death of her husband, occupies no higher social space than the indigent or inebriate immigrant and African. Indeed, Knocky's abandonment signals the loss of a woman's very property in whiteness, a historical set of privileges, opportunities, rights, and exclusivity that set her apart from racial or ethnic others.

In her story of Knocky Luft, Davis gives us a direct glimpse of the paradox that would ground her imagining of a "reconstructed" national whiteness. While Davis wanted a whiteness that would allow for a boundary-crossing inclusiveness missing from the *Atlantic* coterie's imagined national community, her linking of this national whiteness to the grounding authority of feminine purity required a disavowal of female desire, particularly one that would result in actual miscegenation. To be of and speak from the "border" for Davis was to blur categories and overturn racial, regional, class, and gender hierarchies but also to erect new limits against the "common," a material and discursive site of boundary-lessness most clearly symbolized by the "yellow slime" of mixed housing and interracial sexuality. Just as the *Atlantic* group worked to ensure a national cultural leadership through formation of a particular kind of "white" citizen, Davis tries to set up a "white subjectivity" for the reconstructed nation-state. Although Davis, too, in the end, holds on to a fixed racial core of female whiteness, unlike her *Atlantic* "fathers," she sought to complicate the dissociative logic that she saw in New England's "hegemonic" national character.

During the 1860s, the *Atlantic Monthly*'s "civil-izing" war rhetoric functioned to construct a particular race-based national identity for U.S. citizens grounded in a particular privileged New England perspective. By concentrating on a short period in the *Atlantic*'s history, it is not my intent to deny shifts in the magazine's racial discourse but to focus on a crucial moment when its understanding of race was being remade. As Gail Bederman has argued about turn-of-the-century U.S. racial discourse, a rhetoric of crisis often functioned as a tactic to naturalize a preexisting identity that can be said to have fallen into "decline" (8). Through its particular war rhetoric that centered on the fate of the New England "character," the *Atlantic Monthly* sought to discover a manifested white racial subjectivity unfolded within past and current events of history. At mid-century, the idea of race was changing from a historical development of institutions to the progress of an innate and unique character defined through self-government (Horsman 41). As editor of the *Atlantic Monthly* from 1861 to 1871, James T. Fields demonstrated an entrepreneurial instinct for using intellectual and literary trends as a means of defining and shaping popular literary tastes. Among those emergent trends that the *Atlantic Monthly* would have the dubious distinction of helping to identify would be the shift toward a race-based sociology. In October 1866, for example, Fields's *Atlantic Monthly* would be among the first journals to publish Charles Sprague's "The Darwinian Theory" with its application of evolutionary ideas to the progress of societies (Ellery Sedgwick 100). During the debate over the Republican plan for Reconstruction, likewise, it was not uncommon for writers such as E. P. Whipple in the Fields-run *Atlantic Monthly* to borrow racial metaphors to contend that conciliation toward the South would "take America down a step in the zoological scale." During the years immediately before and after the Civil War, the *Atlantic Monthly* had begun to connect the development of societies to innate racial characters, and in its narrative of the "civil-izing" war's national crisis, it sought to lay out the ground for this "innate white character."

In its interpretation of the Civil War, the *Atlantic Monthly* picked up the discursive association between the challenge of slavery and the manifested racial character of the white Republic. Repeatedly, articles discussing the war tended to identify in the current national crisis the "birth," as they argued, of a new nation purified and united in its representative character. In his December 1864 essay entitled "We Are a Nation," John T. Trowbridge ignores, as did most of the *Atlantic*'s other writers, the immediate causes of the war, tending instead to see the battles as symptomatic of a larger historical progress in moral principles and individual growth. Claiming that the nation is in the "birth-throes of a new era," Trowbridge rhapsodizes, "Here at last, Humanity has flowered; here has blossomed a new race of men, capable of postponing persons to uses, and private preferences to public good, of subjecting its wildest passions to a sense of justice,—qualities so rare, that, when they are most strikingly manifested in us, foreign observers stand astonished and incredulous" (771). Building on the language of the march of civilization and liberty's westward progress from northern Europe to England and now to "America," Trowbridge proclaims that America is unfolding "a new Western race" (773). Here Trowbridge does not mean for us to take his trope of race as merely literal. Like many antebellum writers, Trowbridge deploys the language of "race" to designate any group of people whom he sees as having a coherent character, without specifically attributing this classification to a common culture or biological makeup as would leading race theorists such as Robert Knox. Yet it is nonetheless clear that for Trowbridge the Civil War is a contest about the inner development of an Anglo-Saxon character destined to be the embodiment of civilization: repeatedly he avers that the nation must realize its inherited capacity for the Anglo-Saxon values of "self-control" and "self-discipline." In the end, Trowbridge insists, the only danger of defeat could arise from "our own weakness, not from the enemy's strength" (774). In Trowbridge's story of the "nation," the war is reduced to an epiphenomenon, one whose outcome hinges upon the private moral character of the people rather than the effective marshaling of military strength, economic resources, or political leadership.

This figuration of the war as a character contest, one that will eventuate in the revitalization of the New England soul and thus the unfolding or development of the "New American" race, recurs in many of the *Atlantic*'s commentaries on the war. Although this discourse evolves through the various stages of the war, several key motifs are recurrent. From the earliest stages of the conflict, the *Atlantic* ran several unsigned articles declaring secession the beginning of a clash between Southern "Barbarism" and "Northern Civilization." In the appropriately titled "Barbarism and Civilization" (January 1861), for example, the unnamed *Atlantic* author argued that the "traceable lines of affinity" in history show progress as leading to the "invention" of the "American, the greatest novelty of all," and implied that the North needed to prove the superiority of its character against an already effeminate and dissipate South weakened by climate and slavery (52). Now this opposition between Northern self-discipline and Southern dissipation served as an important rhetorical strategy within many abolitionist texts, including Stowe's *Uncle Tom's Cabin*, but in picking up this structuring antithesis, the *Atlantic*, as did a number of other New England civic leaders, turned the war matters into less a question of the fate of slaves than a judgment on the "white" New Englanders' character. In July 1861 the *Atlantic* ran another article, "The Ordeal by Battle," decrying the barbarism of the South and calling for the North not to let the "Anglo-American race" revert back or degenerate from its democratic heights: "The Secessionists have suggested to us a fatal argument. 'The superior race must control the inferior.' Very well; if they insist on invoking the ordeal by battle to decide which is the superior, let it be so" (90). The early articles in the *Atlantic Monthly* on the war rarely mentioned the controversy over states' rights or even slavery. Situating the secession against seventeenth-century British history and the struggle over Cromwell's Commonwealth, they declared the rebellion a "religious war" for the soul of the New England (often read as an Anglo-American) "race": "The most truly religious thing that a man can do is to fight his way through habits and deficiencies back to the pure manlike elements of his nature, which are the ineffaceable traces of the Divine workmanship, and alone really worth fighting for" ("War and Literature" 680).

Given the *Atlantic* editors' propensity to construe the war as a purification of the New England "soul," it is not surprising that among the contributors to the monthly's deliberations would be Ralph Waldo Emerson, whose essay "American Civilization" appeared anonymously in April 1862. Like his contemporaries, Emerson proclaimed that the Southerners lived in a "semi-barbarous state" and argued that "Emancipation" should be less a matter of justice to the men and women under slavery than "the demand of civilization," for the war must cultivate a "new Man," "men of original perception and original action, who can open their eyes wider than to nationality, namely, to consideration of benefit to the human race, can act in the interest of civilization" (508–9). While Emerson's turn to racialized discourse in his later writing has commanded the attention of scholars such as Anita Haya Patterson (138–39), Emerson did not just transform his idealism into racial expressivism. Like many New Englanders, Emerson used his rhetorical condemnations against slavery as occasions in which to fashion a specific racialized performance of a white New England identity. In the process of witnessing the events of the Civil War, Emerson and the writers of the *Atlantic Monthly* sought to reinvent the white character, and his as well as theirs was a particularly race-centered antiracism.[4] In their discussions of the war, Emerson and the *Atlantic* coterie debated less the state of the war, or especially the conditions of the slave or freedman or freedwoman, than the need for the white character to prove its self-discipline and love for liberty. Comparing the war to the appearance of Moses before the Hebrews and to the advent of Jesus, Emerson contends that this holy war's outcome will similarly "carry forward races to new convictions, and elevate the rules of life." In summary, a civilization will be known "by the kind of man the country turns out" (506). Although Emerson tends to reify this white racial New England character as an abstract category, he, too, tends to praise the "civil-izing war" for its advancement of the nation's "racialized" New England character.

To write about the war for James Fields and the contributors to the *Atlantic Monthly* was to participate in the making of a "white" regional identity that would be nationalized as the "American" civilization. Yet the *Atlantic Monthly*'s connection of the war ordeal to racial development also involved a particular style of masculine performance. In arguing that the war was a stage in the evolutionary advance of an Anglo-American culture, writers such as E. E. Hale in the February 1864 issue likewise tied the war's eventual victory to the revitalization of "Northern" or "Anglo-American" manhood. As indicated by his very title, "Northern Invasion," Hale placed the Civil War, as did most of the *Atlantic Monthly* writers, in the long view of civilizations: New England's defeat of the Confederates would only be another historical recurrence of the Gothic defeat of the more "effeminate" and "overly refined" Greek and Roman cultures (245). What ensured this inevitable success would be no economic or political advantages that the North might have but simply the innate manly character of the Yankee: "The rigor of Northern climates produces, on the other hand, in the long run, hardy physical constitutions among men, with determined individuality of character" (245). The *Atlantic Monthly*'s editorials on the Civil War were thus finally racial discourses of hereditary masculine identity: a macho New England nationalism that had as its center the hard white body of male self-government and individualism. The outcome would not be just a federal union or the manumission of the slaves but the right of this white or Northern-based New England manhood to a national leadership claimed in terms of culture as well as politics. While not all of the *Atlantic Monthly*'s writings on the war shared this fantasy of race and manhood, it is important to retrieve this particular narrative of the war to understand Davis's own "civil-izing" war novel. In trying to claim a peculiar and self-contained white New England racial character, the *Atlantic Monthly*'s writers excluded any contradictory signs of indeterminacy and racial ambiguity. Theirs is a version of the Civil War that is a verdict on the white character, a verdict that Davis in her novel will give a different ending.

The Mulattoization of Whiteness

In the typical plot of nineteenth-century women's fiction, Nina Bayn has argued, a poor and friendless orphan struggles against abandonment and abuse—frequently with the help of other strong, unmarried women—to achieve domestic security (30). In *Waiting for the Verdict*, Davis reimagines this pattern of the typical sentimental female bildungsroman popularized by best-sellers such as Susan Warner's *A Wide Wide World* (1851) to trace out the character of events leading to the Civil War. To the suspense about the orphan daughter's achievement of maternal character in the face of villainous and dissolute suitors and guardians, Davis now adds a question about the indeterminate fate of the nation's white racial identity. Specifically in the novel's opening melodrama, Ross Burley, the illegitimate daughter of a deceased working-class Northern mother, Margaret Burley, and an aristocratic Southern seducer, James Strebling, must decide whether she will ally herself with her maternal or paternal lineage. After his legal wife's death, the Kentuckian Strebling returns to Philadelphia to reclaim the abandoned child of his youthful indiscretion, initiating a fight over the paternal control of the motherless child. In the altercation between Strebling and Ross Burley's grandfather over who will raise the orphan child, Davis echoes the Boston-based community's racial nationalism. Examining his illegitimate child, for example, Strebling declares with pride that she could be raised as a proper Southern lady because "[t]here are thoroughbred points in her. She will turn to the ease and delicacy of life as instinctively as a well-bred animal" (25). In refusing to let his granddaughter leave with her returned father, on the other hand, Joe Burley defends his possessiveness by insisting on the dominant force of her Northern white character: "But huckster or not, the gal's face is honest, an' the Burley's blood is clean. I'll keep it so" (24). In Rosalyn's choice at the end of this scene to identify with her absent mother's Northern blood, Davis appears to assimilate the racial logic reflected in the *Atlantic Monthly* editorials on the war: the Northern character seems superior to Southern dissipation, and Ross has chosen Northern self-discipline over Southern aristocratic ease and luxury. The orphan child has seemingly found a home.

But we should not fail to note the ways in which Davis complicates this familial battle on the home front and the racial hierarchies associated with its regional characters. When Rosalyn says that she will not be "made vile and tainted" by succumbing to the dissolute life of her father, this declaration of Northern independence means opting, as her father reminds her, for a life of commerce and labor that places her on the same level as the "Negro": "And you sit in the market! Selling herbs, and radishes—yes? My black people sit in the market" (11). Rosalyn's moment of identification with her Northern white ancestry, her Burley blood, is marked by a simultaneous forced recognition of the indeterminate boundary between whiteness and blackness. While Rosalyn has chosen to claim her Northern breeding, her homeless working-class status equally leaves her, like Knocky Luft, in a shared space with the freed slaves.

To Davis's readers, Ross's course of action would be clear, to deny any association with those whom Strebling spurns as "my black people" lest she surrender her affiliation with whiteness. As David Roediger and Noel Ignatiev have argued, whiteness in the antebellum era for the immigrant and the working class who could not claim Anglo-Saxonism by blood descent depended on a logic of differentiation or a refusal of association with the permanent slave or colored other (Ignatiev 112; Roediger, *Wages* 95). But Davis does not allow her heroine such a race privilege, insisting

instead on her labor alongside the freed slave in the marketplace of Philadelphia. Rather than affirming the Anglo-American moral character in
her prelude to the war, as the *Atlantic* had so determinedly mapped out,
Davis finally leaves Rosalyn's racial identity an ambiguous, fluctuating
matter: the daughter of a Northern mother and a Southern seducer, she
is a character who, against the admonitions of the *Atlantic*, cannot define
herself against the barbarous Southern race, for she carries their blood
within her; nor can she define herself against the African slaves or free
persons, for she explicitly concedes to life among them as a wage laborer,
or as George Fitzhugh argued in *Cannibals All*, to be a marketplace slave
without a master (25).[5] Rosalyn's mulattoization in *Waiting for the Verdict*
encompasses a variety of often contradictory imaginative possibilities,
whereby traditional class and regional boundaries are breached and yet
left tentatively in play as a residual legitimating logic.

Questions of blood and the question of whiteness function overtly in
Davis's fictional history of the Civil War and continue to be a defining
trope in her image of the Reconstruction-era Republican Mother, Ross
Burley. Yet even as Davis raises to the foreground the racial genealogy of
her heroine, she refuses to define this whiteness as a difference from the
novel's characters of color. While Ross initially feels a seemingly "natural
antipathy" to the "dirty yellow skin of the mulatto Sap (Broderip) [that]
made her sick" (10), Davis later indicates that it is this childish disgust
that is unnatural, as Ross becomes an abolitionist on the Underground
Railroad and comes to see her fate as parallel to the slave. In her study of
the Cult of True Womanhood in nineteenth-century American society,
Hazel Carby has argued that the middle-class white woman's glorified
piety, purity, submissiveness, and domesticity depended on the exclusion
of women of color who could not be expected to achieve this ideal image
of motherhood and female sexuality (*Reconstructing Womanhood* 26).
White female influence thus depended on the serviceability of the black
presence to stand in for the promiscuity and the exotic, earthly, and
aggressive character that the white woman could not own in herself.
Although Davis by no means accepted the equality between African and
Anglo-American women, and particularly as we will see in a moment, a
commonality between black and white women's sexuality, she complicates the differential logic on which whiteness grounded itself. Ross carries within her more than "one drop" of tainted blood from her "morally
black" mother and from her choice of "slave" labor in the marketplace,

and thus her background can make no claim to the middle-class true woman's supposed legacy of inborn domesticity. For Davis, the fate of the woman from the border in a society increasingly insisting on a race-based national character is similar to the mulatto passer: both are seeking access to the advantages of whiteness and struggling with the exclusions and denials that such a nomination demands.

Davis further underscores and presses this comparison between the bastard Republican Mother and the mulatto in the language she uses to describe Ross's possible marriage to Garrick Randolph. When Rosalyn tests the tolerance of her suitor by pointing to a poor child in the marketplace and asking if he can believe that "Bourbon blood" hides there, Garrick reproves her by saying that "coarse sights and sounds, such as her class know, leave marks which never wash away, Miss Burley. Vulgar training is the damned spot that will not out, whether you put its possessor in the White House or the Tuileries" (83). For her Southern suitor, the class aspirant, like the racial passer, cannot elude the determinants of her/his spotted heritage, the one or more drops of bad blood that she/he carries upon her/his body like the spots of Lady Macbeth that "will not out." In initially declining Garrick's proposal of marriage, Rosalyn likewise concedes to the Southern aristocrat's imagining of class in racial terms: "There is a fable that all men are born free and equal in this country. . . . It only needs for you and me to stand face to face to prove the baseness of this falsehood. Every man carries the stamp of his birth and breeding as plainly in his soul as on his face" (229). Against democratic equality, Davis discloses a social hierarchy defined by physiognomy, blood, and race, and thus Ross's story, like the mulatto John Broderip's story, unfolds as a matter of passing, of escaping out of or eluding the destiny of her birth.

But if Davis starts her novel with a dispute over the white character of the Republican Mother, unlike the contributors to Fields's *Atlantic Monthly*, she tries to recode whiteness as a miscegenated discourse that will bring together North and South, rich and poor, black and white, into a domestic union. By making the "bastard," working-class, part-Southern woman Ross Burley the Republican Mother, Davis allows for contaminations impermissible in the *Atlantic*'s body politic. Yet such a polluting of the national body is only possible for Davis through a spiritualizing of race, making it more a matter of ideology than genealogy, of proper identifications than hereditary antecedents. We see this disembodiment of race in Garrick's acceptance of Ross Burley. Although Ross tells Garrick that she is a hybrid on par with his slaves, he dismisses her confessions of a race-based impurity of character. Instead, he insists that her femininity is above history, society, and even biology. Refusing to deny her, Garrick in a key scene in the novel contends that whiteness is a matter of ideology and spirit rather than of biology: "There she was, without a name, a true, beautiful soul looking through a true, beautiful body, giving herself to him. She was that, but she was nothing more. There was neither name, nor lineage, nor kinsfolk to marry with his wife" (232). In declaring Rosalyn's soul transcendent of class, race, and region, Garrick articulates the novel's answer to the possible mulattoization of future Republican Mothers who come, like Davis, from the "border": the true soul of white folks does not necessarily descend from New England's Anglo-American elite, and indeed this whiteness can even be miscegenated as long as it consists of a transcorporeal identification with a particular style of femininity. This performance of femininity, which is enacted both in the domestic sphere and on the battlefront, is moreover not exclusive to any cultural group and is accessible, by imitation, even to black women. This possibility is embodied through Anny, the slave woman who was a "born housekeeper" (352) and who escapes during the confusion of the war to find her "husband," Nathan, and to establish a home. In seeking to reimagine whiteness, Davis pictures a racial identity defined more in relation to a set of attitudes and values than created through actual material acquisition; this imagined whiteness is a mobile and traveling subjectivity. As Davis's novel insists, Ross carried "home about with her" in the battlefield (85).[6] To borrow George Lipsitz's terminology, in *Waiting for the Verdict* Davis attempts to redefine whiteness for women not as a matter of blood or segregation but as a possessive investment in an identity, an identity that could serve as nonpecuniary property and that would afford its adherents upward mobility and influence, the power as a participant in the socializing mission of the nation (Lipsitz 2–3).

Now Davis's substitution of domesticity for masculine self-government as the acquirable, if not innate, characteristic of national whiteness makes the feminine household the primary means for the corporealization of that national whiteness. This intersection between the feminine home and the racial body is also evident in the crucial conversion of the Southerner Garrick Randolph under the influence of Ross's bastard yet still white character. While the *Atlantic Monthly* and Emerson argued that the barbarous Southern character ought to be brought under the sway of a nationalized Anglo-American self-discipline, Davis places the uplift of the white Southern race in the nurturing hands of the angel in the house. The novel's initial action sequence specifically invokes the *Atlantic Monthly*'s discourse on the unfolding of the superior white character through the ordeal by battle and yet gains power by overturning and resignifying this ideologically useful racial logic. In the early chapters of the novel, Davis relates the story of Garrick Randolph, the effeminate and bookish Southern scholar who agrees to cross the Kentucky borderland to deliver the secret message of an ambushed Union soldier. Repeatedly during Garrick's trek across enemy territory, Davis calls attention to the transformation that comes to Garrick through his ordeal by battle; for example, Garrick muses while surreptitiously crossing Confederate occupied territory about the hatching of his new self: "the shell was only breaking off which had crusted over him in the old college library, from which he had been dragged, and that a few more touches of the knife would bring all that was in him of good or ill to the light" (48). While Davis taps into the *Atlantic Monthly*'s war rhetoric, seeming to agree that the war would make the effete Garrick a new man awakened to his innate racial character, she also undermines the *Atlantic Monthly*'s narrative. Significantly, it is Garrick, rather than the narrator, who thinks that his courage will prove his racial or blood superiority, but his assumption is mocked as arrogance: "the impregnable conceit of the man, his steely confidence in himself and his race, never were so bare or shameless as in that moment" (48). During the last leg of Garrick's journey, as he flees from pursuing Confederate troops, moreover, it is Ross Burley who, disguised in a "ragged beard and hair" (50), takes command and leads a fainting Garrick.

To this gender reversal, Davis's *Waiting for the Verdict* adds a telling racial ambiguity. When Garrick first meets with the disguised Ross Burley and her Quaker companion, the Underground Railroad worker Abigail Blanchard, the women mistake the Southern gentleman for the mulatto who was to act as their driver in a planned escape. In this scene, Davis overlaps the New England leadership's narrative of recovered manhood with the abolitionist slave narrative and, by miscegenating discourses, marks the Kentuckian Garrick as brother to the fugitive slave, one who needs the aid of these abolitionist women to be freed. Both the fugitive slave and the Southern male are in need of a "matriarchal influence" to quicken them back to life: it is this battlefield domesticity, not the war itself, that makes Garrick a new man. Looking at Rosalyn, Garrick, we are told, reflects that "the girl's education had been different; where-ever her home might be, the air in it, he felt was electric with energy; it was but a focus from which opened fields of work— . . . There was no dormant unused power in her brain; her companions had been men and women who entered the world as thorough-blooded competitors once sprang on the green, springy turf in the grand old games, every natural strength severely trained" (55). In the domestic influence that Rosalyn carried "wherever," she seems to give "birth" to a new race of "thorough-blooded" competitors, and it is this education that brings Garrick to his proper "field of work," a field of work that will involve correcting the sins of his Southern fathers and his divided family.

One of the novel's most extended subplots involves the arrogant Garrick's attempt to undo the sins of his fathers, despite his earlier insistence on their "pure descent" (38), by locating his grandfather's missing will and confessing that it left the family estate to his uncle, James Strebling. Yet Garrick's discovery of his moral character through this repentant action involves his "imitation," just like the freed slave Anny, of Rosalyn's domesticated whiteness. In his altered behavior toward others, including the freed slaves, Garrick is said to be taking on and performing, as if living out the theatrical makeovers of his namesake, the famous eighteenth-century English actor David Garrick, the very "body" of his wife: "The very tones of his voice had somehow (we are told) a tang like those of Ross" (335), and he "returned forever to his true self" as he begins to act and think like his wife under her "influence over him" (332–33).[7] Just as Davis pictures Ross Burley's situation as homologous to the racial melodrama of the tragic mulatto; she makes the Southern barbarian the equivalent object, just like the freedwoman and freedman, of the domestic Northern woman's civilizing agency. Garrick does not become part of the emergent Anglo-American race at the end of the war (as the *Atlantic* prophesized) through his development of masculine self-reliance. Rather, he achieves his racial destiny through his surrender to the influence of his wife's whiteness. If the "civil-izing" War between the States was always a racial epiphenomenon or character contest, its leaders are, according to Davis, less the Captain Markles of the battlefield than the home managers of a feminizing influence. While Davis picks up the motif of "disciplinary intimacy" common to sentimental women's fiction, as described by Richard Brodhead and Lora Romero (Brodhead 18; Romero, chapter 1), her racial text is nevertheless set against the social and literary discourse on whiteness within the public, masculine narratives of the Civil War. Retrieving this historical moment and context in which Davis's Reconstruction novel is produced forces us to call into question the tendency just to read her novel as "manifest domesticity" or a novel in which sentimentality has inscribed within it the same abstracted and translocal masculine notion of racial imperialism.

Yet if whiteness is closely tied to a woman's nature in *Waiting for the Verdict*, Davis was also concerned about the proper training of this white feminine subjectivity, especially in regard to its sexuality; she needed to keep her heroine's association with the other in the realm of metaphor away from the actual commons, the space of miscegenation and fluid sexuality. If the specter of Knocky Luft's fate haunts many of Davis's tales of domesticity, it would be easy to read the secondary plot of the novel centered around the romantic relationship between Margaret Conrad and the mulatto John Broderip as a moral fable repudiating tabooed interraciality. But Davis does not so straightforwardly seek to protect white womanhood against black male aggression. In moments of narrative crises, what threatens to erupt on the surface of Davis's novel is precisely the fear that a woman's instincts may not lead her to fear the "broad rip," this tearing of the virgin territory of white womanhood. In the scene in which Margaret and John escape from the music conservatory during the party, Davis reveals the ambivalence of womanly "instincts":

So they stood side by side in the narrow, dim recess, with its shelving roof. The music had sunk to a low, intermittent sobbing, the unrest of some unhopeful pain. One could find in it the baffled moan of the sea, or the cry of an unloved woman. The man shivered before it like a reed in a cold wind.

Miss Conrad looked at the little figure beside her, at the sallow insignificant mask of a face. Something which looked out through it made her draw back with an undefined alarm. It was a power which she had seen beneath no other man's eyes.

He turned with quick suspicion. "Why do you avoid me, Miss Conrad? I was not Repulsive to you when you first knew me. Why do you fly from me?"

There was an involuntary movement, like a shiver of repugnance, through her slow, firm limbs. (124)

There are many ways that one might read this scene. In speaking of Margaret's "involuntary movement" and "undefined alarm," Davis hints at questions of natural antipathy between the races that were recurrent within the slavery and Reconstruction debate and questions whether such a repugnance is learned and whether it can be overcome (Fredrickson, *Arrogance* 165–97). Likewise, the language that Davis uses to describe the music ("baffled moan") suggests the sexual longing and possible consummation (at least in the shivering of the male reed) and provides an erotic reading of this scene grounded in romantic racist notions of black hypersexuality. Yet Davis's language is overtly contradictory and deconstructs itself, as she pictures John as both aggressively virile and yet "sallow," "insignificant," and "little." In reading this scene, I do not want to level her inconsistencies into a manageable racial statement. The scene is more interesting in the anxiety and affect that it divulges: fears about the influence of the black other on white femininity and the instability of the white racial self. In this scene of Margaret's repressed sexual longing for John Broderip, Davis reveals that both she and her character feared the undisciplined sexual body, for its transgressions, if allowed, would threaten to undo the racial fantasy of a "miscegenated" whiteness that structures the novel. While Davis allows her heroine to be of mixed white blood and even to be of illegitimate birth, the novel's plot suggests Davis always feared the degradation of this "domestic whiteness" into the "common," a chaotic world without boundaries. Davis wanted to ensure the purity and invulnerability of her heroine's investment in a whiteness that was free of sexual longing for an other whose erotic attraction might overpower her own influence.

In the following scene, we see how in Davis's fiction "miscegenation" must remain a gesture of sympathetic identification rather than an actual sexual union, as she reroutes rather than represses black male sexuality, mapping an itinerary within the "higher" realm of a spiritual boundary crossing. When John is back alone again in his room, we learn that he has purloined a number of Margaret's domestic articles—"scissors, thimble, all the fanciful little implements of a woman's sewing, even some half finished bits of embroidery which he had stolen once from Margaret's basket" (127). Playing with these fetishes, John remarks to himself that he had tried to "counterfeit her presence through these things" (127). Although John is not permitted in *Waiting for the Verdict* to possess the body of the white woman (nor she his), he does transfer this forbidden desire to her domestic articles. In a key narrative tactic, Davis argues that the black man may learn to love the white woman's counterfeit presence, the domesticity tied to her highest racial embodiment. Rather than decrying or repressing black sexuality in her novel, Davis reroutes and channels it toward the white woman's metonymic signs. While John cannot possess Margaret physically, he can "know" her counterfeit presence and aspire to the transcorporeal "miscegenated whiteness." Later in the novel, John similarly sublimates his disappointed love for Margaret into a mosaic embrace of his people. We read, "He thought that Miss Conrad thought his coming work as noble a one as did her father" (317) because he had answered the higher calling "to be the leader of a great people out of slavery; out of the ignorance in which they've been bound" (316). For Davis, literal miscegenation must undergo a transference away from the corporal body of the domestic angel to her ethereal ideals.

Although throughout *Waiting for the Verdict* Davis can flirt with a white femininity that transgresses racialized boundaries (whether of region, class, or actual race), her novel, in the end, fears the body of her heroine will become "common." Margaret can love John and challenge taboos, but she cannot forfeit the sexual purity upon which the potency of a feminized national whiteness rests. Instead, she must use her higher character to discipline the body of the freed slave as well as the Southern rebel toward domestic ideals and toward the white racial family constituted through the domestic angel's influence. There is an ambivalence in Davis's challenge to the *Atlantic* group's habits of othering. While Davis, in her depiction of Ross, Garrick, and even now Margaret, repudiates the logic that would have defined whiteness as difference and as a property that could only be owned by so-called white people, she could not countenance the literal embodiment of her more inclusive national community of miscegenated whiteness. Even in the realm of fiction, she could not allow for white women to lose the domestic distinctiveness that keeps them away from the commons, and she preserves their sexual purity. While Davis renegotiates ideological and institutional forms of gender normativity, she could not, in the end, resist social and political controls on female sexuality. Gender was a separate site of oppression from a supposedly natural female sexuality. Davis's miscegenated Republican Mother is finally a desexualized one, and her boundary crossing must be sanitized and transformed into something other than a tabooed attraction to the racial other. However, in moments of narrative crises, as we have seen in the conversation between John and Margaret, a tabooed interracial sexuality threatens to return to disrupt Davis's racialized domestic woman's purity, and Davis finally has to erase this climactic narrative possibility by having John slain during the war. Davis's *Waiting for the Verdict* is a novel that tries to refashion a white "American" nationalism around the "miscegenated" Republican Mother's inner domesticity and transcendent purity, but such a new imagined community must first remove the specter of racial intermarriage as an external threat and then remove the inner threat of a white woman's own fluid and volatile sexual nature.

By continually blaming transgressions of the sexual color line on black women, especially, Davis can reassure her white sentimental readers, male and female, of their natural propensity toward whiteness. Although Davis locates the skepticism about the black woman's virtue in the voices of her minor characters, her fiction never sufficiently allows the black woman to repudiate the charges against her character. Thus while the devoted Anny travels desperately to be reunited with her husband, Nathan, a journey that proves the black woman can embody the domestic ideals of true womanhood, the men in the camps only sneer at Anny's indecency: "Is there no shame or decency left among this people? I believe that virtue is a thing unknown to an African woman!" (280). In response, Davis pictures Anny as unable to comprehend the captain's accusation: Anny "looked at him, bewildered, trying to read his meaning." Davis's unwillingness to let the black woman fully deny the constitution of her carnal body within the white imagination is seen even more clearly at the end. Although Davis allows that Anny can be a "born housekeeper," Anny must assure the readers that there is no danger of actual miscegenation if she is incorporated within the new republican nation: "Dar's no danger of many marriages . . . an' as for mixin' de blood, it's been the fault ob de whites when dat eber was done. Dar'll be less of it when cullored women is larned to respect themselves. O, Missus! Dat talk of marryin' is sech a fur-off shadder!" (355). While Anny speaks out against the faults of whites, she still has internalized the dominant representation of African American womanhood, implying that the crimes of the white slave master were due in part to the carnality of black women. Anny's consent to the idea of black women as fallen women obfuscates and covers up the violence rendered against slave women. By having Anny assure readers that black women will self-segregate from white folks, Davis ends her novel assuring readers that there is little chance of intermarriage. In Anny's self-abnegation, like Hobomok's at the end of Lydia Maria Child's earlier sentimental novel, *Hobomok*, Davis thus preserves the superior transcendent purity of the new "miscegenated Republican Mother."

Yet such an imagining of the white mother's sexual purity involves literally a narrative gap in Davis's novel that discloses the self-contradiction within her racial views. As critics have noted, none of the major characters in the novel have surviving or known mothers (Pfaelzer 163), and John's mother's whiteness, upon which his whole identity as a tragic mulatto descends, is never explained. While we do not know how John obtained his white blood, this whiteness is what the other heroic protagonists in the novel recognize within him. Thus when Captain Markle confronts John over their rivalrous love for Margaret, Markle is said to feel the instinctive mysterious sympathy of race: there "came secretly that healthy sense of satisfaction with which two finely tempered blades strike each other, or one man of the true blood recognizes another, by the masonry of a glance, even in his enemy" (288). Similarly, Davis makes Ross a mulatto whose domesticated whiteness depends on an absent motherly inheritance, which causes all who are influenced by her to feel something akin to the spontaneous sympathies of race. While both of Davis's "mulatto" protagonists' whiteness depends on their maternal lineage, Davis cannot write into her novel these mother's stories because such a representation would simultaneously expose the white woman's sexual immorality, and her vulnerability to the power of the other, with his/her sexual allure and possible reverse acculturation.

While Davis's narrative in *Waiting for the Verdict* developed contemporaneously with an emergent discourse on the manifest destiny of Northern Anglo-Americanness in the Civil War, her narrative of domesticated whiteness is separate from and seeks to inhabit a different sphere from the *Atlantic*'s public and masculine discourse of nation building while attempting to construct a female subjectivity that denies "race" specificity (opening it up to a variety of regions, classes, and races) yet needs the discourse of racial transcendence in order to confer value and potency to female influence. We need to open up our understanding of race within nineteenth-century women's fiction; we need to ask not simply if women crossed the domestic threshold to become agents of imperialism and racism but to investigate whether they, in staying in their separate sphere of feminine influence, constructed ambivalently alternative cultural practices regarding the soul and character of white folks. The verdict that

Davis awaits in her novel is not only the fate of African Americans under Reconstruction but also of an emergent miscegenated white race. Yet her silence about interracial sexuality among white women finally prevented her from completely pushing the nation toward a third space of truly open borders.

3. "CORPOREAL SUSPICION"

*The Missing Crimes of Neoabolitionist Rape Culture in
Pauline Hopkins's Detective Histories*

In the climactic scene of *Hagar's Daughter*, Pauline Hopkins's serialized novel for the *Colored American Magazine* (1901–2), the former slave Aunt Henny testifies in court that General Benson of the U.S. Treasury Department is really an imposter. Although he may appear "civilized," she informs the court, he is really the cruel slave master St. Clair Ellis whom she nursed and raised and who has now, twenty years later, killed his secretary and mistress, Miss Bradford: "He ain't Gin'ral Benson no more'n I'm a white 'ooman. . . . Ise got a scar on me jedge, where dat imp ob de debbil hit me wid a block ob wood when he warn't but seven years ol'" (256). Against the power of the white patriarchal government, Hopkins in this telling scene places the voice and traumatic memory of the slave woman. While the police could not detect the brute beneath the general's masquerade of civility, Aunt Henny knows, as surely as she says she knows herself as a black woman, the criminal character disguised by the general's gentlemanly impersonation. This scene is a symptomatic moment in Hopkins's fiction, one that comments upon her own writerly situation, her political objectives, and the textual strategies in her fiction. While Aunt Henny's witness clearly puts in tension the contending forces of institutionalized racist power and the protest of the black woman, her testimony regarding the specific crime of General Benson against women (Bradford, Hagar, and herself) also arouses a "corporeal suspicion" about the unverifiability of the "white" social character and the visibility of racial identity.[1] Moreover, just as it is the oppositional gaze of Aunt Henny that brings to light what the social order could not detect within its own midst, the culpable public official, it is also Aunt Henny here who attests to the missing everyday crimes of whiteness against women, crimes that reveal the villain to be not just the obvious white supremacist but also the self-avowed neoabolitionist.

In her study of the disruptive horror of the "monster" in Gothic fiction, Judith Halberstam has argued that the grotesque criminals of sensational fiction raise questions about boundaries and their dissolution, particularly the boundaries regulating the normative body. Speaking of "postmodern monsters," Halberstam writes, they are "no longer the hideous other[s] storming the gates of the human citadel. . . . Monsters in postmodernism are already inside—the house, the body, the head, the skin, the nation—and they work their way out. Accordingly, it is the human facade of the normal, that tends to become the place of terror in postmodern Gothic" (162). Although Pauline Hopkins's *Hagar's Daughter* draws upon the generic codes of detective rather than Gothic fiction, her "polyvocality" (Ammons 211) similarly unsettles the boundaries separating the innocent and normative white neoabolitionist body from the monster. While Aunt Henny's testimony discloses the killer already roaming undetected at the heart of the nation's capital, Benson's criminality is finally no different from the innocence of the turn-of-the-century neoabolitionist. After Aunt Henny's testimony, it is revealed that General Benson is really the brother of the detective Henson, and both were former slave owners. By making the hero and villain literally blood relations, *Hagar's Daughter* blurs the boundaries between the while male villain and the white male savior. Thus *Hagar's Daughter* plots out a detective history in which all white folks are implicated in the crime, not only the crime against Miss Bradford but also the missing everyday crimes of a patriarchal whiteness that prescripted it.

The crime that Hopkins puts on trial in *Hagar's Daughter* is less any one specific misdeed, whether the murder of Bradford or the assault on Hagar, than a rape culture perpetuated through an undetected misogynistic whiteness. In "Fighting Bodies, Fighting Words: A Theory and Politics of Rape Prevention," Sharon Marcus has argued that since rape functions as part of the "process of sexist gendering" (391), or a way that a patriarchal culture tries to socialize gender identity in men and women, the prevention of rape must involve the disrupting of society's "rape script" that creates the potential role of rapist and rape victim. By connecting the pre–Civil War violation of Hagar with the murder of post-Reconstruction women, Hopkins's novel reveals that the common ground linking the crimes in the past and in the present is St. Clair/Benson's abuse of women. In writing a detective history to indict rape culture, Hopkins discloses that crimes against women, both white and black women, will be stopped not through the punishing of individual malefactors but only by the eradication of a norm of racial masculinity that defines itself through violence against women. Similarly, in her writing on critical legal theory, Moira Gatens has argued against the courts' tendency to treat the criminal as an aberrant individual, a lone monster and thus the sole bearer of responsibility, for such a habitual stance obscures and leaves unchallenged the larger structural cruelties in the system that encourage and give birth to the "criminal" (40–42). In *Hagar's Daughter*, Hopkins attempts to locate an antiracist strategy that goes beyond the initial step of criminalizing individual acts of white supremacism in order to expose and to alter the linked texts of whiteness and masculinity in a turn-of-the-century rape culture (see Gilroy 46).

In her essays for the *Colored American Magazine* and in her serial novels, Pauline Hopkins repeatedly suggests that in post-Reconstruction America, the nation has become a crime scene: first a site of lynchings, of disenfranchisement, of segregation, and of a peonage laws but second also a capital of missing crimes, of a misogyny and structural racism that are not persecuted, indeed not even detected as crimes, until white folks are forced to recognize themselves in the call from the margins. In *Hagar's Daughter*, Hopkins wants to indict the larger social discourse of whiteness, especially among the Boston-based New England heirs of the antislavery tradition. Hopkins's text positions these white readers so that they must confront their shared racial investment in supposedly unrepresentative hate crimes, and it puts on trial the larger process of racial gendering with which these crimes cooperate. Particularly by creating moments of boundary crisis when white readers must see themselves in the alienating gaze of the black female other, Hopkins's *Hagar's Daughter* forces Boston's neoabolitionist heirs to see how their idealized racial identifications are themselves the culprit perpetuating racism and misogyny. In *Hagar's Daughter*, racism and antiracism descend from the same family history.

Reabolitionizing Whiteness

In the article "Recent Developments in the 'Land of the Free'" for the *Colored American Magazine* (August 1902), Charleea H. Williams eschews a close historical or economic analysis of the race problem in favor of a disclosure, after careful investigation, of the "body" of the criminal. Examining several recent incidents of race violence—a mob riot in New Madrid, Missouri, in which a group of eight or ten white youths attacked a troop of black musicians, and a lynching in Washington, North Carolina, of nineteen-year-old James Walker for reputedly poisoning a family—Williams finds evidence of what she calls a "hereditary white outlawry." While Williams expresses her indignation at the heinousness of these "massacres," she attributes the motivating causes of these crimes to the "produced characteristics" of "inheritance and home education" within white folks. As a result of a history of slavery, the character of Southern white people has undergone, although Williams rarely states the outcomes so baldly, a degeneration and reversion to barbarism.

> These produced characteristics,—which were transmitted and educated into the children of that white people from generation to generation during that long period of slavery, until they became fixed and established characteristics in very large numbers of that people—are now to be found among them in all the walks of life, from the United States Senate down to the most humble occupation, followed by those of the white race—found among politicians and professing Christians. There are, however, many among that people who, it is probable, because of a far better inheritance and home education, even in those dark centuries, escaped the damaging characteristics. (285)

Although Williams is careful to allow for exceptions to the natural law of blood and heredity, she traces current racial incidents to the transmission of white racial characteristics down generations of Southerners. In speaking of such a hereditary character for white folks, Williams offers a tactical reversal of the biologically based arguments for the inferiority and depravity of blacks, such as Frederick Hoffman's 1896 work, *Race Traits and Tendencies of the American Negro*. During the 1890s, social scientists, including E. A. Ross, one of the founders of modern sociology, borrowed heavily from Darwinian-based theories of evolution and heredity to explain and legitimate national and class differences and to validate Anglo-Saxon supremacy. Despite the immediate causes that might incite Southern whites to violence, Williams contends, the germ of such prejudicial action resides in the innate character of whites. The history of slavery has literally been reembodied as heredity, and no whites, regardless of class, are immune to the taint of this possible one drop of selfishness. Just as General Benson in Hopkins's *Hagar's Daughter* passed among the Washington elite, William warns there are degenerate aristocratic whites slipping undetected into the U.S. Senate.

Williams's repeated use of the argument of hereditary outlawry in the "Recent Developments in the 'Land of the Free'" resituates turn-of-the-century discrimination and injustices within the character of whites.[2] While we might today find her preservation of racial distinctions, even as she reverses hierarchies, ethically problematic, Williams significantly turns the discussion of turn-of-the-century race relations back onto the analysis of the white character in ways reminiscent of the plots of Hopkins's fiction. In many Southern whites, Williams implies, lies, to borrow the subtitle to *Of One Blood*, a "hidden self," a habitual unconscious propensity to violence that she names collectively as barbarism. Trying to explain the New Madrid lynching, Williams writes, "That terrible inheritance and an education from the centuries of slavery has so often demanded the lives of a number of innocent Negroes. . . . It seems to have become the practice under the unwritten laws, become a prevailing habit permitted by that Controlling Influence which rules" (287). Left unchecked, as Williams notes near the end of her article, such "barbarism" will "continue[] to cultivate and strengthen those inherited characteristics in the children and youth and many mature people" (292). To fight racial violence and injustice, as a consequence, demands exposing the "hidden self" of passing whites among the controlling powers, lest, if biological determinism is left to take its course, a "continued education" in the "direction" of savagery "eventually result in a general race war" (293). For Charleea Williams and for many other writers of the *Colored American Magazine*, the end of racism hinges on the reformation of the white character, whether by education, by legal action, or by an exposure that will cause an unfixing of white's privileged self-possession.

Hopkins's writing for the Boston-based *Colored American Magazine* has frequently been the launching point from which to begin investigations of her fiction (Carby, *Reconstructing Womanhood* 121). The facts of her association with the magazine founded in 1900 by Walter W. Wallace, a Virginian who moved to Boston to work as a drugstore prescription clerk, are now fairly well known. Initially appointed as editor of the women's section, Hopkins soon became a main contributor, often writing under pseudonyms like Alan Pinkerton, the founder of the famous detective agency, to disguise the extent of her authorship. In February of 1903 her name appeared for one month on the masthead as the editor, and it has been speculated that she served as the editor as well as feature writer during the magazine's last two years in Boston. With the subsidization of the magazine by Booker T. Washington in 1904 and the appointment of Fred Moore as editor, however, the magazine relocated its publishing headquarters from Boston to New York, and Hopkins (most likely because her politics differed from the accommodationist gradualism of the magazine's new financial backer) ended her association with the journal (Bullock 106–9). But this history omits the magazine's complicated relation to white patrons and readers despite the desire to be black owned and operated. Although Wallace started the magazine by forming the Colored Cooperative Publishing Company to solicit subscriptions, he soon ran into financial difficulty. Despite efforts to win advertisers, his success with A&P, Doubleday, and Century Manufacturing never covered costs. At the end of the first year, as a consequence, Wallace reorganized the *Colored American Magazine* with the support of the older established residents of Boston, such as William Dupree, an administrator in the postal service who had fought in the Fifty-fourth, the Massachusetts regiment of African American volunteers. At the same time, Wallace and his associates brought in R. S. Elliott, a white man who previously worked for Lothrop, Lee and Shepard publishing firm to help produce the magazine. It is not insignificant that Hopkins's *Hagar's Daughter* began to be serialized in March 1901, a month after the reorganization of the *Colored American Magazine* under white patronage, and that it was Elliott who encouraged Wallace to publish novels, starting with Hopkins's *Contending Forces*. In the early years as the magazine struggled for survival, the *Colored American Magazine*'s editors looked to the abolitionist descendants of Boston for a renewed alliance to speak out against racial injustice and to support black self-expression. And it was these same white patrons who encouraged the editors to keep themselves afloat by publishing popular fictions such as those that Hopkins would subsequently write.

In 1903 Francis Garrison, one of the three sons of the famous abolitionist leader William Lloyd Garrison, remarked that "Father's belief that the new generation of whites would materially differ from the old, since they would no longer have slavery to tie to, proved too optimistic" (qtd. in

McPherson 373). In this candid reflection, Garrison confesses that many of the heirs of the New England antislavery tradition had failed to live up to their parents' antiracist commitment to justice and equality. In his extensive study of the generation of neoabolitionists, James McPherson has argued that the sons and daughters of the earlier antislavery leaders shifted in their outlook on the "race question," moving through a cycle from pessimism and apathy to optimistic (Washingtonian) gradualism to a revival of militancy with their efforts to found the National Association for the Advancement of Colored People (NAACP) (299). However, at the turn of the century, as their attention increasingly shifted to the issue of immigration restriction rather than antiblack violence, neoabolitionists became increasingly attracted to racialist theories of human character. As Mark Schneider notes, many neoabolitionists who had once believed in the "ability of America to assimilate its immigrants, now began to argue that in fact, 'races' had distinct hereditary traits, and therefore immigration of inferior races should be limited" (21). The "race question" for turn-of-the-century New Englanders referred as much to the decline of the older "Anglo-Saxon race" as to the problems of the color line, and this fear of their own degeneration was intertwined with their response (or often indifference) to current racial prejudice and violence at home and in the South.

There were several shifts within the turn-of-the-century discourse of neoabolitionism that Hopkins, like Charleea Williams, would work to interrupt in her journalistic pieces and serial novels. Increasingly, the heirs of Garrison were rewriting the meaning of "abolitionism" to empty it of its association with the specific fight for equality and justice for African Americans. Historical reminiscences and accounts of the abolitionist movement at the first part of the twentieth century tended to de-racialize Garrison's achievement and motivation and to reenvision him as an "abstracted" man of principle. In his re-creation of Garrison as a latter-day Thoreau, for instance, Ernest Crosby in the 1905 *Garrison, the Nonresistant* praises Garrison as a man who based his message on "abstract morality" as opposed to "man-made" or constitutional law and as one who had an "objective adherence" to "absolute truth" (134). While certainly Garrison did challenge constitutional legitimacy, Crosby makes no reference to the fight against racism or to African Americans. Instead, abolitionism becomes itself an abstracted signifier, the marker of a former New England (and Anglo-American) greatness and of an uncorrupted and uncompromised morality. But this morality, despite its selfless devotion to higher causes, has no specific concern for the lived reality of the freed slaves (indeed, they are not even mentioned) or for empowering the agency of the other. Omitting the contributions of African Americans who worked in the abolitionist movement with Garrison, Crosby even erases their presence as the actual subjects of Garrison's movement. Abolitionism comes to stand for a decontextualized and disembodied sense of justice, one whose moral urgency can be rechanneled for other causes, particularly the shoring up of a white racial difference in the abandonment of the fight against racism. As the journalist Ray Stannard Baker observed in his series of articles investigating the state of race relations in half a dozen Northern cities that was later published as *Following the Color Line* (1905), the "better class" of people in Boston had withdrawn from the "race question." Imagining what Bostonians would say, Baker writes, "We have helped the Negro to liberty; we have helped to educate him; we have encouraged him to stand on his own feet. Now let's see what he can do for himself" (228).

In his account of his grandfather for the Christian Fellowship newspaper, *World Tomorrow*, Oswald Garrison Villard similarly seems to reify abolitionism to a position or a standpoint of higher morality for New Englanders to claim their own hereditary leadership rather than a battle for racial justice. Such a neoabolitionist stand does not demand a real ethical engagement with the other. Like Crosby, Villard recalls fondly the abolitionist conflict as the last "good" war, which was "thrilling as the greatest of moral wars in America" (56). When speaking specifically of Garrison's achievements, he likewise divorces the work of the abolitionist from the struggle for freedom and justice for African American citizens. Everyone admired Garrison, he writes, because "[t]hey soon saw that there was no personal animus, no sense of personal wrong save that which Jesus Himself might have felt at the wronging of one of His fellow human beings. It was the sense of impersonal justice which was the mainspring of it all" (56). Once again, in Villard's account of his famous forbearer there is no reference to black people. Not only does he omit the participation of African Americans, but he fails to acknowledge them even as the object of his grandfather's sympathy or anger. Justice for Garrison was "impersonal" and decontextualized, above persons and above race. It demands no recognition of the call from the margins or cooperation with people of color. In their stories of Garrison, the next generation of neoabolitionists abandoned the question of race so as to figure Garrison as the subject of a contemporary conservative historical consciousness: he is the man of higher moral character not of radical activism; his principles stand in for absolutism against moral chaos, but he is no longer the firebrand and the freedom fighter who might really understand and speak for an African American audience.

In its monthly sketches of famous abolitionists from the heroic past during its first years of publication, the *Colored American Magazine* worked to call New England society back to its fading antislavery tradition. To the *Colored American* writers, Boston's white establishment had not just turned their attention away from the worsening racial oppression in the South to concentrate on their own declining influence at home; rather, prompted by immigration, labor unrest, and the growth of corporate trusts, they had become absorbed in their own ethnic and class distinctions. In his article "Reminiscences of the Life of Harriet Beecher Stowe and Her Family," as a consequence, C. Grant Williams makes a direct appeal for the renewal of the heroic battles of the past: "Today the old battle of the abolitionists must be fought over again on the question of disenfranchisement; happily, we hope, without the horrors of war if only the American people will be persuaded to be just toward a weaker race" (127). As his language makes clear, Williams hoped to elicit the Boston community's collective memory of a heroic past that could only motivate them to fairness and justice. In her own writing about antebellum abolitionist leaders, Hopkins reveals that she, too, shared Williams's urgency in raising the consciousness of the heirs of Boston's famous women and men. In an article entitled "Whittier, the Friend of the Negro," for example, Hopkins concludes her history with a jeremiadic appeal: "We, of this generation, cannot realize the difficulty and dangers encountered by the men identified with the antislavery struggle. Many of these men were poor or had sacrificed their fortune to their principle" (330). By comparing the leaders of the past to the present in the fight to end racism, Hopkins works to arouse in the younger generation a shame about their rewriting of abolitionism as a sign of their moral, and concomitant hereditary, superiority.

Yet if abolitionism was retrospectively being rewritten as a neoabolitionism conferring hereditary genius, this refashioning signaled a crisis within the meaning of Anglo-Saxonism and whiteness among many New Englanders as they were forced to confront the inundation of "ethnic" minorities. In its discussion of the "white problem," the *Colored American Magazine* appealed to this instability in what Matthew Frye Jacobson has called "variegated whiteness" (52), or a whiteness divided into various subracial categories that were frequently coterminous with ethnicity, class, or region. In such a complicated racial hierarchy, an Irish, Italian, or Jewish immigrant could be white and yet nonwhite in comparison with New England's Anglo-Saxon ruling elite. While various members of the native-born Protestant Anglo-Saxon elite turned to hereditary character, one now equated with an abolitionist legacy, to shore up class distinctions and their privileged leadership, the *Colored American Magazine* used this race language to point out that whiteness itself was in a flux. The *Colored American Magazine* emphasized in its articles that whiteness had been pushed into a state of contestation, as southern European immigrants, the Irish, and Russian Jews were challenging and changing what it meant to be white.[3]

Along with its struggle to recover a race history as the basis of a black consciousness, the *Colored American Magazine* sought to repudiate whiteness as a monolithic and stable social entity. In "Queen Victoria—The Friend of the Negro" (March 1901), comparing British and American racial attitudes (a theme prevalent in Hopkins's own fiction), Robert Carter located one cause of the treatment of blacks in the U.S. to the evolution of a new "white" character in this country: "The answer is this: There have been gathered here in the United States the offspring of every nation belonging to the white race. They have found that their race (the white race) is largely in the majority, a majority of numbers, of wealth, of education, of culture, of refinement, of financial power and mercantile activity, with whom they blend in social life and in religious worship" (355). In his explanation of race discrimination, Carter pinpoints what he sees as the "melting" or amalgamation of a new white race in the United States through the confluence of various European ethnic groups. His differentiation between "Anglo-Saxonism" and "whiteness," his awareness of the evolutionary flux through the amalgamation of whites of European descent, hints at an important assumption that circulates as well in Hopkins's detective histories. We can see this same implied narrative about the evolutionary instability of whiteness in an 1904 article, "The Rise and Fall of Peoples and Nations," by Charles S. Williams. As was familiar within the republican discourse of nineteenth-century America, Williams finds in the rise of the old Southern aristocracy a recurrence of the decline of nations such as Babylon, Egypt, and Rome. The white race will fall in a manner similar to the debacle of these former empires because of not just moral but inherited character flaws: "so detrimental to progress and the betterment uplifting to the people, there came to some of this people who, by inheritance and education from the centuries of that enslavement of certain members of the human family, an aristocracy of selfishness, habits of tyranny and in certain types of them so inheriting a degree of cruelty in excess of that found among the uncivilized and past tribes of past ages" (137). What is significant in Charles Williams's discussion of "the rise and fall of peoples and nations," as in Charleea Williams's "Recent Developments," is the class- and region-based analysis of the "white problem." In these articles (which one might speculate were written by the same person using a common masculine and feminine nom de plume), a hereditary line of white barbarism is specifically associated with a particular moneyed power of the Old South. In Charles Williams's, as opposed to Charleea Williams's, account, this racialized white aristocracy is clearly "degenerating"—"leading the descending grade down to the lower plan from which man has been struggling for long periods of time to get away from" (139). However, the class sympathies, as well as the racialized inclusiveness of "white aristocracy," are not unconflicted. By noting that an admixture of Southern aristocratic "whiteness" will bring down even the Northern republican character, and hence the nation as a whole, Williams calls attention to whiteness's fluctuating meaning.[4]

In her article "Munroe Rogers," as a consequence, Hopkins organizes her antirace argument around the neoabolitionist's panic not just about a racialized Anglo-Saxon decline but about the uncertain meaning of whiteness. While reporting the "criminal injustice" against Munroe Rogers, ever present is the "missing bodies" of the former abolitionist leaders whose heirs are failing to live up to their legacy. The overt news story that Hopkins relates is Massachusetts attorney general Parker's intransigent approval of the extradition of Munroe Rogers back to South Carolina on suspicion of arson—a charge Hopkins rails against as false—but the buried referent is the fate of what Hopkins calls the "inherited morals" (26) of the hereditary white character. In this Progressive Era fugitive slave narrative, Hopkins tries to requicken the furor over the earlier passage of the Fugitive Slave Bill and over the culpable compliance of many of Massachusetts's leaders to its injustices. But in rewriting a pre–Civil War antislavery narrative for post-Reconstruction America, Hopkins does not just try to awaken memory and raise consciousnesses; she attempts to challenge the race-based thinking of many of these New England heirs. After reprimanding the old Boston Brahmin elite for their sins of omission, Hopkins shifts her focus to remind her audience of the fictional amalgamation of various minorities under the category of whiteness. At the end of her essay, Hopkins clearly links the discriminations of the color line to immigration restrictions based on racialized hierarchies and notions of a variegated whiteness. Talking back to the Boston elite to indict the "white problem," Hopkins calls for an alliance among all people of color. Since the problem of the day is the exclusionary practices of a hereditary white class, Hopkins suggests the political efficacy of a class-based alliance of all non-Anglo-Saxon folks: the current political conflicts, Hopkins writes, ought to be "merged into one great question involving the herd of common people of whom the Negro is a recognized factor" (26).

To the discussion of the crimes within turn-of-the-century America, Hopkins and the other writers for the *Colored American Magazine* bring forth the "missing question" of the divided body of white folks and, as Hopkins's article on Munroe Rogers makes clear, the inherited morals among the neoabolitionist heirs of the antislavery legacy. Hopkins in particular devised an intellectual strategy that sought to utilize this concept of race (of whiteness) and transform it into a means of political intervention. By drawing on a language of "heredity" and of "blood," Hopkins was able to open up a public space for the "oppositional gaze" of black men and women, one that had the authority to force neoabolitionists to examine the split between their own white identifications and their perceptions by others. In *The Novel and the Police*, D. A. Miller argues for cooperation between nineteenth-century realist fiction and discipline in society, maintaining that the bourgeois novel ultimately brings what is outside the social order under regulatory supervision. In borrowing the popular form of detective fiction, Hopkins, however, uses her detecting fictions to expose what is already inside the social order but has escaped regulatory supervision. But rather than exposing the crimes of individual racists in her detective fiction, Hopkins tries to discipline the racial body of Boston's neoabolitionist heirs, to overturn, by an exposure of their monstrous relation with the racist other, the racialized bodily boundaries by which they see themselves as different from the criminal.

Detecting Fictions

I want to start with the seemingly erroneous comment that Pauline Hopkins's *Hagar's Daughter* tells the story of a crime that is never detected. At first glance it may seem that her melodramatic novel offers us full narrative disclosure, tying up all loose ends into an intelligible whole and providing a final summation in Henson's confession at Cuthbert Sumner's trial of what happened in the past. If the convention within detective fiction is the restoration of the suppressed narrative that provides a sense of the ending and a solution to the crime (Roth 168), *Hagar's Daughter* appears to end bafflement with a satisfying resolution. As readers, we feel that the hero, Cuthbert Sumner, has been exonerated; the outsider, St. Clair Ellis, whose infringement had threatened the "innocent" community, has been expelled if not incarcerated; and all the miscellaneous clues have been rendered meaningful with the opening of Bowen's trunk and the revelation of Hagar's and Jewel's identity. But the apparent containment of the criminal other, of that which threatens to disrupt and destroy the community, Hopkins intimates, is merely an illusion, and the crime, within the community at large, still remains invisible. By ending the novel with Cuthbert Sumner's prejudicial rejection of the octoroon Jewel rather than his acquittal, Hopkins undercuts the overt closure with a final ironic revelation of the missing, or unprosecuted, crimes against African American women and suggests that the hero (the neoabolitionist heir) and the villain are one and the same and maintain the same white racial formation.[5]

In his discussion of the connection between classic detective fiction and late-nineteenth-century culture, John Cawelti argues that the popularity of the genre arose from the particular tension between confidence and guilt within middle-class society. Although confident in the historical progress of civilization and the achievement of their capitalist bourgeois ideals, middle-class nineteenth-century Americans also sustained a guilt about their own suspected moral hypocrisy and possible corruption at the heart of their values. Through the resolution of the detective novel, however, middle-class readers experienced the relief of seeing a clear and meaningful order restored to the "innocent" community and the identification of the criminal as different from themselves. In a suggestive comment, Cawelti continues by noting that the cycles of legislative reform in the late nineteenth century, especially in terms of the inner-city, working-class poor, might be seen as "an exteriorization" of the guilt experienced by the middle class (103). In Cawelti's assertion that detective fiction taps into the same middle-class guilt that incited reform movements and legislation lies a clue for better understanding Hopkins's fiction. At a time when federal antilynching legislation failed to find support, Hopkins sought to "exteriorize" or detect, expose, and re-mediate the hypocrisy at the heart of the northern middle-class heirs of abolitionism. However, rather than reassure them of their innocence, she would appeal to their dread of degeneration and instability in their "superior" moral (white) character.

By splicing the story of the tragic mulatto onto the sensationalized narrative forms of detective fiction, Hopkins starts out with an irony that would have been apparent to her "colored" readers. It is only the murder of a white woman (the secretary Miss Bradford, named after the famous governor of the Plymouth Colony), not the rape, abduction, and murder of black women, that is considered a crime worthy of detection (or of a detective fiction) within Washington society. In such an ideology of "crime," Hopkins suggests, violent anger by white males against minorities is, if not exactly accepted by the northern elite, seem as somehow natural or unalterable behavior due to the devaluation of black women. In *Hagar's Daughter*, Hopkins struggled with the problem of how to make a racialized gender violence legible to a Progressive Era culture that had only a rudimentary language to speak about these domestic crimes. In her account of family violence in Boston from 1880 to 1960, Linda Gordon contends that this violence has been "historically and politically constructed" (3). In arguing that gender violence in part assumes its reality through the language that is used to describe it, Gordon does not trivialize the bruised and broken limbs behind poststructuralist word play. Rather, she suggests that the definitions of what forms unacceptable levels of abuse against women and how that abuse is talked about vary according to current social and political outlooks. In resorting to the popular form of detective fiction to retell the tragic mulatto's story, Hopkins tried to fashion a language to name the undetected crimes against black women, hate crimes that were inseparable from the process of gendering whiteness.

Although Hopkins's plot is convoluted, the main outline of *Hagar's Daughter* consists of a simple romantic triangle functioning as a political allegory: the rivalry between General Benson (the former slave trader St.

Clair Ellis) and Cuthbert Sumner (the neoabolitionist heir) for Jewel Bowen, the daughter of a wealthy California mine owner (the nation's future). In this familiar story of competition for the body of the "jewel" woman, the boundaries of an imagined national community are drawn, as each of these characters within this tale of seduction represents ideas central to the "race problem" unfolded within the *Colored American Magazine*. It takes little stretch of the imagination to see General Benson as the figure of the white racist. Yet it is the character of Cuthbert Sumner within this rivalry for the body of the daughter of the West that is even more pointedly representative. Cuthbert Sumner's name itself hardly disguises the historical reference that Hopkins wished to make to the famous Massachusetts senator, Charles Sumner, who worked first as an abolitionist and, after the war, lead the Radical Republicans committed to the advocacy of black suffrage and civil rights. By naming her central protagonist after this "uncompromising" civil rights leader, Hopkins impugns the neoabolitionists heirs who did not mobilize around the threat to disenfranchisement coming from the post-Reconstruction South. Against the moral commitment and principled heroism of the late Sumner (d. 1874), *Hagar's Daughter* sets the wavering dilettantish ardor of this, as Hopkins writes, "only child of New England ancestry favored by fortune" (85). Hopkins's distaste for the supposedly white hero in the novel and his ignominious character are only too evident at the novel's end in his abandonment of (the) "Jewel" on the discovery of her mixed-race heritage. When Cuthbert contends that the "knowledge of her origin would kill all desire in me," Ellis Enson reprimands the young man in words that we might speculate all too closely reveal Hopkins's own reproof: "And this is the sum total of what Puritan New England philanthropy will allow—every privilege but the vital one of deciding a question of the commonest personal liberty" (271). Concerned only with keeping the "fountain head of our racial stream as unpoluted [*sic*] as possible" (271), Cuthbert Sumner cannot perceive that it is already poisoned from within by a "hereditary outlawry" of which his actions provide an obvious sign.

But Hopkins does not just make the allusively named Cuthbert Sumner a flawed character to decry the sins of the neoabolitionist heirs of New England; she uses the genre form of detective fiction to cast a corporeal suspicion on the white New England "racialized" body. As I have already alluded, what distinguishes detective fiction from the sensational crime novel is the commitment of a "murder of passion," a crime that makes the criminal an insider, as opposed to a professional villain or an outside threat, and this interiority, as it were, initiates the "scandal," the community's loss of its own privileged or innocent self-image. From this fear of scandal arises the community's—and often the readers'—desire to exonerate the hero, to clear him/her of the implications of a crime that also questions the character of the community itself. By having the "only" and representative son of New England accused of murder, Hopkins taps into her white northern readers' anxieties about their own identity and its difference from the other nonwhite immigrants. The suspense that motivates the narrative force of Hopkins's fiction is whether Cuthbert Sumner will be cleared of all culpability. It would not be too much of an inference to suggest that, by having the abolitionist heir indicted for murder, Hopkins found a fictional displacement for her own anger at the immorality of Boston's Brahmin sons. Although Cuthbert may not stand arraigned for racism in the novel, the suspicion cast on his character indirectly expresses the objections Hopkins had to the neoabolitionists' betrayal of their sisters and brothers of color.

In *Hagar's Daughter*, Hopkins develops a voice of protest by casting the New England neoabolitionist heir under suspicion. This corporeal suspicion she extends to the entire white community of representative men. Before the resolution of the mystery in the detective fiction, all of the characters are equally suspect and must be scrutinized for clues as to their complicity in the crime. This universality of suspicion not only allows for Hopkins to question the white character but also serves as a tactic for what might be called an interventionist "defamiliarization." As a result of the anxious atmosphere that follows the "murder" in detective fiction, as Geoffrey Hartman notes, the familiar itself becomes strange, and the casually accepted is now viewed with a critical skepticism: "It is as if crime alone could make us see again" (214–15). While before the murder the white community had seen its own virtue as unquestioned, they now must consider the "character" of one of their own and in turn their own possible criminality. Both the entire white community in the novel and the reader now find themselves under a corporeal suspicion, and the disclosure of the "hereditary outlawry" in the novel's trial scene suggests, as the columnists for the evening paper reporting on the trial noted, the "effects of slavery can never be eradicated, and our most distinguished families are not immune from contact with this mongrel race" (266).

They are not immune from contact, Hopkins implies, because they are the "mongrel race" whose white character can also be inherited.

I want to elaborate on Hopkins interventionist strategy of "corporeal suspicion" by looking at the scene in which Venus visits Detective Henson's office to report her own inferences and intuitions, but first I need to make one more comment about the conventions of detective fiction that Hopkins draws upon to formulate a resistant history. The detective is often someone who steps in to help solve the crime after the failure of the police to identify the culprit. While the police themselves are frequently stupid or corrupt, the amateur detective, often as a result of his/her own detachment or marginal status, accomplishes what the official representatives of the social order cannot do themselves: he/she detects the crime and ferrets out its perpetrator to the exclusion of the police (Roth 62). It is significant, thus, that Hopkins has made the black woman Venus the active agent who finds the kidnapped Jewel, but by making Venus the heroic detective, Hopkins does not just reenvision the stereotypical gender role of the "true" woman. She dramatizes the function of the black woman's voice in challenging the normativity of whiteness. Nowhere is this clearer than in the exchange between Venus and Detective Henson. Although critics such as Kristina Brooks have noted the problems with Hopkins's portrayal of comic black caricatures from the minstrel tradition (Brooks 119–58), Hopkins directs the laughter back across the color line through Venus's antics. When Venus first "chatters" away about her suspicions regarding General Benson, Hopkins seems to position the reader to share Detective Henson's condescending indulgence of this loyal servant's performance on behalf of her mistress. But she soon demonstrates the myopia and discrimination of the detective himself:

"Who do you think sent this, Venus?"

"No one but old Benson."

Again the chief smiled at the quaint answer. But he looked at her still more searchingly, as he asked:

"Did anything of a suspicious nature occur to make you hold that opinion?"

"Well, yes sir, there did. Something I overheard the General Benson say to the old lady."

. . . .

"You do not like General Benson, I see."

"Like him! Who could, the sly old villain. He's mighty shrewd, and—" she paused.

"Well, what?"

"Foxy," she finished. "He tries to be mighty sweet to me, but I like a gentleman to stay where he belongs and not be loving servant girls on the sly." (226)

At first, Henson finds Venus the quaint loyal servant, and he only exhibits a "sign of excitement" in her story, when she discloses that her father is a personal servant to General Benson. While Henson's failure to listen to Venus's opinions until they show what he sees as direct relation to the case testifies to society's trivializing of the voices of black women, Hopkins is also commenting on the racialized reading of "suspicion." In contrast to the white detective, Venus finds signs of criminality in the behavior of white men such as Benson who sexually exploit their black female servants and act without principle. Yet to Henson, such a mistreatment of black women (one that echoes the novel's opening assault on Hagar) is not "anything of a suspicious nature." If Venus is the one who solves the crime in Hopkins's *Hagar's Daughter*, it is because to the white detective the crime is undetectable. Crime is only made legible when it is no longer enacted upon the bodies of black women but assaults white womanhood (the "Jewel") or generates a scandal about white manhood that might alter the reading of "his-story" (the neoabolitionist Cuthbert Sumner's). Although the black character is always under suspicion for his/her possible criminality and inferiority, Hopkins uses the dynamics of detective fiction to reverse this cultural atmosphere to bring the white character equally under the atmosphere of suspicion. To the intended black female readers of this scene, what is underscored is not Venus's sassy and risible pretensions but the purblindness of the detective who is impervious to racial and gender violence perpetuated by the white character.

Throughout *Hagar's Daughter*, such incidents of detection by the black female characters recur repeatedly. In highlighting the ability of all her black female characters (from the seemingly caricatured mammy to the tragic mulatto and wench) to outsmart the white detectives, Hopkins seeks not only to resignify the identity of African American women but to claim a space for the African American woman's witness to the truth of white history. Unlike Detective Henson, who is said to be a man with a "wonderful power of discernment" (188), none of the black women in the novel are duped by the devious or disingenuous games of Major Walker, General Benson, and Aurelia Madison. When Mrs. Bowen hears

Aurelia plead her devotion to Jewel despite her renewed romance with Cuthbert, Hagar/Mrs. Bowen "heard it all but deep in her heart was a doubt of the specious pleader" (136). Similarly, shortly thereafter, when General Benson begins to court Jewel, Hagar eyes him with suspicion, such that we are told, "He felt uneasy in her presence, that under her rather haughty manner a keen sight was hidden that read his motives" (139). While Hopkins's female characters may seem at times too stereotypical, too accommodationist, they are not lacking in subjectivity, if by subjectivity we mean less a realistic, well-rounded psychological depth than the possession of a point of view and a return gaze that acts upon the world and expresses a distinct racial interiority. In scenes such as these, in which the "keen sight" of Hagar is compared to her husband's and to that of the other male characters, Hopkins places into narrative tension two ways of knowing, seeing, and naming the world: the official patriarchal (white) point of view and an alternative one originating out of the experience of black women.[6]

Yet the importance of Hagar's "keen sight" lies in more than her oppositional standpoint to dominant or official affidavits of the truth. In contrast to her biblical counterpart, Hopkins's Hagar returns from the wilderness of the West to disrupt the community that would exclude both a history of crimes against her and the black woman's "power to detect" the violence in the white character. Indeed, Hagar represents what whiteness needs to repress from its own consciousness: the return gaze of the black female other, a gaze that might call hegemonic representations of white character into question. In her turn to detective fiction where all are scrutinized and rendered suspect, Hopkins found a way to smuggle back in what the Washington community and its New England representatives (Sumners) would bury. Within the discursive space of popular detective fiction, the gaze of the black woman could return to testify against the white character and even, as we see in the scene of Violet's witness to Detective Henson, the "undetected" gender violence of neoabolitionists who are blood brothers and sisters to the criminals.

The subversiveness of Hagar's detection lies in her refusal to divide her Washington world into criminals and "ordinary" or "innocent" people. White racism, as George Lipsitz implies in his study of the possessive investment in whiteness, has involved a claim of white innocence, for with this innocence comes a sense of entitlement, power, and a right to subjugate those who are designated as less "innocent" (20). In Hopkins's plotting of suspense in the novel, the mystery raised is not just who is Hagar's daughter but who are the possible white descendants and reincarnations of Walker, Ellis, and their ilk, the perpetuators of a hereditary white outlawry and therefore not innocent. The answer in the novel is that no one is innocent.

Although Hopkins uses the psychological doubling within detective fiction to link her villain (Benson) and the sleuth (Henson), she similarly makes the neoabolitionist heir Cuthbert a race brother to General Benson. Both of them see no problem with seducing and then abandoning the tragic mulatto, even if we are never sure of any sexual consummation in Cuthbert's relation to Aurelia. In fact, Hopkins indicates Cuthbert's secret admiration and identification with this southern rake. Although Cuthbert knows that General Benson is of "suspicious character" (especially in his dealings with women), he would rather remain faithful in his duty to this white brother and keep his membership in the fraternity of white privilege than to warn Jewel. At one key moment in the text, Hopkins even suggests that this effete descendent of the abolitionist crusaders would emulate the criminal's misogynistic dandyish display. On the level of unconscious fantasy, Cuthbert, it is critical to note, is not innocent of the crime of which he has been wrongfully accused but is conspiratorial in the larger rape script. In Cuthbert's mind, he would as easily displace onto the African American female his own sexual violence: "As the thought lingered in his mind (his pity for Jewel to be wed to such a reprobate), General Benson paused beside his desk. Cuthbert could not refrain from giving him an admiring glance nor could he wonder at the infatuation of most women for the handsome chief who stood there drawing on his gloves, his costly fur-lined coat unbuttoned and nearly sweeping the carpet giving an added charm to this handsome face, elegant figure, and gracious manner" (150). Although General Benson is described in terms of the meretricious sartorial splendor of nineteenth-century confidence men, Cuthbert desires to be him, to have the power over women that would come with being him. Cuthbert's crime is his phantasmic identification with a white male "outlawry" that belies his stated adherence to abstract morality and justice. Although the neoabolitionist would stress the otherness of the southern racist, Hopkins creates a moment of panicked self-recognition on the part of her white male readers in which they must recognize their oneness with the serial racist killer because both share in a white male fantasy of empowerment and privilege through a racialized gender violence.[7]

It is not only in the coupling of Cuthbert with the reprobate General Benson that Hopkins reveals the irony of the exoneration of the white New England character for the murder of Miss Bradford. In the narrative climax of the trial scene, Hopkins's *Hagar's Daughter* shows a structural link between whiteness and a symbolic, if not always real, violence against black women. While it is Detective Henson's testimony that frees Cuthbert of suspicion, the plot of *Hagar's Daughter* connects this defense of the "white" character with the degradation and mysterious disappearance of the mulatto, Aurelia Madison, the daughter of the scheming mine owner, Major Madison, and Cuthbert Sumner's former fiancée. To clear Cuthbert's name, no one questions the prudence, compassion, or the justice of destroying her reputation and character, and indeed it is the sensational story of the degenerate mulatto passer that the papers circulate to win sympathy for Cuthbert. While Cuthbert is cleared of murder charges, this declaration of innocence, moreover, demands the "disappearance," possibly even murder, of the black woman. In the aftermath of the trial, Hopkins highlights that Aurelia's fate emerges as another unsolved mystery: "Nothing criminal was charged against Aurelia; in fact, no one desired to inflict more punishment on the unfortunate woman, and when she left the court room that day she vanished forever from the public view" (272). Why, we need to ask as readers, did Hopkins not give us Aurelia's story? Although it might be argued that Hopkins assimilated stereotypes about the tragic mulatto, there is a greater structural intentionality in Aurelia's disappearance. By discursively linking the restoration of the white male character with the ruination (as it were) of the woman of color, Hopkins seeks to expose the real and symbolic violence that is a constitutive part of even an "innocent" white maleness.[8] In exposing that the neoabolitionist Cuthbert Sumner's exoneration depends on the exploitation and abandonment of the woman of color, Hopkins bears witness against the larger rape culture that the legal system does not put on trial. In the supposed closure of the mystery in *Hagar's Daughter*, Hopkins pictures a white identity that exists as a divided subjectivity, a subjectivity that exists by elisions and omissions of fantasy and desire that would expose it as no different from the southern villain of the past, or of the present.

The solution to the mystery and to the truth of the white neoabolitionist Cuthbert Sumner's character requires a literal return to the site of "origins," to the representational space that has been left out of current neoabolitionist renderings of their heroic past: the ruined plantations of post-Reconstruction America. To discover the truth of General Benson's scheme and to find the hostages, Aunt Henny and Jewel, Violet returns to Enson Hall to ferret out the truth. At the plantation, Hopkins's narrator states that rumor held that "the ghost of Ellis Enson 'walked' accompanied by a lady who bore an infant in her arms" (228), and thus in Violet's investigation there she serves to help Henson remember his own crimes against his wife. In writing of the superstitions surrounding the Enson plantation, Hopkins reveals how a counterfactual history kept alive by African American women refuses to let these everyday crimes of gender violence, as well as the slavery past, be forgotten. In contrast to southern writers who used stories of the ruined plantation to invoke the passing of a lost Eden, Hopkins (proleptic of Toni Morrison's description of Circe in *Song of Solomon*) imagines a plantation house in the charge of an "Old Negress" reputed to be a "witch woman" who deals and traffics with evil spirits. Described as a "nightmare of a woman" (150), Auntie Griffin is the monstrous avenger and conjure woman watching over the ruins of a plantation history that has twisted and maimed her life and the lives of women of color who still walk as ghosts with "an infant in their arms."

In Violet's return to Enson Hall and the past on behalf of Detective Henson/Ellis Enson to find out the truth of the neoabolitionist white character in the present, *Hagar's Daughter* reveals that what is imprisoned there are the violated bodies of black women, Aunt Henny and Jewel, the mammy and the tragic mulatto of representational fictions. Once again Hopkins discursively links the white male character and black female identity: Only through the silencing of the everyday gender violence against black women had the truth of the "false" white identity not come out. Such an imprisonment remains possible only through the cooperation of black males with white patriarchal order, since Benson's servant Isaac acts as the abductor and guard of the black women on behalf of his master. It is not insignificant then that it is Violet (Violet disguised as a boy no less) who solves the mystery and breaks the representational encoding. In her investigation, Violet brings to light the "undetected" rape script with its process of sexist gendering.

What is interesting in this scene of Violet's discovery of Jewel's and

Aunt Henny's imprisonment is Hopkins's omission (at least initially) of what Violet sees as she spies through the window. In this telling double-voiced ellipsis, Hopkins seeks to implicate white readers in their own inability to detect the truth from the external clues. After noting that Violet "peers in" through the window after climbing a vine along the wall, Hopkins then skips to say that Violet telegraphs Henson only that "all O.K. Just as we thought" (234). But what is it that "we thought," since at this time a reader does not know what Violet saw. While Henson surely believes that he has solved the mystery and discovered the whereabouts of Jewel, Hopkins indicates that Violet sees something other than we think. Before interrupting the narrative, Hopkins remarks that Violet hears a "sweet young voice" and an "aged Negro voice" endeavoring to "comfort and encourage one another." Yet such a description deliberately does not make clear whether Violet sees Aunt Henny or Aunt Griffith, nor does it indicate whether Aunt Henny is playing the comforting mammy (as a reader might suspect) or whether she is collaborating with a sister of color. Hopkins calls Violet the "lad" in this scene and does not use any gender markers for either of the two voices: they could be male or female, they could be Jewel and Aunt Henny or Aunt Henny and Aunt Griffith. Now certainly on one level Hopkins's omission builds suspense; we need to wait until the trial to discover what happens, but it is also an attempt to open up a space of resistance. While this scene at first glance seems an image from the plantation past, viewed from the revelations of the end it is not a plantation story. Hopkins overturns her readers' expectations, for the hidden voices buried within the repressed past are not those of the mammy comforting the white daughter but of two black women equally imprisoned in a world that doesn't make visible the specifically gendered as well as racial crimes against them. Their freedom can only come through the intervention of another black woman (Violet) who can see their story just as "we thought" and not in the white his-stories.

In this scene, Hopkins puts her white readers in the position of the detective, but they are doomed like the famous Henson to misconstrue the clues. Only the reader who has concluded that Jewel is "Hagar's Daughter" can see this scene and the story correctly. That Hopkins entitles her novel "Hagar's Daughter" is no accident, for she is the missing clue, the daughter of miscegenation and thus the figure of liminality and boundarylessness who exceeds traditional racial narratives of black and white. She is what one would have to know to be able to detect the character of the actors aright and to re-member the particularly gendered race crimes of the past. In *Hagar's Daughter*, Hopkins creates a double-voiced text that reads differently for the knowing black reader and the unsuspecting white audience. What would prevent readers from solving the mystery, as Violet does before the trial scene, is their own identification with a whiteness that displaces onto black women the "crimes" within their own soul. To read the scene accurately, Hopkins forces readers to surrender their racial identity, to see from the perspective of the black woman who can detect the artificial boundaries within a white identity that insists on its difference from the "colored" other.

Hopkins enacts such a traumatic blurring of the boundary between the white self and its other in having the missing corpse of the tragic mulatto, Aurelia, resurface and reappear in the body of the "Jewel" of womanhood, Jewel Bowen. While Aurelia's story at the end is lost so as to restore the innocence of the white character (Cuthbert), the revelation of Jewel's identity as Hagar's daughter once again implicates his criminality. In her opening exposition of the Washington scene, Hopkins had clearly differentiated between the stereotypical "virgin" and "whore" of Jewel Bowen and Aurelia Madison: "Aurelia was a gorgeous tropical flower; Jewel, a fair fragrant lily" (103). In contrast to the dark temptress, Jewel was a representative of the "Saxon type, dazzling fair, with creamy roseate skin" (82). Such expectations, however, Hopkins overturns in the novel's ending by exposing society's ideal embodiment of white beauty as a forgery, as herself the offspring of miscegenation and a victim of gender violence. While Hopkins blurs the binary opposition that society constructs between white womanhood and the racial other, Aurelia's disappearance and reemergence as the "Jewel" has implications that are more than deconstructive. Although this feminine type of phantasmic identification had seemingly been beyond suspicion, Hopkins casts doubts on the social construction of white femaleness itself, such that we can never sure that it ever reflects the purity of type.

Although Cuthbert had insisted that Jewel was his "white angel of purity," while the tropic flower of Aurelia "caused his blood to flow faster," Cuthbert finds himself confronted with the return of a "threatening female sexuality" that he had sought to project and to enjoy upon the body of the woman of color. In the twinned sisterhood of Aurelia and Jewel, Cuthbert must now face those parts of his own white character that he had split off from himself by putting them onto the mulatto siren. While Cuthbert tries to flee from this revelation of his own character, in the seemingly sentimental and trite ending, Hopkins implicates his white hereditary outlaw. In the tombstone of Jewel Bowen that Cuthbert Sumner encounters on his return to Boston, Hopkins provides the sign that will refuse to allow the white character to remain unremarked and undetected. In facing this grave marker, Cuthbert loses the transparency of his own white character.

In Henson's apology to Hagar, we see also another false tactic of neoabolitionist antiracism. While Henson blames himself for his moral failure, he does not question a social hierarchy based on the privileges of whiteness. He would individually extend his sympathies to the wife he loves (the exception to the rule), but he does not see any wrong in his condescension to Venus or the patronage of his faithful servant Uncle William who fought along with him in the war. It is not insignificant then that Hopkins links together two acts: Henson's apology and the death of the abandoned miscegenated Jewel. Henson's apology to Hagar is tantamount to a defense of whiteness: his individual focus does not challenge white identity itself or call for its transformation. Similarly, Cuthbert suggests that he cannot marry Jewel because he cannot both be the representative "body" of New England neoabolitionist whiteness and wed to the transracial future. Within the semiotic encoding of the novel, Hagar's daughter is the liminal figure that is a disturbing sign of the arbitrariness of neoabolitionist's whiteness. But the final message of *Hagar's Daughter* is the failure of current solutions to the crimes of race, for these solutions leave this whiteness unindicted and its gender violence unseen. Indeed, Henson's individualistic act of apology is a sign of whiteness itself and keeps its performance in play.

In *Hagar's Daughter*, Hopkins attempts to show the monstrousness even within white antiracism or neoabolitionism. In "White Anti-racist Rhetoric as Apologia," Debian Marty has argued that white antiracism tends to adopt an apologetic strategy that acknowledges some moral fallibility, at least on a collective level, for past enormities, yet still refuses to examine the privileges of whiteness in terms of rights, benefits, and opportunities (51–52). Among these rights is also one of unknowing, of refusing to know people of color in a way that would require an acceptance of the other as the other knows herself/himself. In order for white antiracism to ethically engage with the otherness of "black folks," Hopkins reveals in *Hagar's Daughter* it must both abnegate the privileges of whiteness and recognize how, particularly its masculinized form, depends on an everyday oppression of women. It is just this reduction of antiracism to a private act of apology or of disavowal, a disavowal that includes a dismissal of the past and present ''look'' of black women, that Hopkins takes the witness stand against in her own detective fiction.

4. UNACQUIRING NEGROPHOBIA

*Younghill Kang and the Cosmopolitan Resistance to the
White Logic of Naturalization*

Amid his picaresque wanderings across 1920s America, the
Korean immigrant narrator of Younghill Kang's novel *East Goes West: The
Making of an Oriental Yankee* (1937) encounters in Boston an African American student, Wagstaff, who works as a "yes-suh" elevator man while putting himself through college. This black Falstaffian wag counsels the
exiled Shakespearean scholar Chungpa Han to "learn the language of
gyp, learn to gyp to. Confess honestly that right is not might, but might
is right, always since the world began. That's the perspective that only a
Negro gets" (274). Throughout his recollections of life as one of the "drift-
ing" Korean resident aliens in America cut off from their homeland after
the Japanese annexation in 1910, Kang inserts the "perspective of the
Negro" and implies a common colonial oppression and displacement
experienced by African and Korean Americans. Resorting to a dream
vision at the novel's close to voice the protest hidden behind barriers of
polite respect, Chungpa once again imagines that he is trapped in a "dark
and cryptlike cellar" in the company of some "frightened-looking
Negroes" as a "red-faced" lynch mob storms their prison/fortress, intent
on burning them all to death (369). But even as Kang organizes memory
in his fictional autobiography in such a way as to open up political ties
of affiliation among historically discriminated groups and to disrupt the
fashioning of a unified Korean American autobiography, he discovers a
difference within their reality as racial subjects in America. As Wagstaff

amid his ironic cynicism prompts Chungpa to muse, "I [Chungpa] was outside the two sharp worlds of color in the American environment. It was in a way true. Through Wagstaff I was having my first introduction to a crystallized caste system, comparable only to India, here in the greatest democratic country in the world" (273).

In reconceptualizing the question of race in nineteenth-century U.S. literature as a "white problem," the last three chapters have filled in some of the voids in our understanding about how antebellum and Progressive Era coracial texts worked to interfere in the reproduction of white bodies. But in opening up a new critical space for understanding the work of immigrant texts from the early twentieth century, we need a "trialectical" approach to the history of whiteness (Soja 70–73), one that complicates our search for a simple emancipatory rhetoric to denaturalize or abolish race thinking. Built into critical studies of minority texts is a certain bifocalization that affords only a crude picture of most individuals' social existence, which often involves an unruly, disorderly, unfixed, and ever-evolving relation not just with a "dominant" culture but with other minority groups in complicated borderland spaces. In contrast, Younghill Kang's *East Goes West* debunks the valorization of "otherness" in minority texts, or the laying claim to a special kind of otherness against U.S. cultural nationalism, whether that otherness is defined positively as an alternative "Korean American" identity or negatively as an "antiwhite," or "antinormative/bourgeois" formation. The difficulty, as Lisa Lowe argues in *Immigrant Acts*, has been in defining a "new type of subjectivity that does not just replicate the racialized and nationalized narratives that ground U.S. citizenship" (70). In restoring the "Negro question" within the personal history of the Korean American, however, Younghill Kang refuses to lock himself into the overdetermined binary logic of a Korean American nationalism that would repress the multiple axes along which identities in the U.S. are, and might be, formed and along which, as well, coalitions might be built with other minority groups. Against the strategy within early Korean American literature to define resistance in oppositional terms to Japanese or Western imperial culture, Kang calls attention to how such a tactic repeats in an alarmingly analogous way the subsuming or erasing of African Americans in the dominant fiction of a reputedly white American culture. Kang's *East Goes West* anticipates and obviates the familiar paradigm of contemporary literary criticism, which focuses on the conflict between white and nonwhite, Western and non-Western, native and colonizer, Asian and American in such a way that other non-dominant groups are rendered invisible. While the current vogue in transnationalism as an alternative mode for writing social identities and agencies in a global context escapes the opposition logic of earlier ethnic studies (assimilation or separatism), its concern with the choice between nation-state identity or transnational identity still eschews a "trialectical" thinking that would explore how people from different diasporas might cross over or out of migratory paths into new multiethnic communities.[1]

By 1937, when he published *East Goes West*, Kang had turned his attention away from the anti-Japanese nationalism of many of his contemporaries, attempting instead to talk back to and challenge the imagining of a pure, monolithic, and naturalized white hegemonic U.S. culture. In his fictional autobiography, Kang avoids assimilating the racialized logic of both colonial and anticolonial groups by calling into question national narratives that would leave the "Negro" and other people of color outside the heterogeneous American scene in which the Korean might find a "home."[2] Between World War I and World War II, American society underwent a significant reconceptualization of whiteness as a system of meaning deployed to determine inclusion in the imagined American national community. While a number of social scientists began to question the naturalness of racial distinctions, especially as applied to ethnic groups, the nation's understanding of race was refigured along black and white lines. In the new dominant category of the Caucasian, Jewish and eastern European immigrants and their children found themselves part of a normative American whiteness, but this inclusiveness depended upon the solidifying of racial conflict as a "Negro problem" (Jacobson 103–10). Now certainly, Asian immigrants did not number among those assumed within the emergent category of the Caucasian, but upon arriving in the U.S., Asian immigrants often acquired the concomitant "Negrophobia" that acted as a strategic anxiety functioning to acculturate the Asian immigrant into Caucasian mainstream society (Hellwig 103). In learning to set themselves apart from African Americans lest they share their marginalized status, Asian Americans were participating in the unfolding of a larger epistemic transformation in the discourse of whiteness. As Wagstaff apprizes Chungpa, despite the invidious prejudices against Asians, nineteenth-century America's complicated and variegated ethnic/racial hierarchies were being "crystallized" into a black and white caste system. This binary understanding of race relations, however, which much of ethnic U.S. literary and cultural studies takes as its universal foundation, itself has a history and one that has often been ignored as an important historical context for understanding the political agency of first-generation Korean Americans such as Younghill Kang.

In his critique of current postcolonial and cultural studies approaches to pre-1980s Asian American literature, Jinqui Ling argues that critics tend to de-contextualize agency, promoting various counterhegemonic strategies apart from the varying forms of social power and oppression that the authors faced within their specific location. Yet as corrective as Ling's comments are to oversimplified models of oppositional identity politics that ignore the complex renegotiations that make a text neither simply radical nor conservative (18), he starts from a standpoint that valorizes the subversive at the expense of reparative and affiliative interventions, thus assuming an orientation that is Westernized. Younghill Kang's *East Goes West* has been so little appreciated because it fails to perform the kind of resistance implicit to the internal structuring of ethnic studies, a kind of resistance that Kang's book implies is coterminous with the twentieth-century politics of whiteness. Since his arrival in New York at the age of eighteen, Younghill Kang felt, like most Koreans of his time period, an exile without a country. At the end of *The Grass Roof* (1931), Kang described Japan's brutal colonial conquest of Korea, which left him as a young man without a place in the world. In his Guggenheim application in 1931, Kang still felt like the sojourner and exile, barred on one hand by U.S. naturalization policy from being more than a permanent alien in America yet "not a citizen elsewhere" since the Japanese dissolved the Korean government (qtd. in S. Lee 376). Rather than look back as did many similarly displaced Koreans, Kang transvalues in *East Goes West* his "citizenless" state into the opportunity for a new transnational and transracial consciousness that would exceed traditional borders and would tie "Negroes" and "Oriental Yankees" together in a cosmopolitan affiliation. In his investigations into "discrepant cosmopolitanisms," Pheng Cheah has argued that contemporary postcolonial criticism needs to reimagine the "cosmopolitan" stance as more than a detached bourgeois aestheticism promoting a global humanity that erases local differences and particularities. What is needed instead is a revitalized cosmopolitanism, one that reaches toward "complex, nonterritorial, postnational forms of allegiance" that cross traditional racial or national borders of identity and that captures the collective strivings and interests of groups from many different locations (Cheah and Robbins 32). Rather than an "abstract emptiness of nonallegiance," Kang's "cosmopolitanism" in *East Goes West* points us toward just such a density of overlapping relationships within a plurality of cultures.

Throughout *East Goes West*, Kang offers a story of consciousness raising that is not the growth and expression of individualized anger but rather of affiliation. Kang is not undergoing what Susan Gubar has called a "racechange," one in which he crosses racial boundaries to imitate or impersonate African Americans, as does Frank Chin's Tam. Indeed, carefully avoiding such mimicry and racial masquerade even as he learns the perspective "that only a Negro gets" (5), Kang attempts to replace the language of "race" and "race consciousness" with a different kind of cosmopolitanism. Starting from an alternative set of assumptions, one that seeks to repair multiracial civility, Kang works to challenge the relational assumptions behind an emerging "white" or "Caucasian" biracial America. To understand Kang's intervention into the "crystallization" of a twentieth-century narrative of whiteness and to the "Negrophobia" such a logic invoked in Asian immigrants, Kang's fictional autobiography must be set against the logic of naturalization evident in the so-called prerequisite cases such as *Ozawa* (1922). In the prerequisite cases, claimants turned to the courts to be declared "white" either to be allowed to naturalize or to avoid extradition. Between 1878 and 1952, the U.S. Supreme Court heard fifty-two prerequisite cases, and in deciding these cases, the courts helped to redefine "whiteness" as less a matter of biology or culture than of "common sense"—or to state it another way, of simply not being "colored" or "black" (Lopez 80–86; Jacobson 236). In prerequisite cases such as that involving the Japanese-born Takao Ozawa, who sued to be classified as white so as to obtain full citizenship, the courts codified two interjoined racial assumptions: first, the twentieth-century notion of a transparent and self-evident whiteness (Flagg 36), and second, the separateness of black culture and experience from an American identity. While these cases demonstrate the function of whiteness as an ideological tool in the assimilation of immigrants, Kang's *East Goes West* is a satire whose intent is to devalue whiteness as a pure property that must be protected. To enact such an intervention into the everyday tactic of whiteness and Negrophobia, Kang authors less an alternative identity, even a hybrid one, than a volume that works to create an affiliative cosmopolitan consciousness that is postethnic.

The Logic of Naturalization

In 1939 Illinois congressman Kent E. Keller introduced a bill in the U.S. House of Representatives to have New York University professor Younghill Kang naturalized as a U.S. citizen. Included in the bill was a collection of statements on Younghill Kang's behalf compiled by the Committee on Citizenship for Younghill Kang that involved such notable literary and civic leaders as Malcolm Cowley, Pearl S. Buck, Lewis Mumford, Maxwell Perkins, and Charles Scribner, among others. The same year Senator Matthew M. Neely of West Virginia offered a second bill to declare Kang an American. Both bills went forward without debate before they were rejected. The failure of Younghill Kang's legislative bid for citizenship might be read as just one more historical consequence of the 1924 Immigration Exclusion Law, which extended restrictions to Koreans and Japanese, were it not for its particular evidence of the legal fiction of "race." In his essay for *Common Ground* magazine in 1941, Kang reflected that he knew "I am an American in all but the citizenship papers denied me by the present interpretation of the law of 1870 under which a Korean is not racially eligible for citizenship" (qtd. in S. Lee 389). While such a restrained comment suggests that he understood that "racism" prohibited his naturalization, it also indicates that Kang knew one's race was a matter of "present interpretation." Who was or was not declared a "free white citizen" or "American" because of "race" or "nationality" had altered over time and constituted no stable entity. In preserving the link between American citizenship and whiteness, those in Congress, it might be argued, were protecting and reembodying their "acquired inheritance" in this racial marker, even as they extended it to previously excluded ethnic groups. Because whiteness as an aspect of identity had been translated within the legal system into an external object of property and a sign of status (C. Harris 104), the naturalization cases were arguments over the meaning and rights to this "white" property.

In *East Goes West*, Kang frames the story of his first years as an exile without a country with brief but telling references to the Immigration Exclusion Act and his failed legal bids for naturalization. It was not until the Immigration and Nationality Act of 1952 (the McCarran-Walter Act) that the U.S. government lifted some interdictions against Asian-origin groups, although entrance was still regulated according to the strategically based quotas of the Cold War era (Chan 140–42). At the beginning of the fictional autobiography, Kang's protagonist, Chungpa, remarks that, when he arrived at age eighteen in America, he "got in just in time before the law against Oriental immigration was passed" (5). More significantly, near the end of his recorded travels, while hitchhiking around New England, Chungpa relates his on-the-road encounter with the "eminent former Wisconsin Senator" Kirby. After Chungpa quips in response to the senator's nativist boosterism that "legally I am denied," the unperturbed senator trivializes this objection by assuring Chungpa that "there are still ways and means of proving exceptions . . . next time I hold government office . . . write me and I will help you" (383). In Chungpa's usual satiric understatement in this scene, a form of what Homi Bhabha has called "sly civility," Kang anticipates his own futile struggle with proving himself an "exception" to the legally codified U.S. race logic (Bhabha, *Location of Culture* 83). But while Kang's self-irony in this scene divulges his own cynical hope about overcoming discrimination, his fictional autobiography calls into question the legal property of whiteness.

Although Kang uses Senator Kirby's shortsighted patriotism as a vehicle for satire, the senator's remarks link the novel to specific discourses within naturalization cases such as Kang's before the U.S. House of Representatives and Senate. Senator Kirby exhorts Chungpa to "believe in America with all your heart," to think of himself as "one of us" because he has the same spirit of "ambitious enterprise" (352). Now the senator's insistence that "America" is in the heart may seem, at first glance, well intended but clichéd and innocuous. He nonetheless taps into the counterargument often made in the naturalization and prerequisite cases that national identity is a "transpositional affective state" rather than a physical or commonsense "racial" sign. In calling Ozawa's defense "transpositional," I mean to suggest that he denies any essentialist or race-based definition of nationality.[3] To be an "American" is to occupy a historically specific "position" or subjectivity not limited by the potential citizen's ethnic background but instead experienced as a set of emotional relations toward cultural objects and practices, from language and education to institutional loyalties. Such a reimagining of national narratives may at first seem transformative, but in the end, the belief that America is in the

heart reinscribes and perpetuates the Negrophobia that whiteness incul-
cates in immigrants.

Two years prior to the 1924 ban on Korean and Japanese immigration,
the Supreme Court had paved the way for this exclusionary legislative
action by ruling against the Japanese-born sixteen-year American army
veteran Takao Ozawa. I want to look at Ozawa's defense in this case and
the Supreme Court's ruling because combined they map out both the
dominant and resistant discourse of naturalization that Kang would perceive as upholding the logic of "whiteness." By contrast, Kang's *East Goes
West* attempts an "affiliative intervention" that transcends the race consciousness of both positions. As part of his eight-year battle for U.S. citizenship, Ozawa composed a legal brief setting forth his argument for his
"Americanness." During his trial, Ozawa had pointed to the skin on his
cheek to indicate the whiteness of his body and had brought in ethnological research to argue that the Japanese were often lighter skinned than
many of the swarthier European groups accepted into American society
(Lopez; see also Ichioka 406–14). Through his ethnological reports and his
own ocular proof, Ozawa indicated what was becoming disturbingly clear
to American society by the 1920s: that racial differences based on morphological traits were highly unstable and often based more on historical
prejudices than direct evidence. But while Ozawa by basing his court case
on the indeterminacy of physiology and while ethnography was helping
to "dis-embody" race (like Kang's character, the naive Senator Kirby), he
also rearticulated national identity as a "transpositional affective state."
Such a transcoding is evident in the first part of Ozawa's brief: "In name,
General Benedict Arnold was an American, but at heart he was a traitor.
In name, I am an American, but at heart I am a true American. I set forth
the following facts which will sufficiently prove this. (1) I did not report
my name, my marriage, or the names of my children to the Japanese
Consulate in Honolulu" (qtd. in Ichioka 407). In setting up an opposition
between name and heart, between surface sign and affective loyalties,
Ozawa attempts to separate national identity from the question of "race."
The final proof of national identity should be "transcorporeal," more a
matter of the heart and soul than of an often ambiguous racial body or
heritage. The narratological complement to Ozawa's earlier dramatic
argument for the slippery nature of morphological or race-based boundaries for national inclusion (from skin to ethnic genealogy) is this reconstruction of citizenship around the "heart." Although nearly a decade

later Carlos Bulosan would entitle his postwar autobiography *America Is in the Heart* and credit Kang as his authorial role model, Kang undercuts this refiguring of national identity, which he saw as a way to preserve the normative value of whiteness.

Despite his challenge to U.S. immigration laws, Ozawa mobilized a defense that finally underwrote the logic of naturalization. To claim that America is in the heart meant that one's right to citizenship in effect arose from the shared cultural values with white middle-class western Europeans. Even though nationality was no longer racial, citizenship still depended upon being nearer white. But such a defense by outcome, and in the *Ozawa* case by intent, renders the African American separate and invisible. This exclusion of the African American is evident in the brief presented by George Wickersham when arguing Ozawa's case before the Supreme Court during the October term in 1922. While Wickersham marshaled ethnographic evidence to prove the "indeterminacy" of whiteness and challenged the meaning of the "uniform rule of naturalization" in the act of 1906, he spent the majority of his brief trying to persuade the Court of a specific meaning of whiteness. As Wickersham states directly at one point in his defense: "white person, as construed by the Court and by the state courts, means a person without Negro blood" (182). Insisting that when the first Congress passed the Naturalization Act of March 26, 1790, they intended only to exclude "Negroes" and not to ban the Japanese, Wickersham repeatedly asseverates that whiteness meant not black, and therefore the Japanese, like the other southern and eastern European groups being assimilated as "Caucasian," ought to be deemed white. Wickersham concluded: "The only safe rule to adopt is to take the term [free white citizen] as it undoubtedly was used when the naturalization law was first adopted, and construe it as embracing all persons not black" (185). As a consequence, the "Japanese . . . is 'white' in color and is of the Caucasian type and race" (184).

The racial logic of early-twentieth-century America involved the strategic positioning of Asian Americans in an ambiguous racial position between white and black (Okihiro 53). If the question of becoming a U.S. citizen involves both acquiring civil and political rights (the right of individual liberty, freedom of speech, association, government influence) and a cultural identity that confers upon the individual a sense of belonging to a social community, Asian Americans were often politically black and (if acceptable) culturally white. Thus Asian Americans could be praised as exemplifying the middle-class white values of self-help, hard work, and resourcefulness while at the same time being relegated to the same marginal economic caste as African Americans. In his statements on behalf of Ozawa's right to naturalize, Wickersham attempts to ensure not just the classification of the Japanese-born Ozawa as a Caucasian, he works to ensure us of Ozawa's white "soul," since, as he notes, "race" designates "qualities of personalities" (184). Yet by evoking the Negrophobic logic of naturalization, Wickersham keeps in place the defining fiction of a new "white" or "Caucasian" American nationalism: to be "white" is to be not black. The inner body of the Asian American, even more so than the external one, essentially shares a sameness with the "American"—a sameness that one proves by dissociation from blacks and other marginalized people of color. To make a case for one's inclusion in America means proving that one possessed the "spirit of the race"—the defining property of whiteness.[4]

Focusing on the "fidelity" of the "heart" as Ozawa does, moreover, renders assent or dissent a private and personal act and participates in the dominant privatization of social problems that precludes any collective racial or interracial resistance. The individual body becomes the source and the scene of oppression and allegiance, and to seek to become an "American citizen" is to renaturalize one's individual body as "white." It is just this a priori precluding of any kind of coalitional or collective action that Kang's novel critiques by avoiding a story of Chungpa's singular growth and development or self-made success. Throughout *East Goes West*, Kang refuses to narrate his protagonist's soul as white, and he refuses to show the proper heartfelt affection that would demonstrate that he shared the ideological spirit and consciousness of a "whiteness" uncontaminated by deviant affinities with African Americans. Although Ozawa had wanted to create a rhetoric that would allow for a transracial nationalism, it is clear from his elaboration that he imagined a solidarity that would emerge between "Asians" and "whites." In contrast, Kang attempts to create a "cosmopolitan" consciousness that exceeds the demands for a voluntaristic assent, or dissent, from one's individual race loyalties. Since "American" culture is sedimented and rooted with the histories and cultures of Africa, and African Americans (as well as Asians, Hispanics, and additional "others"), Ozawa's defense bolsters the enabling fiction that the U.S. stands unmarked by the influence of black Americans and people of color in its midst. In his autobiographical novel,

Kang invokes the panic European Americans feel about their own racial fabrication to pen a counterhistory to the U.S.'s amnesiac national memory. The very omnipresence of jazz, Kang writes, reveals the dividedness and instability within white "American" self-definitions: "it [jazz] had caught up the rhythm of America—this Negro jazz—it had taken possession of the Western planet, working upon all hitherto known cultures and civilizations" (18). By inverting the assumed direction of colonization, Kang calls attention to the unnaturalness of what Justice George Sutherland called the "popular acceptance" of whiteness that buries into the unconscious collective life its own hybrid formation.

The reviews of Kang's *East Goes West* reveal that what was at stake was less the artistic merit of the fictional autobiography than the "whiteness" of his "naturalized" consciousness. In their evaluations, reviewers tended to favor Chungpa's American adventures according to the degree with which they confirmed the mythologized story of the immigrant self-made man, flattening his polyvocal discourse into either (good) assimilationist consent or (bad) separatist anger. Katherine Woods's favorable review for the *New York Times Book Review* (October 17, 1937) identified Kang's novel as a "white" autobiography in the tradition of the nation's mythic heroes—Benjamin Franklin and Horatio Alger. Woods applauds Kang for being a "poor boy who made good" and as a model minority who decided to put "his roots" into America and "to make it his home" (11). Although Woods commends *East Goes West* as keenly individualized, she praises only what is familiar and flattering to nationalist narratives of the "true" American experience. In contrast, Maxwell Geismar of the *Nation* complained that Kang had written a bitter novel of protest. Choosing to focus on Kang's disillusionment in the novel about racial discrimination and mechanized dehumanization in a society run on "efficiency," Geismar muses that Kang has lost his lyric voice within the novel's satire. "Because of this [Kang's expatriation] his work has gained in ironic power, in intellectual preoccupation, in a sense of farce. But these may be used to cover frustration. And Younghill Kang has lost, for the moment at least, the distinguishing trait of the earlier period, a friendship at once discerning and indulgent for the land and the life around him" (482). Behind Geismar's deprecation lies the same logic of the *Ozawa* case, the need for the "naturalizing" American to have in his/her heart a white "soul" "indulgent" of the country's problems, and its discriminations. There is certainly nothing particularly new about Geismar's criticizing the author of color for his "anger": as long as Kang struggled to be nearer white, his work was lauded, but as he assumed a tone that was at once ironic, incensed, rebellious even, he was viewed as an insufficient Asian with an insufficiently white heart, no longer stoical, affably self-effacing, dispassionate. Hence both of these reviews, as antithetical as they may first appear, express the same foundational logic, and both recognize the genuine dissidence in Kang's fictional autobiography, which arises from his push toward a more cosmopolitan cultural merger of African American, Asian, and European voices.[5]

As a number of Asian American critics have commented, the native Eastern autobiographical tradition starts from different assumptions, and the Euro-American genre privileges values—individualism over communitarianism, idealism over materialism, personalism over the authority of the past—that are incommensurate with the immigrant Asian author's social education and rhetorical training (Shen 584). Early Asian authors, such as the Korean-born Il-han New who published *When I Was a Boy in Korea* (1926), adopted the autobiographical form in answer to the forces of the marketplace. In New's case, the publishing house D. Lothrop had been printing an autobiographical series of books recounting an author's boyhood in a foreign land (Kim 25). To satisfy the expectations of his readership, Kang would have needed to emulate the autobiographical voice of the master's language, but in both his story of his childhood in Korea told in *The Grass Roof* and his narrative of Americanization, *East Goes West,* Kang obscures any expected individualism behind indirection and impersonality. As Bhaba has theorized about agency and the postcolonial subject, the native's resistance to the dominant language of colonialism often arises in the temporal disjunctions of "mimicry," or the native's reiteration of the hegemonic codes of the "white" man/woman with a difference (*Location of Culture* 245). Although Kang seems to copy the lyric subjectivism of late romantic modernists such as Thomas Wolfe, his colleague at New York University, or F. Scott Fitzgerald (Strange 37), he invokes and repeats this Western "I" only to transform and renegotiate it. Specifically, he unsettles this unified romantic self by mobilizing a polyglot or multicultural "American" location. By mimicking both the language of Wolfe and the "language of gyp" (the African American), Kang exposes the alien within the supposed pure white racial subjectivity and speaks for all repressed groups as he releases the prohibited anger against the dominant biracial language of naturalization that makes the African American separate.

Third Space, Third Time of Affiliation

Like his fictional alter ego, Chungpa Han, Younghill Kang immigrated to the United States in 1921 as one of the small number of privileged "refugee students" issued passports by the Japanese government of occupied Korea (K. Lee 64). Although Kang along with other refugee students came from the *yangban*, or aristocrat, class in Korea, which alone had the privilege of education, once in America he, like his fellow expatriates, found himself forced into manual labor despite his extensive study. Working as farmhands, houseboys, cooks, waiters, railroad porters, and miners, these students may not have been representative of the typical Korean American immigrant laborer brought together in the work teams, or *sip-changs* (Kim 34), but they would have found themselves better able to identify with the situation of the "Negro in America." This underemployment enables Chungpa, as he implies on several occasions, to empathize with the various black men he meets during his travels who tell him, as the Schmitt's cook, Laurenzo, bemoaned: "Here I am chockfull of education. Still a niggerman" (262). Like Laurenzo, Alfred, Wagstaff, and the other educated black men whose stories interrupt Chungpa's narrative, Kang knew what it was like to find his talents unrewarded with opportunity, to be dismissed as inferior by Euro-Americans. In his autobiographical narratives, by noting the shared subjugation of Asians and Africans, Kang seems to suggest a coalitional habit of thinking through which blacks and Koreans might join to fight against white power. Rather than insisting on his status as a political exile who would work solely to redeem his country (Takaki, *Strangers* 282), Kang sought instead to become a "new cosmopolitan citizen," one who would have as his special mission the resistance to all fixed nationalisms, American, Japanese, or Korean. Indeed, in his own revisionist history of civilization, Chungpa's mentor, Kim, tells a fable about the survival of "African cats" and "Asian rats" in Europe and America, and although the cat and the rat might be considered natural enemies, in Kim's tale they cohabit peacefully in the slums of America, surviving together against the forces that would seek to kill them (256).

One way to approach this question of a "denaturalized" postcolonial

Korean American positionality in *East Goes West* is through the trope of space, which has become so prominent within "ethnic" studies. Central to the fiction of the first part of the twentieth century is the description of an autonomous world indifferent to the middle-class mainstream white American society—whether of Harlem or Chinatown or the Lower East Side—and representative of an oppositional site of cultural reproduction. The formation of an alternative self-authorizing culture was often depicted metonymically as an actual and separate social space—the ethnic or racial "neighborhood"—that made resistance visible as topography. This is not to say that many writers did not find this "ghetto" claustrophobic or tyrannical, but its presence still figured as a location from which even those who wanted to be emancipated from it could deny the totalizing history and vision of a white, Protestant, middle-class, heterosexual America. I start with this observation because it leads us to a salient feature of what is missing in Kang's *East Goes West*, and significantly so. In place of a tale of the ghetto, Kang's fictional autobiography gives us a tale of exile and wandering. It might be argued that Kang's peripatetic narrative form can be explained on the level of genre (he is writing a comic picaresque adventure, a travelogue) or of biography (he is just recounting his own homelessness), but neither explanation identifies Kang's artistic aim. It is after all a bit myopic to see Kang as beholden to the literal facts of his own experience or even to sociological analysis.

One place that emerges in the novel as a mythologized space is Harlem, which as much as Chinatown or Greenwich Village stands in as a "city of refuge" for Chungpa. While Chungpa tends to satirize the Korean nationalists, he often discloses a sympathetic identification with the people of Harlem and in the black community. When he first arrives, for example, Chungpa underscores his close identification with the African American. Trying to get his first job in the YMCA in Harlem, Chungpa is informed that he does not qualify since the position must not "be given to a Negro and Oriental" (19). This equivalence between the African American and the Asian is underscored when Chungpa attains his next job as a domestic (with the aid of Hsun Pak), and his employer insists that she has hired them to replace her former African American help. Similarly, when Chungpa and the other Asian students try to sell Hsun's tea, they find that the only place that they receive a civil welcome is in Harlem: "They peddled it from house to house. Harlem was a favorite selling ground. They did not get kicked out there" (64).

Throughout the episodic structure of *East Goes West*, there is a discursive link between space and race, but ironically it is the black community that becomes an important site of altruism and justice. Chungpa does not just see "blackness" as a political or economic position of exclusion and discrimination that he as a Korean American shares: he accepts blackness as a "race" and cultural consciousness that he and most modern so-called white Americans share. While Chungpa finds greater humanity in Harlem, he also employs Harlem as a metonym for all of modern American culture, or at least New York culture. In contrast to Boston or Baltimore, two other cities prominently featured in the novel, Harlem embodies the spirit of the age. Seeing his first cabaret show when George takes him to Harlem, Chungpa remarks that "in fact the jolly rich, highly emotional atmosphere seemed to caricature New York, as George, Hsun, and I knew it . . . frank love, loose laughter, a lack of discipline, . . . vulgarity, good humor, . . . sheepishness, plenty of smartness, too, and pavement cunning . . . everywhere a nonchalant grotesqueness (to us at least who remembered the formal traditional of Asia)" (75). At first glance this passage may seem to repeat the rhetoric of primitivism so familiar among modernist artists such as Sherwood Anderson, Eugene O'Neill, and F. Scott Fitzgerald. Yet Chungpa's equation of modern America with Harlem actually reverses the differential logic on which primitivism depends. If African Americans often stood as the displaced symbols of what the efficient industrial modern society had given up—sexuality, emotionalism, spontaneity, excess—for Chungpa and his friends *this is America*. In this scene, Kang's protagonist collapses the assurance of separation that the "slummer" felt in knowing he was different from the "other."

Kang attempts not to repeat the primitivist caricatures of Harlemites but to "blacken" the culture of America so as to expose the repression of heterogeneity within white American nationality. In learning the language of gyp, in taking on the black perspective, Kang does not, however, perform a racial mimicry similar to Al Jolson's blackface. In his descriptions of life in Greenwich Village, Kang satirizes the stereotyping of African Americans as exotic others. At his first speakeasy party, Chungpa reports that he has witnessed a brief exchange between an inebriated flapper, Sally, and a "serious-looking young Negro." When Alfred, a black man, offends the revelers with his sobriety, Sally enjoins him to act more like a "Negro": "Throw away all in-in-in-hibitions. D-dance and sing— and be-be a Negro" (163). In his ironic reflection on Sally's romantic racism, Kang indicates that his identification with the African American will not duplicate the Anglo-Europeans' exoticizing fantasies. Although for the villagers the "inside" glimpse at the "New Negro" is one that is invidiously dictated by their own desire to escape sexual and social conventions, Kang strives to break the primacy of the Anglo-European perspective without simply repeating its colonial ideas of primitivism.

Indeed, in *East Goes West*, Kang explores the myriad scenes of 1920s America, but what he continually finds among the avant-garde is a fervent wish to be "black" (to undergo a "racechange") and yet to hide the heritage of Africa in their white face of "Americanness." In celebrating jazz as the crooning spirit of modernism, Kang was picking up the ideas of New Negro writers such as J. A. Rogers, whose in "Jazz at Home" printed in Locke's anthology for the *Survey Graphic* anthology celebrated jazz as a vehicle for democraticization and racial amalgamation (220). While Langston Hughes saw jazz as the "eternal tom-tom beating in the Negro soul," Kang uses it as a motif for the "Negro soul" behind the racial masquerade of whiteness, a whiteness that would conceal the color that would destabilize its own identity formations (692). When Chungpa first accompanies Kim to Greenwich Village, he remarks that "it might have been some kind of temple in which to worship African jazz" (161). Observing the cult of primitivism everywhere fetishized in the Village, he notes in the same vein that all the "distorted drawings" on the wall try to imitate a "pair of African idols" (161).

Kang's reformulation of the usual link between topography and the memory of an "authentic" Asian identity is even clearer in his telling of the story of George Jum, the "Americanized Pagan" who "had left all Asian culture behind as a thing of nought" (31). While George Jum, like other characters such as Kim, acts as a foil standing in for parts of Chungpa, it is significant that this representative of the Americanized Korean is in love with Harlem, or more specifically a Harlem cabaret dancer, June (73). That June is not really "colored" but a white woman who wears dark makeup to appear in the chorus line only underscores Kang's point about the race of American culture. By linking George's Americanization to his love for the Harlem dancer, Kang challenges the white face of America's self-understandings. To say that Kang attempts to criticize the process of Americanization in *East Goes West* is to miss the broader scope of his challenge. He calls into question not just the need to imitate the American but the "commonsense" racial constitution of a "unified white American culture" evident in Ozawa's naturalization case.

To expose this repression of the difference already at whiteness's core, Kang dramatizes the disingenuous Chungpa's response to the racial masquerades and minstrelsy of Cotton Club Harlem. While critics such as Neal Ignatiev, George Lipsitz, and David Roediger have examined "white racial identities" as constructs or ideological positions that arise within specific historical contexts because of their political, economic, or psychological usefulness, whiteness, as the *Ozawa* case pointed out, has not only been unmarked or accepted as natural but has been reified as singular and homogeneous by being juxtaposed against a heterogeneity of colored others (Chambers 145). To see race as defined in oppositional terms permits precisely the obfuscation of complex racial transactions and interdependences that whiteness needs to maintain its narcissistic centrality and purity. Upon first being introduced to June in a nightclub, Chungpa remarks, "Soon he [George] returned with June, who to our surprise was not black but white, white as chalk. So she must be a white girl unless behind that white mask lived a Negro soul. She still looked to us a strange thing and all the more for her simple dress" (76). In this comic scene, Chungpa discovers that the "black" cabaret dancer is really white, and not just white but exaggeratedly pale—"chalk white." But in his musing that maybe she is not really white, despite appearances, for she might have a "Negro soul," Kang interrupts the White Negroes' ontological security in the "inalienable right" to their stable racial property. While the minstrel performer and the Harlem slummer assure themselves that the performance can end whenever they needed or wanted to reclaim their "natural" identities, Kang suggests that the performance is never over and that the foundational mimicry offstage may possibly be of the black soul insisting on its pure white face. Like the Asian American, the white American also has an ambivalent racial identity, being at times, when it is to his/her advantage or pleasure, politically white but culturally and improvisationally "colored." In his description of his first encounter with June, Kang brings together the ideas of identity and masquerade, intimating that gender and race identities are often performances learned under the regulatory pressure of society, and, as a consequence, Kang's narrative suggests there is no natural and unchanging essence behind one's "ethnic" constitution.

In altering the story of Americanization so that Chungpa must be

acclimated to an American society that is black, black not so much specifically in that it is a separate African American culture, though it is that
at times, but black in the sense that all of America may be like June, a
white woman pretending to be black or, more tellingly, a "white" woman
whose real spirit is the blackness that she portrays as "other." In *Immigrant Subjectivities in Asian American and Asian Diasporic Literature*, Sheng-
Mei Ma argues that America is often figured within the unconscious fantasy of the male Asian immigrant as a white woman. Certainly such a
gendering of America recurs throughout *East Goes West* in Kim's and
Chungpa's allied obsessions with the characters of Helen and Trip. But we
should not fail to detect the irony here in at least one of the three romantic plots that constitute *East Goes West*: in representing George's displaced
assimilationist desire for the white woman, Kang makes her not really
white, and by doing so, he calls into question the racialized body of the
white erotic fantasy of the Asian male in order to complicate the color of
America. In finding June a "strange thing," an ambiguous sign of American national identity, either a white actor in black face or a black soul
under a white mask and masquerade, Chungpa pushes his readers toward
the tabooed suspension of clear racial differences that the *Ozawa* and
other prerequisite cases had tried to eliminate. In such a world of "racechanges," the trickster Chungpa seems to ask, what can be (to borrow a
term from the U.S. Supreme Court) the "commonsensical" understanding of whiteness?

While Sheng-mei Ma argues that Asian American writers tried to
reverse their emasculation within American culture by treating women as
objects to be dominated or idealized (65), Kang's Chungpa Han has a
much more complicated relationship to femininity as well as to blackness. In *East Goes West*, Kang points at times toward an alternative narrative to what Dana Nelson has called "national manhood," the tactic
within white nationalized masculinity to define itself through dissociation and the splitting off of the "black" and "feminine" as the defining
rite of passage into the fraternity of white U.S. citizenry (Nelson, *National
Manhood* 11). Kang, by contrast, refuses such a practice of dis-identification within the immigrant history of naturalization, instead turning
toward a third standpoint by imagining a different kind of multiracial
and gender consciousness. This struggle toward a different kind of
identitarian positionality becomes visible on several occasions when

Chungpa draws attention to the fact that his "feminization" is the price he must pay in order to fit into American society. When Hsun Pak, for example, helps him attain his first job as a houseboy, Pak instructs him to "be shy like Korean bride" (61), and later, upon putting on the "white aprons, badges of servitude," Chungpa reflects that "the upper part looked man now, the lower, woman" (63). In this image of the literal whitening out of his penis and the skirting of his legs, Chungpa offers a visual symbol of the Asian male's castration as part of the socioeconomic oppression in 1920s America. But not only is Chungpa reduced to the status of a woman by being confined to domestic labor in the home, he can find manufacturing work only by accepting the employment usually assigned to black women. After Chungpa finds a job as a seamstress in Mr. McCann's factory, he relates the story of how one mischievous coworker would tease him by placing on his head the hat of another girl, Queenie, "to see if I looked like a Negro woman" (123). Once again Kang's symbolic dreamscape is almost too evident in this comic scene, as his wearing of Queenie's hat identifies his economic debasement from a bearer of the phallus to a feminine vessel of receptivity. In trying to sketch out the unimaginable community of overlapping allegiances and identifications in *East Goes West*, Kang connects questions of race and gender. Yet instead of depicting a cross-racial solidarity that depended on a shared misogynistic treatment of women, Kang initiates a cosmopolitan community that goes beyond a shared manhood. Rather than objectifying women to recapture the "phallus," Kang figures this scene of his being turned into a black woman into a self-ironic joke that acknowledges the common economic strivings and anger at discrimination that join Asian males to black women. As he allows for a mutual translatability of their similar, though still different, experiences, Chungpa finds a resilience here in the strategy of the African American, whose distinct humor lies in the ability to find "some funny side in lack of dignity, in losing face" (75). Although to become "naturalized" Ozawa had argued that he was "not black" and did not have the "qualities" and "personalities" of the black other and that his heart was pure, Chungpa performs an ironic minstrel show in which he is forced to take on and yet at the same time is willing, with a sense of humor, to assume the identity of the doubly discriminated against African American woman. He permits himself to be nearer black, and even momentarily female, than nearer white.

From "Genu-wine" Article to Cosmopolitan

When Rev. Bonheure, an African American preacher from Boston, invites Chungpa to testify as part of his ministry, Kang's alter ego seems to deliver Booker Washington's message of self-help and discipline: "Make something of yourselves. Be educated. . . . Don't depend on your leaders. They can't help you. Nothing can, but your own will to make something of yourself" (338). Telling his story before a "black" audience, Chungpa at first reverts to the narrative of the self-made man in the immigrant story of the model minority, yet Chungpa is delivering here less an accommodationist message than an indirect warning to the congregation to distrust "good-time" con artists and ministers who might abuse their trust and need for uplift. The people do not hear his message: they only see the "miracle" of an articulate Korean who does not confirm their stereotypes of the "Chinaman." As one woman cries out: "Chinaman can speak, too!!" (338). Basing their loyalties and their understanding on a simple race logic, they cannot discern the genuine from the false messenger, just as they cannot separate the real Korean from the "Chinaman" stereotype. Kang calls attention to this false association between the "genuine" and "race" in the conversation between Chungpa and Bonheure that takes place after the revival. After lauding Chungpa for giving a "good speech," Bonheure confides that he needs to correct some of the Korean immigrant's mispronunciations: the correct way to say "genuine," he notes, is "genu-wine" (339).

Throughout *East Goes West*, Kang raises disruptive questions about the nature of the "genuine." While it may seem as if Kang is satirizing Bonheure's lack of education, his equal mockery of the insular and pretentiously Dale Carnegiesque Mr. Lively suggests that Bonheure, and his way of speaking, may be no less legitimate—and authentic—than any other American way. In America, all representative men (black or white) tend to be con artists and salesmen (shape-shifting performers), despite the insistence of Justice Sutherland in the *Ozawa* case about the common-sense understanding of the true "qualities of personalities" possessed by the white American. This soul may not be any more genuine than "genu-wine," not without, that is to say, its many different inflections that tend to serve the interests of those looking for profit or power. In his fictional autobiography, Kang works to de-realize, de-normalize, and relativize the white body that Ozawa tried to enact as "genuine" in his own case for citizenship. Rather than taking America to heart, Kang tries to demonstrate that there is only a "genu-wine" embodied whiteness to assimilate.

Kang's oppositional gaze into the "genuine" soul of American "entrepreneurship" and middle-class family life becomes acute in his portrayal of the encyclopedia salesman, Mr. Lively, who, when he invites Chungpa to stay at his home, promises to reveal to his Oriental protégé that "Americans are models of family life" and to show him what a "real American home looks like" (146). In Chungpa's naive agreement to be led into the "holy of Holies of American civilization" (154), Kang traps the unsuspecting reader into a subversive mockery of his/her culture-bound expectations. If readers expect to share the pleasure of witnessing the foreigner's appreciation of one of the great "American" verities, the middle-class family, Kang repeats in excess Mr. Lively's verbal glorification of the "American" way to reveal the huckster's empty bombast. As Chungpa soon learns, Lively's words are merely "sales talk" that correspond only to his self-advertised dream (148). Once in the Lively home, Kang lists details that slowly lift the veil on the simulacrum of fireside contentment. Gradually Kang reveals the tension between the family picture Chungpa deferentially reports (as if admiring) and the exaggerated disingenuineness of Lively's conventional boosterism. Although Mrs. Lively was, Chungpa reports, "perpetually flustered and aggrieved"—often bursting into tears "so much over unimportant things!"—Mr. Lively "always said to [Chungpa] that [he] was lucky to come into a beautiful American home and see the inside" (142). Although Chungpa in his sly impersonality does not name the American housewife as an aggrieved victim of her social prison, he does mock the fictive formula of American domesticity. Likewise, he mocks through apparent obedient repetition Mr. Lively's constant deification of salesmanship as the sign of "manly independence" (142). While appearing to play up to and flatter this "great white father," Chungpa exposes his host's foibles. In his lengthy transcription of the rhetoric of salesmanship, particularly, Kang imitates Mr. Lively's banter in order to expose the ridiculousness of this vaunted and self-aggrandizing white masculinity. By the end of the lesson, Chungpa remarks that in its attempt to make the "customer do what we know is good for her" Western business has the same policy and position as the "Western missionaries" (158). While Chungpa exposes the fictiveness of white American nationalism, whose capitalist adventurism is compared to the sexual domination of women, Lively, by contrast, upon learning about Chung-pa's knowledge of British literature and his reading of Shakespeare, bursts into enthusiasm, for "this fine boy seems the genuine article" (137) from which to make a profit.[6]

Rather than trying to perform in his fictional autobiography a Korean American identity that is the "genuine article," Kang tries to point toward a cosmopolitan consciousness of multiple affiliations (black, white, and Korean). Yet if Kang never does fully name this new affiliative positionality, he identifies the ironic sabotaging of whiteness as the first stage in the constitution of a new interracialism. This undoing of whiteness is most clearly evident in his dramatization of the tragic romance of Kim, the Asian philosopher, and Helen, the American daughter of a prosperous Boston family. As the symbolic name of the idealized woman after the face that launched the thousand ships of Troy suggests, Kang is writing in the romance of Helen a "third world text," which, although it might seem merely personal or private, "necessarily project[s] a political dimension in the form of a national allegory" (Jameson, "Third-World Literature" 69). In Kang's national allegory, this interracial romance, proscribed in many states as illegal miscegenation at the time Kang wrote *East Goes West* (1937), functions as a deterrent narrative about an unbalanced obsession for the beauty of Euro-American white civilization. In Helen, Kim thinks that he has found the perfect complement to his exiled Asian soul: "her difference of ideas was a thrilling stimulation, yet his own innate simplicity of soul—an Eastern quality—found an echo in hers from New England" (222). Although it might seem at first that Kang is arguing for a congruency of hearts and souls that would bespeak the Korean's qualifications for naturalization despite his color, he implies that such a complete whitening finally leads to Kim's diminution and death.[7]

While in the romance of Kim and Helen Kang taps into powerful paranoiac nationalist fantasies about imperiled white daughters of the empire that were used to justify racial violence (Sharpe 4–6), the story of the star-crossed lovers Kim and Helen connects with a more immediate cultural referent. In his defense of his rights to gain citizenship, Takao Ozawa argued that the immigrant's internalization of the "heart" of nationalism could be witnessed in his love for American education, the English language, Western churches, and also white Americanized women. In the *Ozawa* case, racial disputes over the natural body of the true American overlapped with gender, for to prove that America was in the heart, Ozawa abrogated not only his culture, he also erased the abject ethnic body of women of color. Proudly in his public statement, Ozawa reminds the judges that "I chose as my wife one educated in American schools . . . instead of one educated in Japan" (qtd. in Ichioka 407). Since the end of the nineteenth century, as Martha Banta has carefully documented, advocates of cultural exceptionalism associated American society with its Daisy Millers and other New Women. In proclaiming his devotion to the idealized Western female, Helen, Kim, like Ozawa, was drawing upon a long discursive history tying feminine types to distinctive national/racial identities. Kang was well aware of this connection between gender and nationalism. In one of his few documented speeches, he argued (as the *New York Times* reported in 1935) for the further economic emancipation of American women since gender equality was a sign of the U.S.'s advanced national culture.[8] To take America to heart was also to embrace, so the *Ozawa* case reaffirmed, the Anglo-European New England woman.

In his initial description of Helen, Kang clearly equates her feminine body with the corpus of America's premodern New England cultural heritage. On first meeting Helen, Chungpa notes that "I suppose it was that obviously she could never be Chinized! No more than a white meetinghouse. She was quiet, but lacked the feminine stodginess of Mrs. Brown . . . she moved from the higher centers and she had the temperament if not the talent for the realm of higher ideas" (213). By using the metaphor of the white colonial meetinghouse, the site of Puritan religion and Revolutionary War meetings, Chungpa sees Helen as the living embodiment of this spiritual and political American idealism. In a manner similar to Henry Adams's often cited statements about the virgin and the dynamo, Kang uses Helen as the virgin, the Platonic object of love, who motivates a world before the modern machine age with its utilitarian values. Indeed, this is the antimodernist idealism that Kim would perceive in Helen's Western beauty: After telling Helen the story of the plant that found a state of bliss in the land of nonexistence, he remarks that "this has been my philosophy, in utilitarian civilizations wherever I and my muse are not wanted" (216).

Although Kim would adulate the feminine body of Western idealism, it is clear from the conversations and incidents that Chungpa reports that Helen is more accurately the symbol of imperialist and racist manifest destiny. In comparison to Kim, who acknowledges that his "sane pessi-

mism" has driven him to a cultural relativism (227, 236), Helen believes in
moral absolutes, the absolutes of her New England fathers. In his typical
seemingly dispassionate but sharply satiric undercutting, Chungpa
reveals the prudery and superficiality of this idealized New England version of the true woman: "she was bred in an old-fashioned Christian
home which forgot that Adam was ever naked with his wife and not
ashamed in the Garden of Eden" (219). When Kim speaks, moreover,
about the less inhibited African civilizations, Helen can only read such
immodesty as a sign of American cultural superiority: "There! And you
still argue we are not better off than to be in Africa" (225). Although Kim
exalts the noble Helen as the "product of this dominant west—Europe as
well as America. . . . It took all these centuries to make you what you are.
And now you have just the right pattern" (223), Kang, through the naive
narrator Chungpa, reveals the gap between Kim's idealized conception of
Helen and her rigid Puritanical commitment to white supremacism.

But Kim's story is not one simply of disillusionment about the individual object of worship, whether of Helen or America, but an allegory about
the racialized narrative of naturalization. When Chungpa naively
exclaims that "Helen might save Kim if she only would," Kang links
Kim's story with Ozawa's story, with the stories of many other refugee
students and bachelors who have come and assimilated to the Gold
Mountain of America. While Kim has "given up one world" and is search-
ing for another (207), Kang shows that the answer to his restless exile is
not simply to become wed to the centuries-long Anglo-centric/New
England tradition that Helen represents and which often legitimates a
rigid provincial nationalism. As Chungpa concludes, "Kim had no
defense against Helen's conservative background. It intensified the feeling he had all along, that he was an unwanted guest in the house of Western culture" (244). Finally, the Korean philosopher's "idealization" of the
white Western woman takes the form of self-hatred for his own racialized
body. Although Helen makes him more aware of his difference, Kim
believes that a consummate relation with her would allow him to transcend his own ethnic identity as part of some incorporeal love of the
heart. In his love for Helen, Kim would secure (like Ozawa) America in
the heart and reconcile and marry East with West.

By equating the white soul with a legacy of New England Puritanism
and racism, Kang opens up a space for a performative cosmopolitanism
that anticipates the contemporary moment of postidentity thinking (see,

for example, Posnock 9–10). Exposing the lack of genuineness within the purity of the "white" heart, soul, and consciousness of America through the story of Kim and Helen, Kang refuses to see any fixed racialized identity as the endpoint of his fictional autobiography. As a diasporic postmodernist, Kang was aware that there was no premodern or precolonial Eden to rediscover as "home." Literally, as he says in *East Goes West*, writing in the period of Japanese and American expansionism in the Pacific, there was no homeland of Korea to which to return. Korea's traditional culture was disintegrating and passing under the forces of modernization. What Kang finally points out is an insight that Stuart Hall voiced in his own essays on race and culture: identities are more a matter of becoming than being or discovering; they are future oriented rather than backward looking ("Cultural Identity" 225). From his opening poetic meditation on time, Kang grounds *East Goes West* on an understanding of process, that identities are finally in process, the Asian American is in process, being fed by black and white and yellow streams. It was Chungpa muses, a "great age of disintegration and new combinations" (314). Rather than falling into a postcolonial nostalgia that attempts to restore cultural cohesion under the logic of race, whether of whiteness or Asianness, Kang struggles to point to a new Utopia that he is never able to name, but it would be a Utopia of new combinations, of cultural interplays and mergers among different races and ethnicities, that would begin once American society had betrayed the logic of naturalization with its Negrophobic assumption that to be American was to be nearer white.

In his story of the Korean nationalist Mr. Lin, who assassinated Chinwan, the Japanese-educated Korean who "looked kindly" on all Asians regardless of their country of origins, Kang invites Asian readers to reimagine their exile as the starting point for a cross-racial identification with other colonized peoples, particularly African Americans. Kang's criticism of the insularity of Lin's anti-Japanese nationalism is loosely based on the 1908 murder of Durham Stevens, the American employed by the Japanese to downplay for the U.S. government and business community the Korean resentment of Japan's invasion (Takaki, *Strangers* 283). Yet in a telling reversal, Kang makes the Korean nationalist hero Chang In-hwan the victim (Chinwan) of a nationalist zealotry in order to point toward a different kind of postcolonial Asian criticism. While Lin contends that he had to kill the "spy" to prove that he was a "true Korean" (68), Kang in the voice of Chungpa calls instead for a greater sense of cosmopolitanism:

"Here in this cosmopolitan city I saw Lin as living in a narrow world, a small world in a large. No message came back and forth from the large world to the little nor from the little world to the large" (69). Although equally displaced like his fellow Korean Lin in America, Chungpa rebukes the narrow-mindedness of ethnic exclusivity and invites his readers to locate themselves within a third space of fragmented and shifting cosmopolitan affiliations. As Chungpa remarks as he later hitchhikes across America, he was "repeating the life of his grandfather, the geomancer, . . . a roving life of ever new contacts and scenes" (344). Kang's story, as told in the life of Chungpa, is one of continual self-displacement, a refusal not simply to assimilate to America but to settle, to reside in any one tradition. In words that echo the resistance of earlier nineteenth-century non-conformists such as Thoreau, Chungpa remarks as he takes flight from Boston, "We left Boston behind; however the accumulation of puritanic dirt made me uneasy. I would have liked to jump at once into the river, wash off all dirts and send them down to the sea, becoming a child again as I was in Korea" (235). To remain stagnant for Kang's protagonist is to accumulate dirt, to lose one's receptivity to change and growth, and that would be a denial of what he calls in one moment of reflection "the new age of broad communication, cross-fertilization, and the shaking of boundaries" (268). In leaving Korea, in leaving Canada, in leaving Boston, in heading for New York, Kang remarks it was because "I had craved a more cosmopolitan environment" (176). Rather than simply demystifying race- or nation-based ideas of identity, Kang affiliates himself with many different and particular ethnic communities, participating in their point of view and thus opening up translocal affections and solidarities.

In both his lament at his exile and his embrace of this very exile as a trope for a higher consciousness that transcends national and racial borders, Kang anticipates some of the recent writing about diasporic internationalism that Tim Brennan finds in the work of Salmon Rushdie and V. S. Naipaul. His homelessness comes to characterize a frame of mind that is defined by its openness, its tolerance of uncertainty, its contradictions, its freedom, its mixture of curiosity and skepticism, its constant flux and change. Describing his approach to the West, Kang's Chungpa anticipates another ecstasy: "I was eager to feel its life in an unbroken stream pass through my heart-blood. . . . Seen in this way, history becomes not history, but poetry and creative process" (190). Although I do not want to suggest that Kang ever stopped feeling a certain loneliness that came with his alienation—his later attempt to naturalize as an American citizen shows that—in his story of Chungpa Han, this Korean-born exile refuses to authenticate any single location, to signal Chungpa's arrival anywhere. While many of the novel's early critics read the novel's end as an intimation of Chungpa's reunion with Trip, he is, reading allegorically, obsessed by the "trip," by the roving desire itself. To belabor the obvious, in a novel so episodic, the absence of a single place or home set up in opposition to Korea or to America is a narratological clue to the text's theme. But in contrast to the disengagement and rootlessness of privileged Third World texts written from metropolitan centers, Kang's text offers a counterhegemonic aesthetics in which he refuses to act as the tourist exile or spectator in order to reattach himself to multiple sites of participation and belonging.

In the end, Kang preserves the postnational, postethnic "cosmopolitanism" (as he calls it) that Chungpa's mentor, Kim, loses in his surrender to Helen's "white" New England body. When Chungpa confessed his struggles to come to terms with America, Kim had advised his friend not to lose his "proper balance": "I suppose, like myself, you can see without trying to do so the exaggerations and prejudices of the West. But by keeping a well-balanced mind, you will see too the exaggerations and prejudices of the Orient" (278). But Kang's "Oriental Yankee," which the subtitle of his fictional autobiography suggests is in the "making," is not simply one who combines East and West, America and Asia (whatever these abstract locations may mean), but someone who moves toward a more particularized affiliation with the heterogeneous group that constitutes and at the same time disables the fiction of a "naturalized" white U.S. citizenry. Such an Oriental Yankee (unlike Ozawa) is a participant performer of many different points of views, a "genu-wine" cosmopolitan always unfolding in time, never fixed or static but always being, as Kang notes in his closing image, reborn to a "happier reincarnation." For Kang, ethnic and racial identity is a homeland that he has left behind for a life that constantly opens itself up to new additions, new affections for and coalitions with others. It is an exile's journey that has no end, only the trip, and more "reincarnations."

5. Dis-integrating Third Spaces

The Unrepresented in Abraham Cahan's and Mary Antin's Narratives of Americanization

In his famous 1928 study of *The Ghetto*, the German-born sociologist Louis Wirth declared the Jewish enclave in America not so much a "physical fact as . . . a state of mind" (287). As a caseworker with Jewish charities in urban Chicago while writing his dissertation, Wirth had been frustrated with these other Jewish immigrants' failure to assimilate, and he chastised this insular group consciousness, even as he tried to understand their clash of values. While Wirth traces the persistence of ethnic traditionalism to a long history of isolation, both forced by legal persecutions and personal and religious needs for security, he faults this "frame of mind" as a "transitional stage" (129) obstructive to an inevitable emergence into the New World composed of an integrated community. In his narrative of the psychological boundaries externalized in the ghetto wall, Wirth opposes the "parochialism" of the ethnic enclave to the "cosmopolitanism" of the larger American culture.[1] Yet Wirth's foundational contrasting of two different "frames of mind" among Jewish immigrants and their corresponding distinct urban scenes leaves out the possibility of a third space, a space, as we have seen in Kang's autobiography, with its own mental culture that cannot be neatly conceptualized as either parochial or cosmopolitan, traditional or modern. In fact, Wirth himself hints at just such a problematic heterogeneous, multiethnic space when he extrapolates to other immigrant groups in his chapter titled "The Sociological Significance of the [Jewish] Ghetto." In addition to the familiar patterns of assimilation or voluntary segregation, there is what Wirth calls "accommodation." Attempting to explain the coexistence and often overlapping of various ethnic neighborhoods, Wirth describes "accommodation" as "two groups . . . occupy[ing] a given area without losing their separate identity because each side is permitted to live its own inner life, and each somehow fears the other or idealizes the other" (283). Accommodation, he remarks shortly thereafter, is the way people avoid "getting under each other's skins, so to speak" (283). While other witnesses of the "ghetto," especially in the Lower East Side of New York City, described the immigrant settlement as a "polyglot boarding house," Wirth trivializes the "accommodated" or cross-cultural crowdedness of tenement communities and reassures his readers that despite the heterogeneity of many "ghettos," there is no fear of a psychological, or here a literal and physical, boundary loss.[2] In his mapping of the transition between New World and Old, Wirth excludes from the frame of his sociological history any dis-integration of identitarian integrity that might emerge if ethnic groups literally "got under each other's skins."[3]

Theorists such as Homi Bhabha, bell hooks, and Edward Soja have called for the active Third Worlding of the center, a push toward hybridity, and a utopian space of fluid and fragmented identities. In a now canonical essay within postcolonial studies, "The Third Space," Bhabha has argued for a political resistance that will be achieved through the possibilities of a third space of radical openness, of marginality, of liminality, of an in-betweenness for critical rethinking, reenvisioning, and insubordination toward all forms of hierarchy. These third spaces will initiate new signs of identity and innovative sites of collaboration (207–9). But in imagining these utopian, or third, sites of resistance, postcolonial writers tend to forget history to imagine the future. These critics write as if third spaces were not always already experienced by diasporic immigrants and not a new millennial real or discursive space to be opened up and inhabited. In referring briefly to a third "accommodated space" outside the homogeneous ethnic neighborhoods, Wirth points out that even such highly concentrated "ghettoes" as New York's celebrated Lower East Side had Jewish and Italian Catholic immigrants living across the hall from each other. In what follows I want to raise questions about what is largely unrepresented, possibly never fully representable, in Jewish immigrant literature from the early twentieth century because this unsaid is what the immigrant is unprepared to deal with or what exceeds his/her psychic apparatus completely to become aware of and understand. As Daniel Soyer has noted, social historians often overlook the interaction among different ethnic communities, which may have been just as important as their relation with mainstream society (4). The long list of immigrant communities in New York at the turn of the century—Italian, Chinese, Irish, Greek, German, Russian, to name a few—underlines the need to historicize and recover the absent presence of third spaces in early-twentieth-century U.S. literature. There are many different "true" versions of this other space, some liberatory, some disorienting or dis-integrating.

Throughout this chapter I will be concerned with representations of the inner city in Jewish immigrant stories of Americanization in order to restore the sense of disjuncture between the complex social interactions within this third space and the ways these writers constructed their own representations of the neighborhood. My concern is with how these immigrant writers helped to construct their own imaginary territory in urban spaces that were often used for different purposes by dozens of social groups and imbued with divergent meanings and, more important, with how, in creating these texts of memory that would build up a space of ethnic authenticity, immigrant writers omitted a very important part of the immediacy of the experience in these neighborhoods: the way other immigrant groups would have been on the sidewalk, in the parks, across the hall, so that they would have gotten under their skin not only in the sense of being physically dangerous, annoying, or inconveniencing but in having a formative influence in the shaping of their new white American identity.[4] Race in the early twentieth century was being delineated in new and contradictory ways for Jewish Americans, as they were becoming whiter and whiter even as they were still labeled as uncouth eastern European barbarians invading Anglo-Saxon America (Jacobson 75). In studies of early-twentieth-century immigrant literatures, we need to start, then, with the recognition that the process of Americanization, which is taken as the central theme within immigrant literature, is a social construct, and as a result, there are many different and competing versions of the way in which an immigrant becomes Americanized (Radhakrishnan 72). Too often we leave as inevitable and uncontested the absorption of the immigrant into some simple monolithic "American" mainstream culture (a "real" America), and studies of immigrant autobiographies focus on the author's retention of a native cultural heritage or renegotiation of the dominant U.S. culture.

By studying several Jewish immigrant texts for their representations of third public spaces where different ethnic and racial groups mixed in a dynamic interaction, from the marketplace to the embodied sites of exchange located in borderland sex districts, I want to problematize as well the binary logic of the immigrant text between what Werner Sollors has most clearly formulated as the New World of consent (America) and the Old World of dissent/descent (the homeland) (*Beyond Ethnicity* 156–57). This abstracted conflict between two worlds represses, as did many immigrant texts, a feared ambivalence about boundary loss, what I call "dis-integration." Many Jewish immigrant writers felt a simultaneous dread about a catastrophic loss of borders and of impotence in multicultural contact zones and also a fantasy of pleasurable liberation from and transgression of ghetto boundaries. Jewish immigrant subjects were not just alienated from America or their homeland but experienced a transformative indeterminacy in their gender, ethnic, class, and sexual identities. When studying the Jewish immigrant's "urban practices," to borrow Michel de Certeau's term (93), as a result, we must look at how they defined their ethnic performance not only against abstracted national formations (America) but also against something closer to home, something in the everyday lived environment of most Lower East Side Jews: a third multicultural contact zone of disconcerting, open-ended transformative and liminal identities. Pre–World War I Jewish immigrant writers such as Abraham Cahan and Mary Antin struggled to represent the city space out of the chaos and the complexity of New York's interethnic dynamic, seeking to dis-integrate public space or to have it disappear from sight, from memory, and, most important, from the process of ethnic subjectivization. The "public spaces" of "integrated" or multicultural contact, however, were always there marking the limits of their paths and stood as that threat and promise against which mapping of the city took shape. These Jewish immigrant writers removed any disruptive challenges to the master narrative of Americanization, one that presumed the immigrant was caught between two processes: either assimilation into a "white" Western European Christian heterosexual middle-class culture or separation into ethnic exclusivity. But one might also lose one's "skin."

Walking and the Unrepresented Third Space

In "Walking in the City" (here New York City), from *The Practice of Everyday Life*, Michel de Certeau contrasts the privileged vantage point of the corporate "trader" atop the World Trade Center to the lived experience of the "walker" down below on the streets in the city.* While it has become common within recent studies of cultural geography to investigate the connection between the symbolic representations of a place and questions of social power, Certeau's contrast between the trader and the walker directs us to more than an investigation into the contestation over space between ruling groups and marginal members of society. Against the abstracted grids of the corporate trader with his/her view from above, Certeau sets the ongoing, continual, accidental, and open-ended mappings of the walker from below. This peripatetic mapping, as Certeau suggests, operates outside the oppositional paradigms of much current cultural and ethnic studies locked into questions of the individual's relation to the mainstream text of the city. The walker, Certeau argues, is often impervious to the identity that comes from above or from organized countercultural arrangements from the margins. Rather, his/her cognition of the city comes from his/her rendering of space as memorable, through his/her repetition of constantly renegotiated decisions about where to go and how to see (feel, taste, touch, eat, sing) the "real" American city. To begin the explication of the pedestrian mappings of the city by Jewish immigrant writers, we need to broaden our emphasis to include an examination of the forms of self-activity that produce a parallel, or coincident, and not necessarily an alternative, mapping of space from below. This self-activity should not be reduced to some defensive adaptation against the official, supposedly totalizing, culture of the power elite in their Manhattan office towers. Instead, we need to ask how the immigrant writers walking the city rendered their place memorable. In the

---

* Although Certeau's "Walking in the City" was written nearly two decades before the tragedy of September 11, 2001, his essay foreshadowed the symbolic value the World Trade Center would acquire for many who felt marginalized in a world of global capitalism or who resented what they saw as U.S. cultural and economic imperialism. Certeau's essay instructs us about the struggle over the meaning and representation of places, a struggle that can often be violent and can be, as even Certeau did not foresee, catastrophic and deadly. In mourning the tragedy of September 11, it seems to me even more important to remember Certeau's thoughts on the World Trade Center, even if they remind us of what is painful or recall our personal losses.

immigrant writers' rendering of an alternative mapping, they not only invented a new cultural geography, but they also condemned certain spaces beyond their periphery of vision.

While the trader imperially standing 110 floors up above the bustle of the streets views the text of the city with a totalizing eye, organizing and arranging all the city's anarchic excess and movements into systems and wholes, the ordinary practitioner of the city, the walker, has a different relation to space. Let me quote Certeau in full for a moment, because his language draws out implications that comment significantly on what it would mean to have an urban immigrant practice that is a "self-activity from below":

> These practitioners make use of spaces that cannot be seen; their knowledge of them is as blind as that of lovers in each other's arms. The paths that correspond in this intertwining, unrecognized poem in which each body is an element signed by many others, elude legibility. It is as though the practices organizing a bustling city were characterized by their blindness. The networks of these moving intersecting writings compose a manifold story that has neither author nor spectator, shaped out of fragments of trajectories and alterations of space; in relation to representations, it remains daily and indefinitely other. (93)

In speaking of these street-level practitioners, the walkers, Certeau attempts to identify an activity and, I might add, a site outside the hegemonic logic of the city. Certeau's writings have illuminated the ways in which mundane activities or "practices" of ordinary women and men disrupt the dominant system, even if unconsciously so, and in unanticipated, anarchic ways that can never be fully contained or closed off by the master planners of the city or by their symbolic culture (R. Kelley 7). At the heart of Certeau's writing is the familiar question of agency, an agency that is exercised, despite the best utilitarian and rationalizing efforts of the city planners atop the World Trade Center, every time the walker takes a shortcut through the unanticipated spaces off the official map. For Certeau, as a result, there is another "long poem" of the city that is constantly being written (101), one that is a result of individual unplanned "walking" from below that is not simply in conformity to or in resistance against the panoptic vision of the planners. Against the grids of the corporate writers of culture, with their view from above, lies the ongoing, continual, open-ended "mapping from below" (102).

As mentioned, to begin an explication of the pedestrian mappings of the city by Jewish immigrant writers, we need to expand our examination of the forms of self-activity that produce a parallel, de-transcendent, and not necessarily alternative sense of space from below. Even as walkers render through a repetition of familiar paths and occasional wanderings their world memorable, and constantly unrememberable, they are themselves a textual performance that is being composed through the chance encounters and accidental tourisms within the city landscape. Certeau's language is particularly telling in the way it complicates the figuration of third space. "Each body is an element signed by many other, elud[ing] legibility," Certeau writes, and later he asserts that there is "neither author nor spectator" among practitioners from below, only stories of people "shaped out of fragments of trajectories and alterations of space" (93). While using the metaphor of walking as an urban practice that restores agency to the common people on the street who finally live, move, and have their being under and between the clear lines of corporate culture's master planners, Certeau significantly qualifies this "self-activity." The walker, according to Certeau, has no stable self. If the walker is illegible to the World Trade Center planner, and therein lies the secrecy that permits an escape from the policing surveillance of institutionalized powers, the walker is unable to be finally author of himself/herself. The pedestrian from the tenements has no control over his/her encounters, the contacts he/she will endure, the bumpings, the elbow jabs, the saliva stepped in on the streets, the assault of noises, the polyglot discourses floating in the air, the violent assaults in the byways through which he/she attempts to shortcut the official path. Despite his/her best intentions, cautious or cursory movements, he/she is "signed" by many "others" in encounters that are constant, unstructured, shifty, but which often get under the skin and are written into the body in the reflexive responses, the nervous mannerisms, the bold strut, even if the originating encounters are never fully memorable as self-contained, discrete instances.[5]

The walker is always, especially while moving in "integrated" spaces where he/she would find the pressed confluence of many colored bodies and many accented tongues, in danger of dis-integration, a dis-integration on the level of the psyche, since his/her ego must try to process a continual assault of new impressions and sensations, and a dis-integration on the level of identity, since his/her transitional performance is always susceptible to welcomed or unwelcomed touches of others. Although Certeau retreats into a linguistic realm of abstract and universal humanity when he speaks of the city crowd, effacing them literally in a synecdochic language of bodies or generally unmarked authors, the particular Jewish, Korean American, Puerto Rican, and Arab people of New York were the signatures that diversify the city scene. Although, as readers/writers and walkers of the street, twentieth-century Jewish immigrants wanted to control the language of their own speech, actions, and understandings of the other, they were also "blind," or liable to touch words, signs, people, they could not foresee.

Yet, finally, through hints and associations, Certeau's metaphor of the urban pedestrian evokes another kind of "streetwalking," where wandering and desire meet either for pleasure or for profit. The walker, this flaneur of the modern city, is, as Certeau realizes, "blind as . . . lovers in each other's arms." What finally is the "desire" to see the city, the "ecstasy" of reading it that Certeau speaks about when analyzing the urban practice from below? How does the walker's mapping of the city intersect with unconscious desires and overlap with sexual fantasy? What lust structures this urban practice? Part of the city's hidden allure, especially the unofficial spaces wandered into from below, may be precisely that they allow one to forget who one is, at least for a little while. The city walker's wanderings may be exactly an unconscious inner mapping of the urge toward the very self-dislocation that frightens the walker who would conquer unfamiliar territory. If, as Julia Kristeva has argued, the object of desire becomes the very experience or self-shattering, the city, particularly the dis-integrating spaces of the city, tease with their titillating promise, a promise of just such a "jouissance," a resolution of the self into a formlessness, where one is neither author nor spectator, neither subject nor object, but something other that is neither legible nor capable of being objectively presented (Kristeva 22).

In their study of the stories of Holocaust survivors, Dominick LaCapra, Lawrence Langer, and Cathy Caruth have argued that the originary terror and trauma of Auschwitz lies outside the unifying logic of any mimetic representation. In their concern with how traumatic events are reenacted in the psyche and how authors struggle to bear witness to these horrors, trauma theorists have noted that certain historical catastrophes, and the uncompensable losses that accompany them, exceed our capacities to narrate them, remaining "failed experiences" that are unthinkable and unsayable. Yet the failed experiences of trauma, as Judith Herman notes, do not just stem from a single unprecedented event (such as war or sexual violence) that overwhelms one's sense of self and place in the world. Trauma also arises from a repeated and prolonged exposure to stress factors in the environment (120). In their reticence about third spaces, immigrant texts reveal the impossibility of testifying to an "everyday and reiterative trauma." As Hasia Diner has argued, during the 1950s and 1960s as more and more Jewish Americans moved alongside Gentiles in the suburbs, stories of the "Lower East Side" took on a sacred status as a memory of an authentic past (60), but what is omitted in these later sentimental recollections is the possibility that earlier immigrant writers might have had their own "trauma" or existential crisis that would have caused them to fit their histories into a collective story and to repress the multiplicities of borderland experiences within the "ghetto." It is my starting point in what follows that there were complexities and diversities that were simplified into familiar sets of assumptions within the Jewish immigrant text and which we must restore if we are fully to understand the discursive practices of these authors, practices that were as much materializing a new sense of identity and space as reflecting it. What had to be elided in the walker's encounter with the city, encounters that were translated into retrospective memories of their Americanization, were moments of panic about dis-integration within the ghetto's contact zones. While the "trauma" of the immigrant in the multicultural city is of a different type from that of the survivor of historical catastrophes such as the Holocaust, immigrants, too, experienced an everyday violation, one about which they would have felt at times no escape or recourse because their repertoire of responses allowed them little understanding.

The story of the over two million Jews who left Europe for the U.S. between 1881 and 1914 has been told by cultural historians such as Irving Howe in *The World of Our Fathers*. Coming mostly from the Russian Empire of eastern Europe as well as from Galicia, Hungary, and Romania, these immigrants crowded into a twenty-block area of the Lower East Side that had once been dominated by the Irish and Germans and that was bounded by the Bowery and the East River and by (longitudinally) Market Street and Fourteenth Street. But if by 1910, 542,061 Jews were crowded into the tenements of the Lower East Side so that the population density in some tenement areas surpassed the highest known foreign aggregation in Bombay, India, with 800.47 people per acre (Binder and Reimers 69–70), these immigrants were neighbors to Italians on Mulberry, Mott, and Elizabeth Streets; Irish settlers on First and Second Avenues; "Asian peoples" in Chinatown; as well as dispersed Greeks, Arabs, Syrians, Gypsies, and some remaining German and Dutch residents (Maffi 67). As Jacob Epstein recalls in his autobiography, "Within easy reach of each other, one could see the most diverse life from many lands, and I absorbed material which was invaluable" (9). In acknowledging that he "absorbed" invaluable material from other ethnic groups and races that were in "easy reach of each other," Epstein hints at what is a telling absence in many immigrant texts and which suggests that the process of assimilation was a more complex phenomenon than memory, a memory often mediated by predominant generic codes, admitted or even allowed. While immigrant writers often framed their stories within the rehearsed script of the conflict between two worlds and diluted their individual stories in the impersonal terms of the public debate over assimilation or cultural retention, they often experienced a sense of displacement that was personal and psychological and that caused ambiguities and contradictions within the immigrant text (Kramer 130–31).

While the multiethnic dynamics of immigrant third spaces frequently eluded narrativization in Jewish immigrant texts, Henry James's *The American Scene* (1905) confronts the multicultural contact zones of New York City directly to develop a particular narrative of white privilege. James's *The American Scene*, while written by one of the most canonical of U.S. writers, sheds light on the way cultural memory is materialized in representations of space in Jewish immigrant writers such as Mary Antin and Abraham Cahan. In 1904, at the age of sixty-one, James returned to his "homeland" from his expatriation in Britain to survey the transformation the U.S. had undergone during his twenty-year absence (Edel 289–90). Although someone whose intellectual training and class background positioned him as a member of the empire builders housed in Certeau's World Trade Center, James through his travel narrative nonetheless adopts the standpoint, or should I say moving point, of the "walker," hoping to wed such an intimate spectatorship with an Olympian abstract and summarizing vision. Yet the walker, as Certeau reminds us, can have no more than a transitory standpoint, one already stepped outside of as soon as it is identified. So James's effort to reconcile the subject position of the "trader" and the "walker," as he himself comes to learn, is as impossible as uniting fixity with perpetual motion or consolidating the taste of the wealthy with those who act without "class." I want to look at several passages from the walker's reflection, in which James must traffic with the "alien": first, as he peregrinates along the upper reach of Fifth and Madison Avenues, the thoroughfares being mapped by the architects of Stanford and White for traders such as J. Pierpoint Morgan and James Frick, and second, as he strolls on a Sunday in Central Park where the "fruit of the foreign trees [has] shaken down there with a force that smothered everything else" (84). As an excursionist, James is not unaffected by the nativist's prejudices; however, these prejudices may be complicated by his cosmopolitan and aesthetic love for the colorful exchanges of commodified national characters in an evolving international market that will bring "brotherhood" (as he opines, briefly) in the second generation (86). But my concern is less with James's predictable racist indiscretions than with how his walking extends Certeau's theory of urban practices to the fashioning of a racialized white identity.

When on the "long residential vistas" of Fifth and Madison James first encounters an "alien" whose ethnic origin remains undecipherable, he is shocked by the incongruity of the man's presence. He would have expected the appearance of such an "alien" on the Lower East Side, in San Juan Hill, but not in the "residential" space of New York's overclass, and this "meeting" unsettles James's received boundaries regarding the correct location of the native and the foreign and the boundary that separates the classes. Although urban journalists such as Jacob Riis had clearly mapped the city in distinctive neighborhoods, or ethnic enclaves, James finds this reassuring spatial arrangement of cultural pluralism fallacious, for "the alien is as truly in possession under the high aristocratic nose, as if he had had but three steps to come" (84). The proximity of the "alien," quantified as a mere three-step walk and unavoidable as an olfactory annoyance, threatens to turn Madison into a tenement district, where the privileged individualism of the trader may be taken possession of along with the land. Yet while James starts his walking encounter with an overly familiar paranoia about "alien" invasion, James is too self-reflexive to leave his tendentious speculations unexamined. Immediately he ponders (switching pronouns from "I" to the impersonal and the "you"): "why, the alien still strik[es] you so as an alien, the singleness of impression, throughout the place, should still be so marked" (84). In answering his own question, James resorts to a telling displacement of culpability that speaks directly to his performance of the self in this urban practice of walking. As James remarks, "the alien *himself fairly makes the singleness of impression. Is not the universal sauce essentially his sauce, and do we* not feel ourselves feeding, half the time, from the ladle, as greasy as he chooses to leave it for us, that he holds out?" (84, my emphasis).

Now there are many levels on which to understand James's answer to why the "alien" fails to be assimilated within the consciousness of the walker/trader, and we should note here the positing of the overriding question for James is not why the immigrant fails to acculturate but why James fails to assimilate the other. In his expansive anecdote about another encounter with a digger, to which he compares this Madison Avenue meeting, James clearly faults the immigrant for his self-separation: the ethnic refuses to make himself known to the native, although due to no want of trying on the part of the representative American. James in his walking vents his epistemological frustration, but his intellectual hunger for knowledge of the other must sate itself on only what is offered from the "greasy" spoon. James's imagery here is telling, for it discloses both the self-congratulation and revulsion he feels in his own "desire" to know the other during his walking. To reach out to the other requires an unhealthy hygienic contamination. Yet it is clear from James's narrative that the "love" that propels his walking is a desire for this soiling encounter. Speaking of his earlier walking on the Jersey shore when he attempted to converse with an obstinate digger, James writes, "to pause before them, for interest in their labour, was, and would have been everywhere, instinctive, but what came home to me on the spot was that whatever *more* would have been anywhere else involved had here inevitably to lapse" (85). In his linguistic indirection, James alludes to more than his class- and race-based presumption that the immigrant ought to want to speak to him and want to know him. Why is the man of leisure's desire to quiz the laborer about his work to be assumed as "instinctive," and instinctive in such as way as to be recognized and responded to by the digger? Or has James linguistically tried not to fall into his own hole and yet slipped: is not his own instincts, his own desires for the ecstasy of reading and meeting the other, a sublimated if not overt homoerotic overture, one that is rebuffed, so that he is left to mourn the ambiguous "whatever more" that might have been. What has inevitably to lapse?

My intention in looking at James's erotics of walking is not simply to point out the homoerotic subtext that shapes James's cross-cultural encounter. It is instead to flesh out the "body," which Certeau argues is "signed by many others" while "walking." While James finds one ostensible lesson in the irony that in America class lines are more rigidly drawn against easy conversation among "excursionists," in contrast to Italy where there would have been an "easy sense . . . of a social relation with any encountered type" (85), his walking he finds, much to his alarm, leaves him with a fear of narrative failure, and it is because of his inability to explain that he feels so vulnerable to the other's allure. Although James's witnessing of the presence of the "alien" might have caused him to further question what is an American, James as the walker, rather than the trader secure in grand speculations, stumbles upon a more immediate and bothersome loss of both questions and explanations: "The challenge to speculation, fed thus by a thousand sources, is so intense as to be, as I say, irritating, but practically beyond doubt, I should also say, you take refuge from it—since your case would otherwise be hard . . . and you find your relief not in the least in any direct satisfaction or solution, but absolutely in that . . . blest general feeling for the impossibility of them" (86–87). As Certeau notes, the walker in the urban scene cannot be an author or spectator since he/she is constantly susceptible to the alterations of space and persons. While Certeau leaves such alterations mere generalities, as James's "outing" testifies, the alterations of the body that threaten to dis-integrate the ego of the spectator are precisely those prompted by "aliens" unknowable and refusing to be known.

Although James initially attempts to translate his misfortune into a crisis of the imagination prompted by being unanchored and alienated from familiar urban landscapes that can be rendered memorable, he resorts to a strategy of narrative salvaging that once again renders him invincible (and invisible) to the other. Unlike Certeau, James knows that he can end uncertainty and doubt by opening up speculation, by making the walker and the trader the same "representative man" of the American scene. In the paragraph that follows, James refurbishes the individualist ethos of nineteenth-century liberalism by wedding it to the consumerist free play of the marketplace. Rather than mourning the loss of identity and fixity, James's autobiographically engendered viewer will refigure his self, his white self, into a permanent tourist, someone who will redefine his class and white status as the ability to view everyone and everything as a commodity to be intellectually traded in and to excite the observer's passive consumption. "He doesn't know, he can't say, before the facts, and he doesn't even want to know or to say: the facts themselves loom, before the understanding, in too large a mass for a mere mouthful; it is as if the syllables were too numerous to make a legible word. The illegible words, accordingly, the great inscrutable answer to questions, hangs in the vast American sky . . . it is under this convenient insight that he travels and considers and contemplates, and to the best of his ability, enjoys" (87). While originally in the dis-integrating spaces of this new American scene, James had experienced a trauma about that which is unsayable—he could find no legible word to be author and master of his domain and lay open to a delicious, self-shattering "alien" possession—he escapes out of himself into the impersonality of the trader. He will realign his vision so as to see all the world as moment by moment unpredictable but, in the larger scheme of things, all designed for his intellectual trading and consumption. James's excursionist can trade in seeing while imagining any encounter with the other does not involve an exchange of looks. Despite the fact he no longer controls the American scene, he will take enjoyment in constant novelty and in intransitive consumption of the many "aliens" who, though they may not speak to him, he can still aesthetically enjoy in the never-ending city scene. The way to avoid "flat fatigue," to no longer feel the loss of the personal relation, James remarks, is to throw oneself into the immensity with no "diminution of quantity, even by that inch, [which] might mark the difference of his having to recognize from afar, as through a rift in the obscurity, the gleam of some propriety of opinion" (88). James knows, as he states at the end of his meditation, that as a privileged white male he can avoid the anxiety of his lost self by shattering it himself or by constantly expanding himself to include novel delights so that he does not have to miss any longer the fact that he does not have a settled standpoint while walking. He can, in short, trade and bargain in the aliens of the world because he does not have to be down in the ditch digging.

Throughout James's *American Scene*, he translates the polyglot scene of New York City's dis-integrating third spaces into a trader's marketplace of endless, unfixed speculations unconnected to the earth and thus inoculates the middle-class nativist walker from being signed and consequently rendered illegible to himself/herself by so many others. While the immigrant "walker" could not be a "trader" like James, could not at times even be an excursionist but only a plebeian walker in the American landscape, he/she often tried to deal with the interethnic transactions in the city's third space in a manner similar to James. Although written as a serialized autobiography for the readers of the *Atlantic Monthly* on the eve of the

First World War with the intention of performing the ideological work of assuring Americans of Jewish acculturation and patriotism (Shavelson 162), Mary Antin's *The Promised Land* reveals that the mapping from below, the walking of the ethnic writer in the city, can involve an urban practice that dangerously aligns itself with whiteness. In terms of the urban practice of the walker, Antin's text traces out the narrative contradictions that appear in a number of Jewish immigrant autobiographies. *The Promised Land* is a self-deconstructing work in which gaps in the text, demarcating their own repressed discursive space, threaten to overturn and repudiate the patriotic story of Americanization. Unable to accept the everyday trauma about the possible dis-integration involved in her journey toward a white American self, Antin develops a strategy for containing the other that is similar to James's effort in *The American Scene*.

Mary Antin's fictionalized autobiography, *The Promised Land*, is at first glance the story of the model minority's Americanization. While the first half describes her parents' and her own early life in Polotz, Poland, and the persecution and economic deprivation they experienced, the second half often reads at times like one long patriotic pledge of allegiance. As Antin traces her rise through hard work and education to achieve the American Dream of success, she presents herself as the "show pupil" of her teachers (239) and of immigration initiative and love of one's adopted country. Yet the narrative gaps and inhibitions in Antin's text show that it was not so easy for her to keep her feet on the long, "undeviant" road of Americanization, not just because the fulfillment of the promise of education, opportunity, and success was not easy and her life was not free of racist discrimination, but because the seams in Antin's story show that there is a third space. This place of cross-ethnic contact is constantly being written out of her narrative, written out because she must remove this threatening third axis that would upset the delicate narrative lines from Old World to New World. It is in the interstitial spaces of Antin's autobiography that a disjunction opens up among her often contradictory representations of her New World neighborhoods.

In her account of life on Dover Street, Antin seems torn between the proper narrative of Americanization that she must tell to perform the truth of her experience. At first, Antin reassures her American audience that any initial tribulations and hardships she experienced in her "ghetto" did not belie the mythic image of America as the land of milk and honey with streets paved with gold: "I was not unhappy on Dover

Street, quite the contrary. Everything of consequence was well with me. Poverty was a superficial, temporary matter; it vanished at the touch of money. Money in America was plentiful" (297). However, shortly before this burst of boosterism, Antin had offered a far less sanguine account of "slum" life, so that her later cheery optimism about the "smiling aspects of life" and its easy money seems disingenuous or a deliberate denial and silencing of pain:

> Still I had moments of depression, when my whole being protested against the life of the slum. I resented the familiarity of my vulgar neighbors. I felt myself defiled by the indecencies I was compelled to witness. Then it was I took to running away from home. I went out in the twilight and walked for hours, my blind feet leading me. I did not care where I went. If I lost my way, so much the better; I never wanted to see Dover Street again. (292)

Now the incoherences in Antin's immigrant autobiography reflect the constraints of the minority writer's voice when addressing a white mainstream audience. But, as importantly, in her railing against one of the many "slum" streets—Arlington, Wheeler, Dover—on which the family lived, Antin complicates the neat division between Poland and America, New World and Old World, that structures the immigrant story of Americanization into an acceptable whiteness. Although here Antin speaks abstractly of "vulgar neighbors" and "indecencies," elsewhere she is less evasive about the details of this third space that is neither Old World or New, a space that is not the homogeneous ghetto found in official accounts. This is the third multiethnic/racial space she must run away from and, in the writing of her autobiography, translate back into the expected story of becoming the "white" respectable middle-class American. Yet her need to walk, shall I say run, away from the clear narrative lines of her autobiography (literally to "lose herself") reflects a double voice, resisting and yet reaffirming whiteness. While her peregrinations reflect her resentment of having to be the dutiful daughter of the American success story, what she desires to escape, precisely like Henry James, is the integration of third spaces rather then either "America" or the organic ethnic communities of the New World. Her later retreat into the mythology of success can be read not only as a deference to the demands of the literary marketplace but in part a "walking" into whiteness as a way of avoiding the dis-integration of the ethnic body. Yet in attempting to run away from the third space, she has eliminated its potential as a site of dissent to Americanization and to the acculturation into whiteness.

If Antin physically runs away from vulgar neighbors, in writing her autobiography, she nonetheless develops a homologous narratological tactic of evasion and distancing. To contain the interethnic conflicts and mutual exchanges that might question her entrance into the promised land of whiteness, Antin reifies and objectifies the "unassimilable" people and social realities of her urban environment into an impressionistic spot of time in the tradition of romantic writers such as Wordsworth. In the end, Antin's response to walking in the mixed crowd of the city is not that much different from Henry James's commodified aestheticism. While she dutifully records the interracial conflicts among the Chelsea folk, such as her father taking a "great hulky colored bully to court" to punish the "evildoer" and the street boys taunting the "Chinky Chinaman" at his laundry, Antin transcribes the race wars back into a spectacle of pleasing variety in the American Scene: "For I have always loved a mixed crowd. I loved the contrasts, the high lights and deep shadows, and the gradations that connect the two, and make all life one. I saw many, many things that I was not aware of seeing at the time. I only found out afterwards what treasures my brain had stored up, when, coming to the puzzling place in life, light and meaning would suddenly burst on me, the hidden fruit of some experience that had not impressed me at the time" (262). The particularities of "interethnic conflict" that lead her to a "puzzling place in life" are impressionistically subsumed and erased in this passage of Antin's text that could be mistaken for a formalistic analysis of an Ashcan artist's canvas. Conflicts, even possible friendships between Irish and Jew, black and Jew, Chinese and Jew, are now "high lights and deep shadows." Yet in replacing impressionism for "realism," shape for individual detail, Antin shows that she alleviates another pressing ethnic trouble that occupies the third space: the pure reproduction of her own identity. By making the identitarian transformations that Certeau has reminded us are possible when walking on the streets merely "impressions" to be stored up and reflected on in tranquility, Antin assures her own control of her ethnic performance: it cannot really be touched and altered by racial and ethnic others because she maintains an aesthetic distance from them. In her own "American scene," Antin responds to the carnival of alien bodies in an analogous manner to James. The mixed public space becomes a dis-integrating space, one that disappears from the text through Antin's discursive repositioning of herself within whiteness, a whiteness defined for the walker (who could also be a trader) as the consumption of multicultural "colors."

Yet Antin, unlike James, cannot so easily elude an awareness of the street's reciprocity, and her chapter ends with her ruminations about the "destiny" within the contact of third spaces.

> I wonder—I wonder. A million threads of life and love and sorrow was the common street; and whether we would or not, we entangled ourselves in a common maze, without paying the homage of a second glance to those who would some day master us; too dull to pick that face from out [of] the crowd which one day would bend over us in love or pity or remorse. . . . Small sin it was to annoy my neighbor by getting in his way, as I stared over my shoulder, if a grown man knew no better than to drop a word in passing that might turn the course of another's life, as a boulder rolled down from the mountain-side deflects the current of a brook. (263)

Despite her awareness that, as Certeau remarks, the walker can be neither wholly author nor spectator but is always in a dialogic flux with the many peoples and events who might reroute, redirect, and recode her performance of self, Antin retreats from the disruption of the third space by refusing to imagine its authorial dis-integration. Her awareness of interconnection and even vulnerability to the mastery of others in the tangled maze soon slips into a sentimental romance that changes the other into a lover, presumably a generalized white, colorless lover. The "encounter" on the street is sanitized as the romantic meeting with a stranger, yet Antin's awareness of the sin of her backward glance at a passing "unnamed" grown man, and of her longing for someone to "turn the course of her life" as irrevocably as a landslide's destruction, uncovers the desire for psychic dis-integration that her romantic comedy would overcome. In the end, as in James's walking through the third spaces of the American Scene, we are left with an unintelligible, or in this case unnamed, "dropped word," a word that could constitute a revolutionary change but one that Antin deflects in her removal of her self within the impersonal reference of "another's life"; thus Antin leaves her own desire/terror of the "word" of this imagined other ambivalent by telling us the man who speaks a possible "transformative" word "knew no better." In the *Promised Land*, Antin demonstrates that she does know better, removing the words of the multiracial third space to restore the necessary binary logic of Old World versus the New and whitewashing the New World's multiaccented constituency.

The Ghetto's "White" Slavery

In rejecting the first draft of *Yekl: A Tale of the Ghetto*, the editors at *McClure's* complained to Abraham Cahan: "You portray only Jews. . . . According to your book one could believe that in America there are no other people but Jews" (qtd. in Chametzky 67). While the editors' criticism displays a not too subtle anti-Semitism—"Americans" could not be expected to identify with a novel with a completely Jewish cast—they point out what would became, especially by the time Cahan wrote *The Rise of David Levinsky*, a characteristic feature of Cahan's writing: Cahan's representation in his fiction of no other people in America, or at least in the Lower East Side, than Jews and a Jewishness made visible by the occasional appearance of Anglo-Gentiles. In many ways, this exclusivity seems unsurprising, given Cahan's need to create a sacred soil for Jewish American identity as a continuation of his work as editor of the *Jewish Daily Forward* and also given William Dean Howells's promotion of Cahan within the political economy of local-color fiction. Yet such a focus is not so inevitable in the immigrant's fiction of Americanization and signals a marked contrast between Cahan's fiction and his journalistic and nonfiction writing. In the second part of his autobiography, *The Education of Abraham Cahan*, entitled *The Golden Land*, Cahan writes, "The most dangerous lawbreakers inhabited the bowery. Criminals and outcasts made it their neighborhood and the cheapest prostitutes strolled its sidewalks. Nearby Chrystie, Forsythe, and Eldridge Streets were no better in the evenings. Irish, Germans, and American lived there along with a few Jews and no Italians" (220–21). Through his discursive association linking racial and ethnic intermixture and lawlessness, Cahan evokes the numerous representations of the other half penned and documented by Anglo-American "traders" in the city scenes. But what is interesting in Cahan's postwar description of the Bowery is less its surrender or resistance to the Progressive Era's dominant ethnological discourse than the complete absence of such cross-ethnic encounters in his tales of the ghetto. Although in *The Rise of David Levinsky* David, on first arriving in America, "slept in the cheapest lodging-houses on the Bowery" (140), Cahan makes no mention of the multiethnic border world there that he depicts in *The Golden Land*. Likewise, although in *Yekl* Mamie lives on Chrystie Street and Jake and Mamie converse standing out on the public sidewalk, Cahan rubs out of the background any hint of the Irish, German, and Italian walkers crowded within the setting. Although Cahan had no reservations about depicting the "immorality" of these borderland sex districts, noting both Jake's and David's visits to prostitutes and dance halls, his fiction remains reticent about another kind of promiscuity, that of racial and ethnic interaction.

In Cahan's first novel, *Yekl*, his forging of a Jewish national identity (recalling his "Bintel Briefs" for the *Forward*) depended on a generative act of repression, the repression of the abject specter of the Jewish American "soul" dis-integrating within an in-between third space. Although in many ways an "ardent assimilationist" (as Sanford Marovitz notes) and a secular socialist, Cahan remained a Jew and retained his father's fear of conversion as the ultimate horror (Marovitz 27, 47). But Cahan's relation to the Gentile New World was complex. In *Beyond Ethnicity*, Werner Sollors reads *Yekl* as a paradigmatic text of the immigrant writer's conflict between the culture of descent, the Old World (represented by Gitl) and the national culture of consent (the New World figured in Mamie). In his use of the word "descent," Sollors implies that this retention of ethnicity represented a "dissent" to Americanization, which required the immigrant's assent (and hopefully ascent) to the consensual culture of liberal individualism and capitalism (157). As convincing as Sollors's interpretation is, there is another overlapping and unconscious political allegory within Cahan's first novel, an allegory that "troubles" the schematic neatness of this narrative conflict between New and Old Worlds. Sollors's analysis arises in part from an unexamined understanding of the immigrant's passage as without multicultural linkages to other ethnic groups. In Sollors's reading, the immigrant can only be alienated from his/her native community that has provided him/her a sense of belonging or be marginalized in America. While I do not want to refute the material reality of this alienation, I do want to add to its psychological conceptualization. The immigrant writer's experience might more fully be seen as a dislocation, exile, or displacement, as Salman Rushdie argues in his "Imaginary Homeland," rather than an alienation (19–29). Not simply a figure caught between two worlds, the dislocated "walker" that Rushdie describes is one whose identity is in unstable transition.

In *Yekl*, as a consequence, to add on to Sollors's argument, there is a second, albeit unconscious, political allegory. Less the immigrant caught in transition between Russia and America, Jake is the dislocated "walker/ excursionist" who doesn't know how to perform identity right, not simply his Jewish self but also a proper American subjectivity. Drawn to neither of the two worlds, America or the Jewish ghetto, this walker gravitates to the third space of Chrystie Street and to the promiscuity that Mamie inhabits. There Jake is seduced by a desire (like James) to map and be mapped by the other. In *Yekl*, Cahan creates a novel that finally is as much about the character's need for dis-identification with excluded body images as it is about the acculturation to a Jewish American self. To position his readers so that they, too, will locate themselves as proper new white Jewish Americans, Cahan in *Yekl* draws upon the popular genre of the white slavery novel, incorporating this tradition as a deterrent shadow narrative that will preserve the character's subjectivization within "authentic" ghetto life. In this second buried narrative, Mamie represents a promiscuous ethnic femininity of an interzonal third space, while Gitl is less the Old World character than the pure character of Americanization, a master narrative that Jake knows he should love but about which the novel finally expresses ambivalence.

In its description of the Lower East Side, Cahan's novel calls attention to the ethnic identity in process there, invoking an anxiety about the fluidity and liminality of an immigrant self whose gender, racial, and class identity has not yet been rendered "memorable." After describing the crowded tenement world of the Jewish neighborhoods, which had become a staple within journalistic accounts of the other half, Cahan remarks that the tenement house "harbors in its bosom specimens of all the whimsical metamorphoses wrought upon the children of Israel" (14). Picking up on this familiar trope of transformation, Cahan's novel describes "one social caldron—a human hodgepodge with its component parts changed but not yet fused into one homogeneous whole" (14). For Cahan, the end product of the ghetto's melting pot will be the rise of the Jewish American, an individual who will be part of a larger ethnic community. But by emphatically claiming the generation of a new community of Jewish Americans, Cahan in turns calls attention to and denies the feared opposite outcome. Although Cahan throughout his fiction will struggle to determine the exact nature of this hyphenated identity (how Jewish? how American?), this uncertainty was only one part of a larger dread about the failure to "produce" a Jewish American identity. What if the immigrant became something completely other, neither quite Jewish nor mainstream middle-class American nor even something in-between, but remained a "human hodgepodge" who is multiple, divided, fragmented by contact with many different races and ethnicities, not just white America?

While Cahan's description of the tenements invokes the fashioning of a new Jewish American identity in the Lower East Side, his initial description of Jake reveals the protagonist to be precisely the "human hodgepodge" of indeterminate character that Cahan boasted the tenements guaranteed as no more than transitional. Jake, as it is clear from Cahan's exposition, is not just a conflicted hyphenated American Jew, he is someone who contains multitudes. In describing Jake's speech, Cahan notes that his eponymous protagonist spoke an imperfect Yiddish that attests not to two worlds but to many: "He had a deep and rather harsh voice, and his r's could do credit to the thickest Irish brogue" (2). Not only does Jake speak like a Boston-bred Irish Catholic, he also wants to imitate its local hero, the boxer John Sullivan. Indeed, as the language of Cahan's representation of Jake lets slip out, the fear is less that Jake will become an unorthodox Jew but that he will become no such "thing," not any "one thing" at all. Discussing Jake's face, Cahan writes, that his eyes were "strongly Semitic naturally, they became still more so each time they were brightened up by his good-natured boyish smile. Indeed, Jake's very nose, which was fleshy and pear-shaped and decidedly not Jewish (although not decidedly anything else), seemed to join the Mosaic faith, and even his shaven upper lip looked penitent, as soon as that smile of his made its appearance" (3). Although his description of Jake begins with the nervous disclosure of his protagonist's wandering identifications, raising questions about whether the Jewish American acts more like a Bostonian Irish Catholic than a Lower East Side Jew, Cahan seeks to preclude the misculturation of such a monstrous "human hodgepodge" by emphatically marking Jake's body as Jewish: Jake is "strongly Semitic naturally." Yet despite trying to close off Jake's tabooed identification by arguing that he can never betray his indelibly marked body, Cahan confesses that his character's nose was "decidedly not Jewish." It is in the parenthetical interjection that Cahan admits into the text the fear that is symptomatic of the novel's larger unconscious bewilderments about a potential catastrophe. Although Jake might not always act Jewish, he cannot act or be—the narrator offhandedly remarks—"decidedly anything else." But of course the resolution to the question of how to perform a "New World" identity is not decidedly so, unless one links ethnic culture to a biological body or transcendent spirit, connections Cahan attempts to make in *Yekl* and later in *The Rise of David Levinsky*. The problem is that there is often "decidedly" no such clear shift from Russian Jew to American or to white Jewish American. The immigrant might get waylaid in a third space, which is no clearly drawn hyphenated borderland in between Old and New Worlds but something undecidedly other.

In his description of Gitl's Americanization within the tenement cauldron, Cahan alludes to her transitional liminality, as a figure who might not perform her assimilation as a Jewish American correctly. Although in leaving off her wig and binding herself in a girdle, Gitl becomes a "brand new wife" (68), and at the divorce proceedings, Cahan's heroine has the "noticeable" "peculiar air of self-confidence with which a few month's life in America is sure to stamp the looks and bearing of every immigrant" (83). Gitl's reembodiment literally as an American with the right look and bearing is contradicted by passages hinting that she may not recite her hyphenated identity properly. In casual allusions to Gitl's "misidentifi-cations," Cahan brings up the specter that lies as a buried referent unsaid in his immigrant novels: the immigrant body's narrative incoherence. We first see this incoherence in the process of Americanization in Cahan's description of Gitl when she lands in New York, for Gitl appeared as neither American nor Jewish but had the "resemblance to a squaw" with her sunburned dark complexion, high cheek bones, and black wig (34). When later, Jake, hissing "some Bowery oath," forces his wife to replace her wig with a kerchief, Cahan writes that "Jake thought that it made her look like an Italian woman of Mulberry Street on Sunday" (37). Although still a pious Jewish woman, Gitl is a promiscuous sign, someone who has no clear identity, especially one that can be marked and sustained on her ethnic body. The work of the tenement then will be thus to assure that Gitl undergoes a proper metamorphosis into a Jewish American.

If within *Yekl* the hidden dread is that the Jewish immigrant in his/her journey toward becoming an American might wander into some forbidden third space of protean identities, the question then becomes how Cahan represses an alternative story of Americanization in *Yekl*, the story hinted at in Gitl's first arrival in New York but then quickly forgotten. In order to ensure that his readers perform a proper story of Americanization, so that they do not walk or wander into a borderland where Jewish Americans might speak like Irish Catholics and pious Jewish wives wear scarves like Italian madonnas, Cahan weds the story of Jewish Americanization to white slavery fiction that circulated as a popular genre during the Progressive Era. The mythologizing narrative of white slavery in both early-twentieth-century public debates and fiction featured sensationalist stories of young women being drugged and seduced into a captive life of prostitution by "cadets" (or pimps), either as they first arrived on Ellis Island, as they ventured alone in the city, or, in the favored minatory versions, as they frequented dance halls in the Lower East Side. In her study of the white slavery debate that lead the U.S. to ratify an international treaty banning the white slave trade in 1905 and to pass the Mann Act in 1910 preventing domestic traffic in women across state lines, Ruth Rossen argues that many of the stories, although they may have had some factual basis, expressed the tensions, fears, and conflicts within American society about immigration and the changing role of women (112–37). To say that young women were coerced or tricked into degradation allayed fears about the New Woman taking control over her body to make sexual choices, and picturing dark-skinned eastern European and Mediterranean pimps externalized the threat of immigration to the pure, white body of America much as the black rapist figured similar racial fears against African Americans. In short, as Kevin Mumford observes, through the white slavery debate, middle-class white America sought to regulate racial, gender, and sexual boundaries, using the debate to discipline women and immigrants who deviated from middle-class norms (14–17).

Yet the white slavery debate from its beginnings was particularly linked to the increase in immigration of eastern European Jews. Although grossly exaggerating the demographic ratios, racial nativists argued that 70 percent of prostitutes during the Progressive Era were Jewish women, concluding that this fact proved that Jewish women as a race were more immoral and loose in character than women of Nordic descent. It is not surprising then, as Edward Bristow argues, that the Yiddish theater as well as early Jewish American tracts and novels turned to the sensational theme of possible white slavery. Two years prior to the publication of Cahan's *Yekl*, the American journalist Lincoln Steffens had generated the narrative codes of white slavery fiction in his "Shloma, daughter of Schmuhl," whose heroine allows her love of finery to lead her into prostitution ("Es ist besser wie packin pants"—it is better than hauling pants) (qtd. in Bristow, 41). In his writings for the *Jewish Daily Forward*, Cahan would also lament that those who lived in the Jewish ghetto could not avoid that fact that Allen Street had become the commercialized red light district (often with the district protection of Tammany bosses). So widespread did the practice of associating white slavery with Jewish immigration become that by the time of the 1911 Dillingham Immigration Commission Report, Jews were singled out as both the victims (young women from the ages of twelve to thirty) and perpetuators of the trade:

> The Jews often import or harbor Russian, Austrian, Hungarian, Polish, or German women, doubtless usually of their own race. . . . There are large numbers of Jews scattered throughout the United States, although mainly located in New York and Chicago, who seduce and keep girls. Some of them are engaged in importation, but apparently they prey rather upon young girls whom they find on the street, in the dance halls, and similar places, and whom . . . they deceive and ruin. (qtd in Friedman-Kasaba 140)

In the Dillingham report about the white slave trade's Jewish cast, native-born Americans sought to shore up racial and ethnic boundaries and to police the behavior of unmarried working-class ethnic men and women. That the report exaggerated the Jewish involvement in the trade suggests its attempts to scapegoat the new immigrant class.

At the heart of the white slavery debate and its fictional representation was the borderland space of the dance hall, and in their attempt to police racial inclusion and gender behavior, the Progressive Era reformers identified this often multiracial and ethnic space as in need of careful surveillance. In an investigative story in *McClure's* magazine in 1909, "Daughters of the Poor: A Painful Story of the Development of New York City as a Leading Center of the White Slave Trade," Police Commissioner George Kibbe Turner singled out the dance hall as the place where the white slavers preyed upon young women. Like many other Progressive Era reformers, Turner believed that Jewish women made up nearly three-fourths of the women in the sex trade, although these disproportionate numbers did not reflect reality but rather alarm at the behavior of Jewish women who were often at the forefront of organized labor unrest in the garment industry (Friedman-Kasaba 140). "But the largest and most pitiable field for exploitation of the girls of the East Side is in procuring them for the white slave trade. The lie of swindling is in itself specialized. Formerly its chief recruiting grounds were the public amusement parks of the tenement districts; now for several years they have been the dance halls, and the work has been specialized very largely according to the character of the halls" (57). Since the dance hall was a space where the new urban woman most clearly denounced her domestic confinement and sexual purity, it is not hard to understand why the reformers would attempt to cast opprobrium on them by associating them with white slavery. But if this narrative sought to restrict the freedom of young women in the city, it also sought to reestablish eroding racial lines. Many dance halls, especially those along Allen Street in the heart of the Jewish "ghetto" of New York City, served as sites of interracial and ethnic mixing and miscegenation. While some "coethnic" societies ran their own dance halls to keep the young segregated and to guard their morals, the borderland world of the dance hall would have been, for many, a place where normal racial, gender, and sexual lines were transgressed.

In his description of Jake and Mamie's encounter at the dance hall, Cahan imports the panic over white slavery into his story of Americanization. Seeking to link Jake's infidelity to his wife with deviation from the formation of a proper Jewish American identity, Cahan uses language that evokes Jake as both working-class gallant and "cadet," a term used to designate the young man who would recruit or impress a young woman into sexual servitude. When Jake arrives at the hall, Miss Jacobs asks Jacob to serve as a panderer, playing up to Mamie in order to get the "aloof" young girl to dance with the young men. Although such a resonance with the white slavery hysteria is at first subtle, in the conversation between Mamie and Jake, Cahan calls attention to the associations. Mamie asks: "Vill you treat?" And Jake replies, "I like to shpek palin, shee? dot'sh a kin' a man I am" (I like to speak plain. That's the kind of man I am) (20). In Mamie's inquiry whether Jake will "treat," Cahan uses the slang term for an informal payment in return for sexual favors (Peiss 76). Although in treating, as opposed to literal prostitution, the young woman accepted only gifts, treats, or a good time in return for sex, Cahan's use of the word would have coded Jake and Mamie's encounter as an exchange of a specific character for knowing readers. In this scene, Cahan taps into fears not only about sexual license but of ethnic uncertainty. The relationship between sexual crossing and ethnic uncertainty discursively links promiscuity and cross-cultural ethnic identification. Once again Jake proves himself a "wandering" unorthodox Jew, taking off his cap to Mamie, whom he compares to a crucifix, or *getzke* (20), a gesture of Christian homage a "good" Jew would have found sacrilegious. The importance of this profane gesture is not simply that Jake is losing his faith, but within the racial and sexual associations of the dance hall Jake is literally becoming an "adulterous" Jew. As an imitator, Jake desires the other in this third space and fails to recite or repeat any kind of proper Jewish American identity. At the end of this initial exchange, Cahan's language is loaded with irony: Jake insists that his performance—mock chivalry? satirical Italian Catholic? honest soul?—is the kind of man that he is. Yet the underlying emotional structure of this scene is precisely the fear that Jake, and we the readers, don't know what kind of man he is. Certainly he is not speaking plain, for not only is he lying by withholding from Mamie his marital status, but he is not forthright either about his desires for Mamie: he does want sexual favors from her. Jake is a "cadet" in the white slavery literature (even if not intentionally so) because he is trying to seduce her, and later, assuming the prerogatives of a pimp, he convinces her to run away and support him on her earnings. The origins of Mamie's money are, moreover, never explained, and it is questionable that a young girl could have accrued so large a savings from the less than subsistence wages most garment workers, especially those who were women, made. It is as if Cahan's text speaks and yet refuses to speak plainly about what kind of man Jake is, and through this indeterminacy *Yekl* opens up his story of Americanization to interpretations of white slavery.

This subtext of white slavery that overlays the story of Jake's Americanization is even more pronounced at the conclusion of the dance hall episode. With the arrival of Fanny, Jake finds himself "treating" both women, yet he boasts of his chivalry: "'Once I am treating, both ladas must be treated alike, ain' it?' remarked the gallant, and again he proved himself as good as his word" (23). Cahan's insistence that Jake is "as good as his word," that he once again speaks plainly, recurs here with increased comedy: a man who has spoken words of "true love" to two women is not beholden to his words, but, more important, the reader is positioned to ask what are Jake's words and what are their origins. A mixture of Yiddish, English, Irish, and Italian, his words are never pure. Jake goes on to say, "'Vot elshe you vant? A peench?' He was again on the point of suiting the action to the word, but Mamie contrived to repay the pinch before she had received it and added a generous piece of profanity into the bargain. Whereupon there ensued a scuffle of a character which defies description in more senses than one" (23). The consummation of Jake's and Mamie's and now Fanny's flirtation, Cahan finally refuses to "represent"; indeed, he asserts that it is beyond representation "in more senses than one." But how is this scuffle beyond representation? Certainly since the chapter's climax defies the turn-of-the-century moral order, Cahan's silence can be explained. In the language of "bargaining" and "repayment," Cahan hints to the reader familiar with the white slavery debates another way to explicate this scene: it is because theirs is a behavior that is not appropriate to the Old World or the New World, to Lower East Side or Uptown Manhattan. This behavior played out in the dance hall has no character—moral or ethnic. Recalling Mary Antin's *Promised Land*, *Yekl* depicts Jake as having a longing and a revulsion for the third dance hall space in which he can lose himself and where he can promiscuously try on many different identities. There in the dance hall identity is all play, never more urgent or efficacious than the moment. Indeed the "foreplay" between Mamie and Jake is unrepresentable because it is, by its very motivating impulse, an escape from the burden of ethnic or American representation. Jake here is lost (and happily so); he has departed into a third space, feeling the exhilaration of leaving his known world and identity behind. Able to transform himself into this "other," Jake takes his leave of the ethnic world of belonging. In his first novel, Abraham Cahan hints at what will become unrepresentable in his later works such as *The Rise of David Levinsky*: the randomness, the promiscuity, the lack of clear binary opposition within the immigrant transformation. Such an indeterminacy of walking in the city where one is touched by so many others, literally realized here, means that the immigrant is not in control of the process of Americanization.

If Jake is mistaken for a white slavery cadet in this scene, it is an exegetic suspicion that Cahan fosters and underscores by having other characters in the novella share the belief. When Jake arrives to pick up Gitl on Ellis Island, the officer thinks at first that Jake has come to recruit her for the trade: "The contrast between Gitl and Jake was so striking that the officer wanted to make sure—partly as a matter of official duty, and partly for the fun of the thing—that the two were actually man and wife" (35). In bringing in the shadow narrative of white slavery, which had been used to regulate who ought to be assimilated and how they ought to be assimilated as proper gendered American citizens, Cahan's *Yekl* gives narrative shape to the fear of a perverse Americanization. One can, of course, as we see in the character of Bernstein in Cahan's tale, dissent to middle-class American life by retaining one's ethnic identity. But what if one's character becomes illegible as American or as Jewish and becomes merely a promiscuous performance and imitation of many different languages? What if one's identity becomes loose, lost in the border zones, the world of the dance hall and Bowery vices? To contain Jake's wandering outside the ghetto and to inscribe on his body a different mapping of the city, Cahan raises the deterrent specter of white slavery. To preserve the oppositional structure within the narrative of Americanization between the Jewish homeland and a monolithic Gentile America, Cahan invokes the double of the cadet, this fictional villain, who may or may not be Jake. Yet finally Cahan's intertextual raising of this specter represents a "walking" into racial nationalism from below, a recognition that the allure of race and its white narrative form is its promise of psychic and cultural integration.

This discursive link between Jake's possible involvement in white slavery and ethnic boundaries can be seen in Cahan's lengthy description of Jake's "walking" in the ghetto. Feeling trapped in his marriage to Gitl, Jake contemplates a desperate departure with Mamie in order to get away and become lost once more to his representative self: "In his abject misery he thought of suicide, of fleeing to Chicago or St Louis, all of which passed through his mind in a stream of the most irrelevant and the most frivolous reminiscences" (73). Jake ponders this escape, moreover, while peripatetically wandering the Lower East Side. Yet despite wanting to "disappear" (to kill himself figuratively if not literally), Jake cannot escape his own boundaries: "Having passed as far as the limit of the Ghetto he took a homeward course by a parallel street, knowing all the while that he would lack the courage to enter his house" (73). What mapping does Jake's walking give us of an immigrant's "urban practice"? What are we to make of this contradiction between wanting to depart yet being unable to leave and to walk outside the ghetto? Although I do not want to minimize the actual danger that people in the Lower East Side felt from the anti-Semitic violence from other gangs when they left their territory, Cahan does not name this as Jake's confining fear. Jake's walk maps for us the dialectic between the immigrant's desire not for Old World and New but between running away and having a home, between remaining lost and accepting the process of Americanization and becoming some kind of Jewish American. While Cahan wrote his stories from the point of view of "traders" such as William Dean Howells in which the "conflict" in ethnic immigrant literature was to be or not to be American, the speech act uttered in Jake's wandering feet is a fear of wandering into

a third space, a space where the whole question of racial and ethnic identification and imitation is without any teleological closure. Is it all an
accident of aimless walking.

In his essay "The World and the Home," Homi Bhabha refers to the
"unhomely" world that is halfway between, that is undefined, that exists
outside the binary opposition between Old World and New World (456).
Cahan's fiction finally sabotages and deconstructs the possibility of such
a longed for yet dreaded unhomeliness (an unhomeliness that he fears
as only exile) by making this place the same as "home." With deliberate
contradiction, Cahan's novel makes Mamie (the maimer and the
mammy), a representative both of infidelity to unified ethnic identities
and of the "motherly" figure of domestic and ethnic confinement. While
Cahan's Mamie lives on Chrystie Street, the site of what he saw as a promiscuous ethnic interaction, he also describes her in terms of her excess
of the "mother tongue," of a garrulity and flamboyancy of dress that
refuses to be either German or Polish Jew or American: "With nervous
volubility . . . she spoke with an overdone American accent in the dialect
of the Polish Jews, affectedly Germanized and profusely interspersed with
English, so that Gitl whose mother tongue was Lithuanian Yiddish, could
scarcely catch the meaning of one half of her flood of garrulity" (50).
While here Cahan ties Mamie to the dangers of that which is outside the
language of ethnic identity, he later alters his picture of her, making her
a motherly figure who will restrain Jake's flight from the ghetto world.
When Jake contemplates going "to Chicago, or to Baltimore, or better
still to England" (73) and attempts to cajole and seduce Mamie into such
a prostituted life with him, she checks his wandering. In a telling domestic scene amid the pillowcases and underwear of the laundry strung out
across the rooftop, Mamie, no longer the dance hall flirt, suddenly treats
Jake with a "motherly harshness" rather than with the wiles of the
coquette (75). Getting Jake to swear by the same memory of his father
that earlier had driven him from the dance halls back to Gitl, Mamie is
transformed into the bearer of the "mother tongue" and ethnic memory.
When Jake asks, "How else shall I swear?" Mamie answers "by you father,
peace upon him" (79). If the third space and borderland world of the
dance hall and Mamie had been defined against the domestic space of
the ethnic home and the Anglo-American mainstream, at the end of *Yekl*
Cahan finally erases such space by transforming the figure of "maiming,"

of ethnic mixture, into the mammy, making it seem finally that nothing can exist outside the "mother tongue," the ethnic body.

Although Cahan sets up an opposition between Mamie the promiscuous woman of the interzones, of the dance hall and Chrystie Street, and Gitl, the figure of the proper Americanization into a Jewish American identity, in the end Cahan's Jake has no choice: all the women would lead him back to a proper narrative of the Jewish American ghetto. While for a moment Jake is in danger of transforming into the cadet, the abject shadow figure that haunts the tale of the true "ghetto man," Mamie, like Gitl, would also domesticate Jake, having renounced her dangerous "street-walking." Yet even as Cahan contains troubling alternative stories to Americanization in the panic about domestication that Jake voices, Cahan fails to bring the two contradictory narratives of the ghetto tale into a settled resolution. Taking the streetcar to wed Mamie, Jake feels a masculine crisis that overlaps with ethnic panic: "But in his inmost heart he was the reverse of eager to reach City Hall. He was painfully reluctant to part with his long-coveted freedom so soon after it had at last been attained" (89). In describing Jake as a "defeated victor" (the title of his last chapter in the novel), Cahan represents Jake's remorse about divorcing Gitl and breaking away from his life in the homeland. Yet Cahan finally fails to give even this regretful, unambiguous moral ending. As Jake rides the streetcar to wed Mamie, he feels a lurching in his heart as he wants to retain his freedom, a freedom ostensibly from married life but also from ethnic representation confined to the ghetto space. Jake himself finally becomes the "white slave," the slave to the collective story of the white Jewish Americanization.

While the ending of *Yekl* makes escape finally impossible and equivalent to a return to the ghetto, by the time of his 1917 novel, *The Rise of David Levinsky*, Cahan would find another means to contain the transformations of America. While Cahan's 1917 novel chronicles the conversion of the Antomir-born Talmudic scholar David Levinsky into a cloak-manufacturing capitalist baron whose Social Darwinism causes him to break the unions, Cahan's novel finally refuses to accept the physical, economic, and even religious evidence of change within his protagonist. Despite the fact that David has learned a new language, dress, secular habits, and even bodily manners, becoming "conscious of the whole performance" of what it means to be an "American" as he says when suppressing his propensity to speak with his gesticulating hands (329), Cahan frames his novel by having David insist that "I cannot escape from my old self" (530). In *Our America: Nativism, Modernism, and Pluralism,* Walter Benn Michaels has argued that the early twentieth century saw the rewriting of race from biology to ideology. As part of this shift away from vulgar racism that depended on morphological or "bodily" differences, race was reimagined as a soul or a consciousness that exceeded visibility. This spiritualizing of race provided Cahan with a deus ex machina to placate his fears of the Jewish American's possible conversion to a "human hodgepodge." However radical may be the transformations, Cahan suggests in *The Rise of David Levinsky,* even if the man or woman of learning becomes a strike-breaking Horatio Alger, no loss of the Old World or change of self is ever finally complete, ever finished, not simply because of lingering childhood habits or genetic differences but because there persists a racialized memory and spiritual inner identity that cannot be rebaptized in any "alien" ways. In the ambiguities and contradictions in the "traumatized" text of *Yekl,* however, Cahan bore witness to the "maiming" of the ethnic self when the other got under one's skin.

6. WHITE DISSOLUTION

Homosexualization and Racial Masculinity in White Life Novels

In April 1954 the John H. Johnson–owned *Jet* magazine raised the titillating question in its cover story, "Are Homosexuals Becoming Respectable?" With the recent arrest of civil rights activist Bayard Rustin along with growing rumors about "famous faculty at southern Negro colleges," the black popular press seemed to share the country's fear of the homosexual menace. As John D'Emilio has argued, the post–World War II witch hunt against lesbians and gay males worked to position same-sex desires outside the formation of a stable national identity during the Truman and Eisenhower eras (see also Chauncey 9–10). The postwar period was a time of sexual and gender regulation, as American society sought to restore a normative patriarchal and nuclear family. But this white lesbian, gay male, bisexual, and transgendered history is not the same as black gay male history, and there is a need still to describe, explain, and theorize how homosexuality operated as a constitutive discourse of black identity and community in the era of integrationist optimism before the murder of the fourteen-year-old Emmett Till in 1955 helped usher in a new era of civil rights protest and nationalist separatism (Alexander 91). While *Jet* magazine raised the specter of the homosexual passer, the hidden deviant of color amid the black community, what is particularly striking in the fiction of this period is the recurrence of the figure of the white homosexual dissolute who evokes the national sex crime panic that linked the homosexual with the "pervert." Certainly

144

there is nothing new in the homophobic ridiculing of gay men (black or white) as scapegoats for the constitution of group identity, and the attribution of homosexuality as a "white thing" would act as a common rhetorical strategy in 1960s black power movements. But the figure of the white dissolute in integrationist-era "white life" novels functioned as a much more complicated discursive practice that sought to intervene in postwar representations of white and black masculinity.

In the decade after the Second World War, many major African American writers, including Zora Neale Hurston, Richard Wright, Ann Petry, Chester Himes, William Yarby, James Baldwin, and Willard Motley, wrote fiction with an all-white cast. These white life novels evolved out of a momentary integrationist optimism following the war when President Truman's Second Commission on Civil Rights recommended the integration of the military (1948) and the Supreme Court decision in *Brown v. the Board of Education* (1954) declared in principle, if not in fact, segregated education illegal. Accompanying this ideological change in climate was a "poetics of integration," as W. Lawrence Hogue notes, promoted from within and outside the black community as testifying to the writers' artistic reach and ability to emphasize "objective" and "universal" themes.[1] In a special forum appearing in the winter 1950 issue of the literary quarterly *Phylon*, Thomas D. Jarrett pronounced that the "Negro Novelist's Coming of Age" could be achieved only through an overcoming of "racial hypersensitivity" and a "growing social consciousness and a universality in the treatment of themes."[2] In late-twentieth-century histories of African American culture, however, these "nonracial" novels, as they are pigeonholed, are frequently dismissed as fashionable and negligible experimentations by their otherwise talented authors or as insufficiently black texts because they did not abide by the traditional rules of racial protest or nationalist representation (Tate, *Psychoanalysis* 7–9). While literary critics tend to read literature by and about blacks as full of racial meanings, these postwar fictions portraying all-white casts have been interpreted as largely free of racial content, but this whitewashing of difference so that whiteness is unmarked, whereas blackness is a contested social or political identity, has enabled Western Europeans to avoid examining the privileges and discriminations afforded by their racialized subject position. In contrast, the white life novels of the integrationist era do not permit whites such an unexamined complacency about their supposedly neutral subjectivities. Neither aberrations from racial intervention nor simply trendy, these midcentury integrationist novels operate within a long tradition of representations of whiteness in the black imagination. Wright's *Savage Holiday* (1954), Hurston's *Seraph on the Suwanee* (1948), and Demby's *Beetlecreek* (1950) can all be read as activist texts that disrupt the regulatory fictions that govern the gendered and racialized reproduction of white male subjectivity. Yet these texts are finally not simply oppositional in offering counterimages of whiteness; these white life novels also disclose a joined concern with the insecurity of the boundaries of black masculinity.[3]

One of the recurring narrative strategies in these white life novels is the homosexualization of the white male or the recurrent deployment of a predatory white gay male character. This "dissolute," as he is designated here to suggest the way his depravity is not solely sexual but is intertwined with other pathologized or criminal behaviors, signified in a literal and metonymic way the horror of racial oppression according to the shifting ideological imagery of Cold War America.[4] In contrast to the later feminized gay male in nationalist rhetoric, the homosexualized dissolute in white life novels often served to remasculinize the white male body in order to find a way to imagine the historical violence against African Americans. Yet if Undersecretary of State John Peurifoy's disclosure in 1950 of ninety-one government-employed homosexuals as security risks started a "pervert inquiry" that lead to the expulsion of sixty federal workers a month and almost two thousand military personnel in the year 1951 alone, the panic Cold War Americans felt about homosexuals centered not only on their recalcitrant presence but, as Lee Edelman (162) and Robert Corber (*Homosexuality* 61) have argued, on their indeterminability. The scapegoating of homosexuals during the McCarthy era undermined, brought into "dissolution," even as it fought to shore up, the slippery definition of true heterosexual white masculinity. Since these sex deviants could pass, no one could be sure to detect definitively those who were not "normal." In their representations of homosexual characters, as a consequence, African American white life novelists sought to recruit homosexuality as a signifier of the instability within masculinity.

In recovering how these "integrationist" writers used their white realist fiction to intervene in the dissolution of white male subjectivity, I will be drawing on the ideas of "mimicry" from Homi Bhabha and other theorists of performativity. Bhabha's ideas about "ambivalence" apply equally to dominant "whites." In "The Postcolonial and the Postmodern," Bhabha argues for a subaltern agency that arises in the "disjunctive temporality" of any recitation of cultural identity on the level of everyday lived experience. Despite his/her attempt to repeat within his/her own body over time the dominant image of whiteness, the colonial subject, Bhabha contends, inevitably fails to reiterate this identity fully and properly. Underneath the formation of colonial subjectivities (and even those of whiteness) is thus always a set of omissions, gaps, and fissures that the apparent stable representation covers up (*Location of Culture* 177). The black look on the crisis of white masculinity in integrationist fiction is one of disclosure, a showing of the contradictions and divisions behind the unstable performance of white masculinity. The new visibility of the homosexual within the nationalist imaginary pointed toward an obvious site of incoherence and ambivalence within white masculinity that, for different reasons, these integrationist writers seized upon.

In making the white dissolute a threat to the security of the black "family" state, these writers, however, could not avoid the incoherence within the supposedly stable gender of the black male. It is this tension between outing the white dissolute who is a danger to the community and having to probe the unresolved homosexual cathexes in their own male identity formations that we see in integrationist writers such as William Demby.[5] The function of the white dissolute will finally be many layered in integrationist fiction, serving as both a novelistic intervention questioning the formation of a naturalized and universalized white maleness and as a vehicle for preventing narrative failure precisely at those moments in which homoeroticism would erupt as constitutive of black male community and unsettle the foundational splitting at the core of black male identity. Demby's *Beetlecreek*, in particular, explores and affirms intimacy between and among black men yet also attempts to manage how far this intimacy might reach by appealing to the national specter of white homosexuality. Although Hurston's *Seraph on the Suwanee* is also about the production of white male subjectivity, Hurston treats interracial homosexual desire as having the potential to disrupt the system of representations underpinning white and black hierarchies of race and gender.

Reembodying the "Savage" State: Wright's *Savage Holiday*

In his 1954 travel piece, *Black Power: A Record of Reactions in a Land of Pathos*, Richard Wright failed to identify with a race consciousness or an African vision of the world, despite his stay among the people of the Gold Coast (Fabre 402). While he had attempted a personal pilgrimage to his point of origins, he discovered, instead, how Western his outlook and affiliations were. There is one moment in which Wright does not just observe his American difference but disturbingly refuses any identification with the men of the Gold Coast, for the "sight of it provoked in me a sense of uneasiness on levels of emotion deeper than I could control" (110). The "it" that so disturbed Wright that he found himself losing "control" was the spectacle of young men dancing together at the outdoor area called the Weekend in Havana, "each with his arm tenderly about the waist of the other, their eyes holding a contented dreamy gaze" (108). If Wright here seems predictably homophobic, given the Cold War panic about perverts within the national state, the trauma that his recognition of "homoeroticism" among the natives elicited unsettled his already ambivalent racial, gender, and national identitarian formations. Although Wright had sought some authentic black self among the Gold Coast citizens, he discovered this alternative "nation" perverted, too, by the enemy within. At first, Wright struggles to position this same-sex intimacy outside his imagined African state: he imputes this "vice" to the British who must have "brought homosexuality to Africa" (108). Through further conversation with his American-educated guide, he discovers that such behavior arises out of native practices of segregating male and female activities. Trying not to sound like a prudish or provincial American, Wright snaps at his increasingly defensive guide: "Look, I'm no moralist; I don't care what they are, . . . [b]ut I want to make sure" (109). In wanting to ease all "interpretive anxiety," Wright rearticulates the Cold War panic about the illegibility of the homosexual passer who might pervert innocent others. Yet in *Black Power*, Wright finds instead that this sexual indeterminacy may even apply to the racial state and his own masculine body: might he also (as he is doing here) lose "control"? After he remarks on how the "African seemed to feel that . . . he had to share it [his joy]" and after he describes the physical movements of one of the dancers who "cajoled with his arms, said yes with his hips" (111), Wright tellingly ends the chapter with ellipses. Suddenly, for Wright, the public questions about race and nation have become intertwined with unconscious fantasies and fears, and the narrative breaks off interruptus. He cannot allow himself to revert to this savage state.

This episode from Wright's failed journey back to Africa transfers and amplifies the same themes about the union of racial and sexual identity that permeates his "sensational" white life novel, *Savage Holiday*, published earlier in the year (1954) as a dime store paperback by Avon Press. Although Claudia Tate has argued that *Savage Holiday* inscribes and exaggerates the "primary text, the ur text" of maternal or female betrayal (*Psychoanalysis* 89), it may be a mistake to read *Savage Holiday*'s protagonist, Erskine Fowler, too closely as Wright's alter ego, despite the similarity beneath the white face to Wright's own misogyny and matricidal desires. After all, Wright declared his central character "foul," if not "foul-er," and his actions are not just violent but absurd, cowardly (fowl-like), and latently homosexual, so that Wright's relation to this character is deliberately distancing, amid the important unconscious identifications. Read as a complementary ethnographic exposé to *Black Power*, Wright's *Savage Holiday* narrates a psychological journey into the heart of darkness of the white corporate state. In *Savage Holiday*, Wright turns the black gaze back on a particular formation of white male subjectivity, what was at the time referred to, borrowing the title of Walter Whyte's sociological study, as the "organization man," to expose the lies and the violence that this identity represses. Wright's *Savage Holiday*, like *Black Power*, is an ambivalent text because it attempts to unmask the ways of white folks behind its WASPish minstrelsy, yet Wright was unable to maintain his necessary distance from the other because of his intense identification with a character who shared his fears of masculine castration and sexual instability. Within its aesthetic disjointedness and inept and mechanical psychological characterizations, *Savage Holiday* reveals Wright's inability to keep himself from losing control and identifying with the novel's "savage white" character.

In writing a hybrid problem novel, pitched as a potboiler about the masculine anxieties of the bureaucratic white man in the gray flannel suit, Wright was attempting to address the question of race within the larger context of social change. As part of the Fordist regime of capitalist accumulation in Cold War America, as Elaine May, Stephanie Coontz, and David Savran have written, white middle-class men (organization men) were encouraged to see themselves as interchangeable parts in a bureaucratic corporate system and to define themselves as consumers and breadwinners in the home (May 178–82; Coontz 58–67; Savran 6–9). This new style of masculinity created a crisis among many men who worried about their feminization as they reorganized their identity around consumption, domesticity, and obedience in the collective workplace. While the U.S. cultural imaginary still upheld the values of a precapitalist or working-class masculinity—toughness, independence, self-reliance— middle-class men found society no longer afforded them an opportunity to live out these ideals. Angry and frustrated about these conflicting messages, middle-class white men often displaced their own feared effeminacy on the homosexual male, and the man in the gray flannel suit assured himself of his difference from the "sissy." As a result of the rise of the middle-class white-collar corporate world, as George Chauncey has documented, the meaning of masculinity changed, being defined less by gender traits than by exclusive heterosexuality (26). The unease with which this reformulation of masculinity as embodied in the organization man took place expressed itself through a panic about same-sex desire. Yet racism, too, was exacerbated by the rise of the organization man. Resistant to their declining status as consumers and breadwinners in Cold War America, many white men channeled their anger and frustration with the corporate order into renewed violence toward women and African Americans as well as toward gay men.

Although there are no black characters in *Savage Holiday*, Wright did not exclude racism against blacks altogether from the field of "representation" in this novel. Following a practice that Michael Rogin has detailed in relation to postwar Hollywood films such as *Gentleman's Agreement*, *Crossfire*, and *Home of the Brave*, in which directors assumed a commonality and substitutability among victim groups—gays, blacks, Jews—Wright uses the child Tony as a stand-in for the colored recipient of white male violence (231). Wright's novel is a true crime potboiler, but we need to inquire more specifically about what crime the novel invokes in its sensationalism. Although Clinton Brewer's 1923 matricidal murder of Wilhelmina Washington, mother of two, is often assumed to be the germ of Wright's pulp novel (Fabre 376), Wright equally draws upon the particular inflections of a renewed sex crime panic that peaked in the mid-1950s.

To many during the McCarthy era, the "homosexual menace" was tied to a broader sex crime panic that included the molestations of young boys and girls. Frequently in middle-brow presses such as *Colliers*, the *Saturday Evening Post*, and the *American Mercury*, sensational stories linked the homosexual and the perverted sex criminal as interchangeable and synonymous "monsters" infiltrating and threatening the family and national public life (Freeman 97–103). At a time when gender roles and sexual values for men and women were changing rapidly, the twinned homosexual psychopath and potential child molester loomed as a useful figure to shore up slipping norms. In a two-page review of J. Paul de River's "factual, scientific" book, *The Sexual Criminal, Newsweek* (October 10, 1949) contributes to the hysterical association of all "nonnormative" sexuality as a criminal queerness: "The sex pervert, whether a homosexual, an exhibitionist, or even a dangerous sadist, is too often regarded merely as a 'queer' person who never hurts anyone but himself. Then the mangled form of some victim focuses attention on the degenerate's work" (52). By educating its audience about how to respond to these "perversions" and citing de River as an authority, *Newsweek* urges draconian measures in which the "sex pervert [should be] treated, not as a coddled patient, but a particularly virulent type of criminal" (54). As the first stage to such a policing of the "enemy within," de River argues that society, especially the psychiatric community, must work to identify, without any equivocation, "perversions," "to spot the particular type of personality that would commit a specific sex crime." In its panic about sex crimes that needed to be eradicated by a clear naming of "deviant types," *Newsweek* divulges the rhetorical strategies that Wright would also invoke for his own purposes in his true crime novel. By telling the story of the accidental death of six-year-old Tony, Wright taps not only into sensational stories about matricide but also into mainstream cultural anxieties about child molestation, which complemented and reenforced the Cold War–era fear of male homosexuality.[6]

The plot of *Savage Holiday* follows the life of a forty-three-year-old insurance representative, Erskine Fowler, during the sixty-hour period after he has been dismissed from the company in order to make a place for the boss's son. The next Sunday morning he unintentionally locks himself out of his apartment while retrieving the newspaper, and, since he is naked, as he attempts to climb back into his apartment through the bathroom window he scares the neighbor child Tony into falling over the balcony. The accident that sets the plot into motion is his inadvertent encountering Tony and causing him to fall ten floors to his death. The remainder of the novel revolves around Erskine's attempts to cope with his guilt and to displace the ultimate blame for the child's death on the bad mother, Mabel Blake, who has neglected her child and traumatized him by allowing him to see her having sex with numerous "boyfriends." In the end, Erskine kills Mabel, punishing her for her "sins" and forcing her to submit to his own unconscious sexual desire. At the same time, Wright implies, Erskine's confession to the police acts out the ex-insurance representative's denied dream-wish to kill his unloving mother. As this brief synopsis suggests, *Savage Holiday* is a psychiatric hodgepodge, almost as labile as its main character, but not simply because Wright did not get his psychoanalysis right or perhaps got it too right that he bootlegged in every mechanical Oedipal complexity. Wanting to make the Freudian family romance a racial melodrama as well, Wright substitutes Tony for the absent black man in order to explore the unconscious fantasies that provide the shaping tension within the more public discourse about race.

Through Erskine's relation to the child Tony, Wright restores to the manifest content of the white life novel the homosexual attractions and loathings that, as Robyn Wiegman has shown, often played a role in the spectacle of lynching (98). In order to deny their identification with and longing for the hyperphallic black man who inhabited their own stereotypical national fantasy, white men often sought to destroy the naked body of the black male by burning, hanging, and finally castrating him. The white male subject has always been in a libidinal relation with the oppressed other, and his racial fighting has often been a form of repressing, while physically expressing, the opposite reaction, desiring. In Wright's *Savage Holiday*, the traumatic memory that sets the action in motion is Tony's childish belief that having sex and "fighting," as he calls it, are the same, and he admits to the father-figure Erskine that "I don't wanna fight. . . . I don't wanna fight ladies like my mother" (99). Although Wright could have borrowed Tony's nightmare directly from Freud, who held in his *A General Introduction to Psychoanalysis* that a child who witnesses his parents' lovemaking often presumes they are in "combat" (Gounard and Gounard 348), Wright complicates such a simple application of psychoanalysis to Tony or Erskine's sexual "hang-ups" by intimating that Tony's conceptual knotting of sex and fighting is not just an illusion. Tony's "misrecognition" that the naked Erskine is trying to rape him, and not just sneak back into the locked apartment, is not completely unfounded. Wright never makes it clear that Erskine's repression of his sexuality is not a cover for same-sex desires of some sort or even a sadism toward the weak child. Indeed, Erskine's unprompted dread that people will think him "queer" and assume "he'd gone deliberately onto the balcony like that nude . . ." (61) (a significant elision) suggests that

Erskine has previously feared that others regard him as the "deviant" pictured in popular accounts of sex crimes. His preemptive protest is in the novel all too implicating.

Wright's *Savage Holiday* begins clearly enough as a social commentary familiar to middle-brow readers of Sloan Wilson's *The Man in the Gray Flannel Suit* or even to audiences of Arthur Miller's *Death of a Salesman*: the novel's opening scene invokes the pathos, if not the tragedy, of the common (at least middle-class white-collar) man. The self-made Erskine Fowler, who rose over the last thirty years up the ranks of Longevity Life Insurance Company, is tossed away like an orange peel to make way for university-trained professionals with modern ideas and techniques, particularly the boss's well-educated son. We are invited to pity this latest victim of economic dislocation and downsizing as Wright describes Erskine as "outdated," "deadwood," "old-fashioned," "standing on the sidelines, rejected, refused." Yet even as Wright's white life novel sounds the universal themes of loneliness, humiliation, and rejection, Wright racially marks Erskine's caricature. This tragedy of the "common man" may be no more than the story of white male outrage and panic about being forced to relinquish occupational advantages that never were accepted as normal for black men. In Wright's *Savage Holiday*, there can be no full sympathy across racial lines: at the opening farewell party, Erskine is described as "a six-foot, hulking, heavy, muscular man with a Lincoln-like, quiet, stolid face, . . . he was the kind of man to whom one intuitively and readily rendered a certain degree of instant deference . . . with no hint in his attitude of apology for himself or his existence, confidant of his inalienable right to confront you and demand his modest due of respect" (14). This portrait of a self-confident and self-possessed Erskine seems completely disconnected to the later characterization of Erskine as an often ridiculous, unsure, and obtuse neurotic. But Wright's inconsistency in the psychological realism of Erskine's character is telling, suggesting that Wright sought to provide a satiric imitation of whiteness. The novel's statements that Erskine was a "man whom one intuitively and readily rendered a certain degree of instant deference" and one who had a confidence as an "inalienable right" mark him according to his privileges as the middle-class white male. If Erskine's joblessness might signal a plea for workers' rights that transcend the color line, Wright never lets us forget his protagonist's white body, Lincoln-like, that looms presuming rather than earning respect.

After the opening scene of Erskine's retirement banquet, the novel shifts from Marx to Freud, from capitalist critique to psychoanalytic case study precisely to tell the natural history of the white male body released from the corporate superego. The "holiday" of Erskine Fowler is a psychological journey into the private life underneath the public character of the white-collar bureaucrat, a journey that invokes only to ridicule some of the foundational myths of the organization man's masculine individualism. Despite Whyte's prefatory disclaimers to the contrary, *The Organization Man* is built around a nostalgia for a lost innocence and for the self-reliant man in his prebureaucratic, group-identified, natural state. In Whyte's narrative of historical shifts in the American character, men in the precapitalist past, before the predominance of megacorporations, were more self-reliant, self-regarding, inner directed, and dedicated to personal realization and fulfillment rather than conformity to group life. Whyte's *Organization Man* is an all-too-familiar complaint that echoes turn-of-the-century U.S. Republican discourse about the decline of moral character in a life of effeminate ease and luxury, including Teddy Roosevelt's alarm about the weakening of the national/racial character in the absence of a "strenuous life" (1–24). While Whyte's sociological study bears only the residual reverberations of these earlier racialized narratives of degeneracy, he continues to equate a particular historical formation of masculinity with the white man's natural/ideal state. In his imprecation of the modern bureaucratic white-collar workplace as a hostile, confining, collaborative environment that prohibits the American male from being himself—from being an individual—Whyte tends to see the presocialized individual male as one rationally directed toward his own self-interest. It is the modern social ethic with its prison of brotherhood that cooperates with the bureaucratic state to incite one's willing consent to the loss of individual initiative, creativity, and action. As Whyte writes, "In current retrospect the turn of the century seems a golden age of individualism, yet by the 1880s the corporation had already shown the eventual bureaucratic direction it was going to take. . . . One of the key assumptions of the Protestant Ethic had been that success was due neither to luck nor to the environment but only to one's natural qualities—if men grew rich it was because they deserved to" (16). But such a romanticized formation of white male subjectivity in its preorganized state omits, as Wright's novel shows, the unconscious desires that exceed individual choice.

In a renegotiation of Whyte's false binarism between the good natural state of the individual and the bad corporate bureaucratic self, Wright argues that it is the "bureaucratic life" that actually keeps the white man from savagery. Although Wright begins his novel with a sympathetic portrayal of Erskine's economic exploitation, he soon attempts to "reembody" the psychological reality behind the tragic life of the white organization man and thus to overturn the prevalent figuration of white male subjectivity. In his transcription of Erskine's meditations after leaving his office farewell party, Wright offers a counternarrative to the white crisis of masculine individualism:

> Work had not only given Erskine his livelihood and conferred upon him the approval of his fellowmen [*sic*]; but, above all, it made him stranger to a part of himself that he feared and wanted never to know. At some point in his childhood he had assumed toward himself the role of a policeman, . . . dragged himself off to serve a sentence of self-imposed labor for life, had locked himself up in a prison cage of toil. . . . How could he suppress or throttle those slow and turgid stirrings of buried impulses now trying to come to resurrected life in the deep dark of him? (33)

Wright's odd characterization of Erskine here is telling. By saying that Erskine is a "stranger to a part of himself," Wright implies that white male subjectivity is a performance that involves splitting off unacceptable unconscious desires and constantly supervising oneself against any possible return of that self-division. Work becomes more than simply a way of making a living or defining oneself; work becomes a way of imprisoning or disciplining the "buried impulses" and dark "stirrings." While Wright's analysis is not particularly nuanced or even original with its warmed-over Freudian reading of business (if not civilization) as the white male superego, the novel's sudden distraction into a Conradian journey into the white heart of de-organized darkness pictures the inner divisions at the core of white male subjectivity. Against a white manhood continually validated as "independent," "rationally self-interested" (even if at times violent), and "innocent," within the rhetoric over the crisis of the organization man, Wright forces readers to see themselves in the mirror of another story.

In telling this other story of Erskine Fowler, Wright uses a tactic of accumulated suspicion that never ties Erskine's crime to a single meaning but keeps it always in excess of a final explanation. At the end of the same interior monologue, Wright opens up the implications of Erskine's story in terms of the organization man's repression: "now, to avoid the commission of what crime—or had the crime already been committed, and was he trying to escape its memory?—was Erskine hankering so anxiously to imprison himself? What had he ever done—or what did he fear doing?—that made him feel so positively that he had to encircle himself, his heart, and his actions with bars, to hold himself in a leash?" (34). The syntax here, an obvious attempt at stream of consciousness verisimilitude, is convoluted, but, more important, the language is ambiguous, as if in the hesitations of the sentences Erskine cannot say that which he denies—the crime. Wright teases us by implying that the "crime" may already have been committed, a statement that is more than a foreshadowing designed to generate suspense. By the end of the novel, we as readers may think we have the conundrum unriddled and finally know the crime Erskine buries from his memory, his matricidal urge as a child. But by leaving throughout the course of the novel the crime unnamed, Wright opens up multiple readings of Erskine's culpability. This deliberate indeterminacy about the source of Erskine's guilt allows the reader to take as Erskine's crime a desire to harm Tony. Continually after Tony's accidental fall, Erskine frets not just about whether he will be apprehended but why Tony had recoiled from him and by so doing toppled over the balcony: "One aspect of the accident bothered him above all; why had little Tony been so frightened of him as to lose his balance when he'd come running nude onto the balcony? Tony knew him, admired him; then why had he gone into such a panic . . . ?" (80, Wright's ellipses). In a Cold War climate in which rhetoric about the homosexual predator committing sex crimes functioned in the constitution of white heterosexual national subjects, Wright's invocation of a similar suspicion in regard to Erskine would have had a significant resonance. Although Wright later closes off this suspicion by offering all too formulaic Freudian symptoms, in the end he has already implicated the organization man for his repressed "savage" desires.

While both Wright and Erskine try to normalize his sexual identity by triangulating it through the mother/whore, Mabel Blake, Wright's novel cannot maintain the psychological distancing necessary for a straightforward race critique. In depicting Erskine's fear of and anger against the strong, sexually liberated—and thus to him, "castrating"—woman, *Savage Holiday* slips into a cross-racial masculine identification. Although the novel attempts to "reembody" the excluded savage self of the white organization man, it allies itself with midcentury fears about the feminization of the white-collar organization man. Repeatedly, Erskine reveals that he shares the postwar panic about a woman's gender nonconformity and that he once more would like, now that he has lost his economic status, to reassert his authority by dominating Mabel. After realizing that he ought to ask Mabel to marry him, Erskine considers, "His lips parted as the idea swam luminously in his consciousness. She'd obey him! she was simple; and above all, he'd be the boss; he'd dominate her completely . . ." (134). Wright's statements in regards to Erskine's desire to dominate Mabel (including once again the telling ellipses) are so often voiced and expressed so directly that at first it seems as if he is self-conscious in condemning this misogyny and resentment against the mother. Wright, it would seem, uses psychological paradigms to glimpse the inner division that leads to patriarchal deprecations of women. Unable to reconcile the opposing images of women as either virgins or whores, Erskine confesses, "He yearned to believe that she was as inno-cent, as good as a boy believes his mother to be, but her manner told him that that was impossible. His desire for her was so close to his rejection of her that he couldn't separate the two. . . . When ever he sought a compro-mise of his love-hate struggle, he grew distressed" (138). Yet Wright's anal-ysis of how the child splits the imagined ideal of the mother into the madonna and the whore finally never goes beyond an awareness of how deep injuries in the child's psyche leave lifetime scars. By making Erskine's attack on Mabel finally an acting out of his anger against the "bad mother," Wright leaves in place this conceptualization of women as to blame. Wright's awareness that whiteness is a racial construct orga-nized around a series of repressions and displacements finally did not allow him to see gender as similarly so constituted. There is, according to Wright, something universal about the family romance at the center of masculinity that transcends race.

If Wright's open-endedness about Erskine's crimes has allowed him to entrap his white audience into seeing their sexuality as incapable of being contained in stable heterosexual representations, the text of Wright's novel, in a state reminiscent of the inner conflict in *Black Power*, found itself too drawn to the troubled and troubling protagonist of *Savage Holi-day*. Although Wright's characterization of Erskine "forced him to con-front his own attitude to his mother" (Fabre 378), this identification concealed a more primal repression in Wright's novel. Just as Wright in

Black Power insisted that he "wanted to make sure" how to read the men dancing, Wright's *Savage Holiday* tried to find a plot that would end its homosexual panic. The very illegibility of Erskine's sexual identity caused Wright finally to insist on naming his character's "savage" (precorporate) state. If Wright invokes the generic matricidal urges of the Freudian Oedipus complex, he does so in order to repress something that, like the earlier sight of the dancing men in *Black Power*, "provoked in me a sense of uneasiness on levels of emotion deeper than I could control." To restore personal and narrative control through his white life novel, Wright turned it ironically into just another story of the very masculine crisis that he sought to undo. The novel finally reinscribes as natural the racial masculinity that he had exposed as a cultural fiction, and Wright reverses the trajectory of his critique by making Erskine just another organization man who fears his domestication by the castrating woman. While Wright's *Savage Holiday* could permit into the consciousness of the text the love and hatred for the mother, it could not speak of the conflicted polymorphous desires that Erskine's story might arouse. In the end, just as Erskine confesses his crimes to the police, Wright stages his protagonist's confession to close off any indefinite meanings to his sensational tale. He was writing, as he told his agent, Paul Reynolds, a story that "deals with just folks, white folks." But as Wright disclosed in his novel, to write about whiteness is to speak about the way race is sexed, even the racial identity of black men.

The Open Secret in the Family

In response to a symposium of essays in *Phylon* in 1950 on the postwar state of "Negro literature," Alain Locke argued that an integrationist-era concern for respectability ought not to introduce a revived aesthetics of self-conscious inhibitions and repressions. The new "New Negro" writers of the Cold War years ought not to fear a bold, broadminded self-expression, particularly out of concern for how they will be seen by the dominant white society: "I am far from suggesting that even a considerable part of this revelation will be morally risqué or socially explosive; some of it will be, of course. But I do sense a strange and widely diffused feeling that many of these situations are Masonic secrets—things to be talked about, but not written or officially disclosed" (394). In speaking of "Masonic secrets" and "risqué" exposés, Locke links the African

American's coming of age and 1950s' sex conformity. In a push toward an aesthetics of integration as a sign of arrival, Locke implies there has been a loss of any acknowledgment of racial and sexual differences. While some African American writers have let an inner tyranny silence them, Locke praises, in contrast, William Demby, who in 1950 published a short bildungsroman novel, *Beetlecreek*. Although Demby consciously patterned his work after that of "universal" modernists such as Sherwood Anderson and Carson McCullers, Demby's depiction of the alienation and loneliness of the sensitive individual in small town America also enters into the contemporary debate about racial segregation and the possibility for integration.[7] When thirteen-year-old Johnny Johnson from Pittsburgh goes to stay with his aunt and uncle in a small West Virginia town, he enters a world divided by color. Once there he befriends a white hermit, Bill Trapp, while attempting to win, at the same time, initiation into an all-male "black" gang, whose members are suspicious of Johnny's delicate "pansy" sensibilities. In the main narrative line of the novel, the climax is built toward the choice that Johnny must make between his friendship with the white man and his allegiance to his black brothers.

To such an overly predetermined didactic plot relocated to a West Virginian Winesburg town, however, Demby adds the specter of queer sexuality, which, as Locke intimated, threatens to exceed either the white or black hegemonic social order. In the last third of the novel, Bill Trapp is accused of being a pedophile and potential child molester after he gives an integrated children's party and the black child Pokey returns home with a "nude" picture torn out of an anatomy encyclopedia. Suddenly, to the black townsfolk Bill Trapp is no longer "surely nice" (67), and Johnny is not only a youth of suspect racial loyalty but also the reputed recipient of white homosexual friendship. To prove simultaneously his racial pride and masculinity, the gang forces Johnny to burn down the house of his white friend as his initiation into the gang. Although the black town wants to imagine its sexual innocence against the intruding presence of this queer white predator, Demby's novel asks its readers to rethink this dominant model of black identity and community in relation to "deviant" others. While Richard Wright invoked the specter of the homosexual pervert in the sensational fiction of the Eisenhower era, Demby offers a much more conflicted representation of same-sex desire. Like the black popular press, Demby's novel wrestles with the realization that the black male social order may already be studded with its supplemental excess of homoerotic desire that threatens to overturn its strategic identity formations (Warner 12).

If Demby's attention was turned to the excess of queer desire in the black community in *Beetlecreek*, this author was only picking up the obsession within widely circulated organs of the black press. In the postwar era, the Johnson-owned *Ebony* and *Jet* frequently carried stories about the homosexual passer. Since the founding of *Ebony* in 1945 to promote, as John H. Johnson proclaimed in his inaugural editorial, "the success stories of famous black Americans," the Johnson-owned publishing empire helped to reflect and constitute the values of a slowly emerging black middle class. With its parade of celebrity figures who embodied the lifestyles of the rich and famous, from Dorothy Dandridge and Eartha Kitt to Harry Belafonte and Jackie Robinson, *Ebony* and *Jet* sought not to represent the "noble Negro," as had the earlier highbrow *Negro Digest*, but a collective fantasy of middle-class ease and consumption. Yet as the accompanying sensational stories about those classified as "impersonators and perverts" testify, this formation of an "integrationist," if not always integrated, middle-class black American in the years after the war initiated an accompanying sense of insecurity and self-doubt about the erosion of traditional forms of manhood. Amid its parade of celebrity images, *Ebony* and *Jet* ushered in a new style of black male performance defined in terms of consumption. In contrast to the later macho nationalism of 1960s activists, *Ebony* and *Jet* flourished in the 1950s by offering commercialized images of a new middle-class black male. Like his white counterpart who had also been redefined as a consumer, this new middle-class black male increasingly exercised power through his exaggerated heterosexuality and dominance over women, gays, and other minorities, especially since he lacked many of the traditional means of political and social control. In its frequent running of stories about gender deviants, the black popular press sought to recoup black male adequacy, setting up clear boundaries between the effeminate male and the masculine and clearly heterosexual race man.

One recurrent type of article that ran in *Ebony*, *Jet*, and *Our World* in the early 1950s to demarcate gender and sex deviance was the exposé on impersonators and "perverts." In the ten-year period after the Second World War, these monthly stories on impersonators and perverts made homosexuality in the black community suddenly an "open secret." By saying that homosexuality became "open," I do not mean to suggest that there was a general tolerance or unspoken acceptance for sexual nonconformity. Rather, a particular style of homosexuality moved out of the private closet to attain the status of public recognition as the necessary defining opposite to heterosexuality (Miller 168). In part, this outing of effeminate homosexuality, but not "straight-acting" queerness, in the black community operated as part of a national public debate about purging the American government and psyche of infections of queerness. However, in contrast to the mainstream white press's figuring of the homosexual deviant, the black press's discourse on impersonators and perverts assumed a decidedly different tone and inflection. While the leaders of the Harlem Renaissance during the 1920s had debated whether a middle-class respectability or bohemianism was the appropriate image of the New Negro, *Ebony* attempted to reconcile and merge these two opposite perspectives by bringing them together in the celebrity spectacle.

To defuse the disorienting and transgressive power of the drag queen, *Ebony* described her as a "passer" who remained a part of her family and of her race. This representational makeover of the drag queen as family man can be seen in *Our World*'s feature story on Phil Black, who performed in New York's Black Cat and Morocco Clubs. As Phil's symbolic stage name suggests, the overriding question that lurks as the buried referent beneath *Our World*'s behind-the-scenes profile of the infamous Hamilton Lodge Ball heir is whether this brother can really be a lover (phile) of "blackness". Can she really be "real"? While black nationalists of the 1960s and 1970s would argue that the homosexual male's refusal to identify with his "biological nature" was equivalent to the self-loathing black man's refusal of his race, *Our World* diverts attention from questions of the essential black body to appeal to the discourse of the family. Throughout the story, *Our World*'s reporter fits the female impersonator into the familiar language of the hard-working self-made Washingtonian black man. Against the popular image of the queen as a heavy-drinking, sexually promiscuous party-goer, *Our World* transcribes Phil's comment that "I don't join the many parties that take place after some clubs close and I have very little use for alcohol. I have never been married chiefly because of my mother. She has no other means of support and has been living with me for 18 years" (P. Black 19). Although he may wear women's clothes, Phil's private life is "normal," adhering to all the middle-class values and domestic pieties of the most respectable of role models. While postmodern critics such as Judith Butler have argued that the drag queen's parodic performance reveals the imitative nature of gender (Butler 135–37), Phil's body is compelled to signify a "natural" racial body, a body that, if it can pass as another gender, still remains true to the family and the race.

In the critical period of the early 1950s, one of the most sensational accounts of female impersonation that *Ebony* and *Jet* carried involved the revelation that Georgia Black had lived "30 years as a woman" within the Florida community of Sandford, only being discovered as a biological male on her deathbed. Although the authors recognized that the reader's initial reaction might be to label Georgia a "fairy" or a "freak," the story overturns these reflexive condemnations by citing the respect of the townspeople and family members for Black, who participated actively in the Women's Missionary Society and raised her second husband's nephew as her own son. As *Ebony* concludes, "Black's true sex made no difference," and Black's neighbor, Mabel Clark, insisted that "I heard lots of nice things about her. As far as I'm concerned, her life is her business" ("The Man Who Lived 30 Years" 93). As in the case of Phil Black, the female impersonator's gender and sexual deviance, while not condoned, did not preclude her inclusion in the "family" as long as she did not betray her race. As her adopted son would testify in a follow-up article ("My Mother Was a Man"), Georgia Black "lived the respectable normal life of a typical Southern churchgoing, God-fearing, home-loving housewife and mother" (Saab 25), and since she remained "true" to her "family," her sexual "abnormality" ought not to be a matter of public surveillance and censure. Although *Ebony*'s article is sensational, and as such implicitly singles Georgia out as a freak, the reader of such a piece would have registered a different concept of male subjectivity than that depicted in the white media. The black male closet formed in the *Ebony* article was less one that demanded a constant self-policing of private gender behavior for "deviance" than a moral urgency to preserve and protect the black family. While a male reader of *Ebony*'s story would not have felt his sexuality affirmed in the coverage of Georgia Black's story, he also would not have had to confront a particularly demeaning psychotherapeutic image of himself. In its coverage of Georgia Black, *Ebony* remains relatively tolerant of alternative male gender identifications.

In discursively tying the homosexual to the passer, the middle-class black press was displacing its own panic about the place of femininity in the marginal masculinity of the celebrity spectacle. Stories like those of Phil Black and Georgia Black pushed homosexuality as an open secret so as to resecure a symbolic order organized around fixed sexual differences at a time in which they seemed to be slipping away. To make Georgia really a "woman" in a man's body was to insist that there were really only two possible subject positions: that occupied by the heterosexual man or homosexual woman who was really a man in a woman's body and that associated with the heterosexual woman or homosexual man who was, like Georgia Black, a woman in a man's body. The complex images of celebrity manhood in the material fantasy world of *Ebony* and *Jet* in which one could display all the virile symbols of hypermasculinity but lack other traditional determinants of male power, citizenship, upward mobility, and property ownership, caused an insecurity about the woman within. The female impersonators and passers absolved black male subjectivity of the plague of femininity. The more outrageous the impersonator's womanliness, the more distant the proximity of the "real" black male from this identification. At a time when males, both black and white, were trained to police themselves against signs of latent homosexuality, one did not have to worry about the "woman within" under the masculine masquerade as long as "femininity" meant "drag." The drag queen turned off the black reader's homophobic monitoring because she equated homosexuality and deviance with gender rather than with sexuality.

While the "female impersonator" could now become an open secret in the black popular middle-class press because she assured black men that they had not accommodated themselves to the femininity within, the text of *Beetlecreek*, by contrast, plays upon the fear implied in the popular press that the male members of same-sex groups may actually desire each other, desire the very men and ideal of male masculinity that they posit as the race man. Demby's work shows that black masculinity is a site of "volatile identification and ambivalent anxious desire" (Harper 147). Traditional psychoanalytic models of male growth and development have centered on Freud's dissociation, as Diana Fuss notes, between desire and identification. As part of a successful completion of his Oedipal struggle, the healthy male child, to put it simply, learns to identify with his father and to direct his desire outward to the other and away from his "narcissistic" impulse toward the same (46). However, as Demby depicts, while the black family would attempt to install homoerotic desire and attraction toward the same sex outside the "family" of racial brotherhood (the homosexual Bill Trapp), this same-sex desire already functions within the group bond despite its presumed heteronormativity. Indeed, in Demby's *Beetlecreek*, the distinction between desire and identification is blurred and exposed as a cultural fiction, for homoerotic desire not only passes within the family, it can help to constitute its very solidarity.

When Johnny goes to his first meeting of the "secret society" or gang with its unnamed "Leader," he witnesses the ritualistic exchange of "dirty" homophobic jokes that bonds the group together: "Baby Boy was half leaning on Johnny's shoulder while the Leader told them a dirty joke '. . . and when the fart jumped in with her, he found out hers was bigger than his!'" (37). Later, too, when Johnny wavers in joining the group, remaining aloof at home during the day, the Leader taunts him that "he's been stayin' in the house like a pansy" (104). If *Beetlecreek* shows the tactical use of homosexuality as the structural transgression that constitutes the borders of the all-male social bond, it likewise disrupts and renegotiates this sexual boundary. Although the gang would exclude the homosexual male, and more largely homoeroticism, as a contaminating exterior to the group's inner identity, *Beetlecreek* reveals how interior is this "deviant" sexuality to the brotherhood. As part of their regular group ceremony, the boys stand together, while clothed, masturbating before "dirty" cartoons and pictures of women torn from magazines: "The red-necked boy had his hands in his pockets and was rubbing them back and forth nervously, at the same time he shimmed up and down the floor" (36). As if to disguise their obvious homoerotic nature behind the Freudian symbolism of this ceremony, the boys share a cigarette after the ritual's consummation: "But when he [Johnny] saw the amused looks the others were giving him, he accepted the brown-stained butt the boy was handing him and gingerly put it in his mouth. He kept his lips as dry as possible because he knew Baby Boy hadn't washed his hands after what he had just done" (37). By taking the "brown-stained butt" in their mouths, the boys act out the repressed wish for a connection with and penetration by their black brother that would make them the disavowed pansy.

In contrast to the discursive strategies of *Ebony, Jet*, and *Our World*, Demby does not keep into play the false binaries between the passer, or impersonator, and the true man, between questions of private sexuality and the public question of the race. The true nationalist black man (the Leader) is not purified of homoerotic desire any more than the pansy, and questions of "private" sexual identity are not simply something that lie outside, separated from, the fashioning of racial unity. In its description of Johnny's dream, moreover, *Beetlecreek* seems to confirm a possible homoerotic component of nationalist and racial fantasies of brotherhood and unity. In setting up an ideal man as the source of identification for individual members, the utopian racist tends to play upon a homoerotic attraction for this image of revolutionary possibility. Similarly, when Johnny dreams about the return of his deceased mother, her image soon slips into an image of a Christ-like Bill Trapp, who in turn, when Johnny looks right into the deep, strange eyes, is the "sly and young" face of the Leader (14). Later, even more clearly before he decides to "belong" to the gang, Johnny reflects that "in some way, when he is dreaming about his mother, when there came over him a hot melting urge to cry, he knew that Bill Trapp was mixed up with what he was feeling for his mother. In the dream, they were one and the same, and about each, he remembered feeling very sad" (154). In *Beetlecreek*, Johnny's feelings for Bill are associated with a taboo longing for the feminine world of the mother. The Oedipal break into masculinity becomes one of identifying with the powerful black man (the Leader). Here the maternal regression is equated with a homosexual longing, for the town has now read Bill's friendship for Johnny a pedophile's en(Trapp)ment of a fourteen-year-old boy. But *Beetlecreek* breaks down any such antimony between identification and desire. Although the group would resolutely insist on a masculine self-identification articulated through the abjectification of femininity (Johnny's mother) and homosexuality (Bill)—here tantamount in Johnny's dream—to ally with the ideal Leader is only a mere fantasy of escaping the excluded taint of deviant psychical identity formations. In the fluid circulation of desire in the novel, neither identification protects Johnny from his own inchoate desires, which in his first meeting with the group caused him to flee the headquarters. If Fanon had argued that white racism (Negrophobia) is really repressed homosexuality, *Beetlecreek*, by contrast, offers no comforting allusion to its male readers that the homosexual is outside their parameters. Same-sex desire also circulates as an unacknowledged excess among black men.

To become the "new Johnny" (162), Johnny must immolate all traces of the homosexual by burning down the house of the other and thus denying it within himself and his group. But *Beetlecreek* complicates what might have been a simple tale of scapegoating the "white man" as a homosexual menace (as we saw in Wright's *Savage Holiday*), for the novel indicates, on one level, the town's accusations about Bill Trapp's "sexual" deviance are true. Although not the pedophilic child molester the rumors paint him, the language of the novel does suggest that his friendship toward Johnny is not totally without homosexual longing. And even the anatomical picture that the town holds as evidence of Bill's perversion is the remaining artifact that he still owns from his ambiguous "partnership" with an Italian circus performer. In the opening voyeuristic scene in which Bill watches the boys trespass on his property, for example, Demby's wording suggests the erotic overtones and recalls Sherwood Anderson's own characterization of Wing Biddlebaum in *Winesburg, Ohio*: "His heart beat fast as it always did. Always when they came he would look into their faces. He would be filled with uncontrollable excitement knowing that he was seeing them while they couldn't see him. . . . For almost ten minutes he watched. Soon he felt the familiar itchy nervousness coming" (7). Of course, on one level, this "itchy nervousness" is the timidity of the socially avoidant personality, but Bill's accelerated heart rate when staring at the boys is also that of the lover. In showing the "latent, often explosive passions," as the original cover of Demby's novel said, below the surface of a small town, Demby reveals that unstable excess of desire that circulates everywhere and most importantly exceeds the "color" line, even though both white and black communities might try to scapegoat the homosexual.

As in *Ebony* and *Jet*, questions about sexual identity are deflected into public questions about race. Although Demby uses a religious language that suggests Johnny enacts a Judas-like betrayal of Bill Trapp, who "looked more like a Sunday school picture of a saint" (129), he makes it clear that Johnny had no unencumbered self that could choose his own identity apart from the aims and obligations imposed by his race. Once the town has reimagined Bill Trapp as a symbol of racial injustice (because his alleged molestation of Pookey goes unpunished by the "white" law), Johnny has no choice but to come out against Bill and to repress his "wayward desires," whatever their manifestations, for his race. At first his new sense of belonging elates him: "For the first time he felt himself to be a member of the gang, felt eligible and equal" (132). Yet Johnny's responsibility to his race, as Demby shows, is finally a Pyrrhic victory that leaves him fleeing from his own desires. After Bill Trapp "hugs" Johnny even though he burned down his house, Johnny must fight to free himself from this embrace. When he pummels Bill with the gasoline can, Johnny is not only trying to avoid his guilt, shame, and anger but his own confused identity, an identity that has a deviant affection for this recluse and, more immediately, a deviant identification with the transgressive gender and sexual behavior that Trapp represents. At the end of Johnny's story, we are told, he "ran and ran and ran." Just as the black popular press both tried to make the homosexual an open secret and contain it within the family, Demby's novel retreats back to the racial family as a source of stability where one can keep complicated homoerotic and interracial desire private.

But for Johnny there is no escape; there is no escape not because he cannot elude his "true" self but because queerness is not, according to the logic of *Beetlecreek*, some marginal sexuality that stands against a normative heterosexuality of true black manhood. Queerness is already, as we have seen, inside the social bond of the young brothers' gang. Although the town members would lock homosexuality into some essential opposition between normative and deviant sexuality (which could then be used to police racial categories), homoerotic desire circulates in complex and often latent forms in human relationships in a way that does not conform neatly to one's political agenda. In *Beetlecreek*, what we are left with is a destabilizing ambiguity that finally eschews and annihilates the identitarian categories. Johnny's desperate flight toward the railroad tracks is a collapse of his own identity that tried to keep queerness in the family by making it a private matter against the public performance of racial loyalty. But such a self-division pushes Johnny into a borderland that finally leaves him lost, torn between contradictory desires with competing values and responsibilities that are not so easily reconciled. To come of age, whether he remains in a segregated or in an integrated world, Johnny must see the queer already in the social order as well as inside himself.

Misogyny and the Homosexual Menace

In her "quasi-fictional, quasi-historical" autobiography, *Dust Tracks on a Road*, Zora Neale Hurston tells the story of an unnamed "white man" who aided in her birth. Arriving at the crucial moment before the midwife, Aunt Judy, could be fetched from Woodbridge, the white man wields his "Barlow Knife" to cut the "navel cord" linking Hurston to her weakened mother (29). Upon seeing the operation performed without her doctoring, Aunt Judy "grumbled for years about it," claiming that Hurston would have as a result a weak back and incontinent bladder until she reached "puberty." Such, indeed, Hurston tells us, was her anatomical fate. In reading Hurston's account of her birth, it is not hard to discern the allegorical implications of this "contested" birth. The white man's intervention separates Hurston both from her mother and from the folk world represented in the midwife, and through such a severing of racial connection Hurston states that she has been left "de-formed," literally unable to stand upright. Yet without the frontier individualism, here symbolized in the white man's barlow, Hurston equally implies that she might have choked on the maternal umbilical cord and thus lacked the necessary differentiation that allowed her to be free and to "spread[ ] her lungs all over Orange County" (29). This image of the split subjectivity of Zora Neale Hurston's speaking voice offers us a hermeneutical key for interpreting her white life novel, *Seraph on the Suwanee*. While in *Seraph* Hurston turns her gaze back upon the dominant southern white fathers who have "de-formed" her self-making, she in turn challenges the repressive racial and gender power system in her own black community that would stifle one's voice. If Hurston adopted, as Barbara Johnson contends, only a "provisional interlocutory stance" that allowed her to trespass back and forth and speak on both sides of the color line, she does so in order to bring into representation what was hidden, repressed, and denied within normative models of both black and white identities (283).

Although race and gender have been examined in Hurston's fiction, they have often been isolated from questions of the postwar construction of "queer" sexuality. In the past, critics such as Susan Meisenhelder have looked closely at Arvay's neurotic repression of her sexuality in *Seraph on the Suwanee* as a product of a southern patriarchal economy (100), but Hurston offers us an inscription through elision of cross-racial same-sex desire that challenges the postwar rhetoric of the homosexual menace and talks back to the exclusions enforced for the preservation of racial boundaries that we saw in William Demby's *Beetlecreek*. While Hurston does challenge the oppressive regulatory fictions of postwar female identity, she specifically links this misogyny to denial, to the denial particularly of a troubling same-sex desire within masculinity. In Jim Meserve's control of Arvay, Hurston witnesses that it is precisely the instability within male identity and the accompanying panic about an "effeminizing" loss of power to the racial other that causes the oppression of many southern women such as Arvay. In contrast to Wright's and Demby's white life novels, Hurston's *Seraph* treats homosexuality as a subversive form of identity that has the potential to disrupt the system of representations underpinning the fashioning of white masculinity in the new plantation south of suburban *Southern Homes and Gardens*.

In a letter to Burroughs Mitchell (December 5, 1947), Hurston acknowledged that she hoped to write in *Seraph on the Suwanee* a bestseller that could be marketed by book clubs and adapted into a Hollywood film. Because of this statement, critics have tended to read Hurston's novel intertexually against such white-authored popular fiction as Marjorie Rawlings's *The Yearling* or Margaret Mitchell's *Gone with the Wind* (Meisenhelder 115). But the question of what literary precedents Hurston had in mind for her depiction of Arvay and Jim Meserve may be less important than why and how she *genders* the ideology of whiteness and discursively ties a possessive investment in it to women. Although Arvay is the victim of a patriarch, Hurston makes clear that it is she (not Jim) who mainly perpetuates exclusionary ideas of whiteness. When Jim hires the Portuguese Corregio to work on his citrus farm, Arvay finds her understanding of white racial identity challenged: "Arvay was annoyed. . . . Jim had said that they were white folks, but the man turned out to be a Portuguese, and his name was Corregio. That made them foreigners, and no foreigners were ever quite white to Arvay. Real White people talked English and without any funny sounds to it" (120). Later on, when Arvay fears that the Corregios' daughter, Felicia, will marry and take her son, Kenny, away from her, she muses to rationalize her hurt: "Felicia and her mother were nothing but heathen idolater and not to be treated white. Arvay proceeded to set up images of them among the African savages and heathen Chinee. They were not fellow-humans, nothing of the kind" (242). At the center of the Arvay's story, then, are the questions who is a fellow human being, who is white, and what is the meaning of this racial formation? As the "white trash" daughter of turpentine still workers from Sawley, Arvay has anxiety about her own class and race position, and feeling that Jim and others "would look down on her as the backwoods Cracker, the piney-woods rooter" (130), she, as a consequence, frequently appeals to a "shared" whiteness to assure herself of her fitness for Jim. In her story of Arvay, Hurston depicts the treacherous route that women take to becoming a woman, or in Arvay's case of not becoming a woman, who is in contact with her own body, sexuality, and psyche. But Hurston connects Arvay's dispossession from herself, and her body, to her investment in whiteness. Arvay's false gender and racial identity come into existence only in relation to one another and are dynamically joined. The more that Arvay submits to the violence that naturalizes her role as a woman, the more that she insists upon her status as white.

In contrast to Arvay, Jim is an errant plantation son who, despite his upper-class credentials, does not choose to preserve the inherited racial hierarchy. He represents the manhood of a New South, whose commercial and entrepreneurial energies were actually bringing in the first slippages in inherited racial boundaries. In the language in which she describes Jim, Hurston calls attention to his difference from Faulkner's southern aristocrats with their faded glory. Although his "ancestors had held plantations upon the Alabama River before the War" (7), Jim Meserve represents the entrepreneurial "individualism" (me-serving energy) of the New South. As Jim himself reflects to Arvay, "I had too much sense to follow their lead. While my old man was sitting around reading and taking notes trying to trace up who did what in the Civil War. . . . I shucked out to get in touch with the New South. So far, I don't think that I have made out so bad" (203). In *Making Whiteness: The Culture of Segregation in the South, 1890–1940*, Grace Elizabeth Hale has investigated the role that the commercialization of the South had in breaking down traditional notions of whiteness. As the economy increasingly came to depend on consumer spending for mass-produced commodities, the country store became the "vulnerable point in the culture of segregation" (285). Even while store owners and entrepreneurs may have wanted to or felt compelled to uphold and maintain the privileges of white supremacy and solidarity, they realized that they needed black customers and that discrimination was not good for business. In telling the story of the new entrepreneur of the New South, Jim Meserve, Hurston contrasts his marketplace orientation to whiteness against the more traditional self-definition of poor white southerners such as Arvay. At the end of the novel, Hurston even notes, Jim hires both blacks and whites based on merit to serve as captains and workers on his shrimping boats, thus creating one of the novel's few integrated spaces where men of diverse races work and socialize together.

In *Seraph on the Suwanee*, Hurston exposes the fissures and the contradictions in white male identity and its history of entrepreneurial (self-made) success.[8] Specifically, she returns to visibility an erotic commerce between men that exceeds the control of white patriarchal ideology: what had been ghosted out of existence in the tales of white manliness building a New South through black and white friendships. A counterreading of Hurston's *Seraph on the Suwanee* might focus on how the odd complications in the love story between Arvay and Jim Meserve rarely involve a third woman but instead Jim's close friendship with black men. In both occasions in which Arvay gives Jim an ultimatum to choose her or another, Jim must decide between his wife and his black male friend. Quarreling over Kenny's friendship with Joe's daughter Belinda, Arvay hints that Joe and Jim have a similar "romance": "Look like Joe is the boss on this place" and "got more influence over you than I have" (113). Jim's evasive response is linguistically coded: "You're my wife, the most precious thing that I got, and nobody don't compare with you. What's between me and Joe is something different altogether and I wouldn't want you to take a pick at him" (113). Although Jim's language attempts to reassure Arvay of her priority, his contrast between his ownership of Arvay and his intimacy with Joe seems to deconstruct its own surface message. The reader, like Arvay, remains insecure about what exactly this "something different" could be. Earlier Arvay has tried to fit their bond into the familiar racist language of the Old South: the close friendships between black and white men could be explained as the relation between a master and his "dog": "Joe is your pet, I'll bound you," Arvay had interpreted for Joe, trying to "bound" the relationship into the hierarchy of man and animal, when he could not relate his feelings for the man (60). Yet in this novel it is his relation to Arvay that Jim bases on property, and later he calls her "my damn property" (216).

The possibility of a different kind of "friendship," of homosocial ties if not homosexual identities, is thus continually raised in Hurston's *Seraph on the Suwanee* but never quite named, and Hurston attempts to reveal a psychological strategy of "compensatory domination" of women that allows the homoerotic ties between men to hide behind the cover of normal manly conquest. Jim's trafficking in women as property is what keeps the novel's men's club unmarked as "queer." Because of a reassuring difference between men and women, the possible same-sex desire remains unnoticed by both the characters and readers. This buried queer text is most evident in the scene of Jim's failure to control the "snake," the scene that precedes Jim's decision to separate from Arvay until she learns to "serve" him. When Arvay fails to help rescue Jim from the rattlesnake that has coiled around and started to crush his body due to her phobia of them, Jim decides that she does not have a woman's true self-sacrificing love. However, Jim informs his wife that Jeff, Joe's son, "knowed all the time how dangerous it was and that he had a chance to lose, but he was a man in love, so he took the chance. . . . That was really what happened out there today" (261). That this scene has a latent homoerotic text is even clearer in Hurston's description of Jeff's struggle to unwind the "phallic" snake from his white master's body: "And Jeff, his prominent behind setting far out, had grabbed the snake by the tail. His strong white teeth, bordered by blue gums were snarled back in fear and rage as he threw his strength into pulling and unwinding the coils by stepping rapidly backwards around Jim and destroying the purchase of the snake" (255). Now one does not have to be a particularly careful excavator of Freudian symbolism to note Hurston's odd attention to Jeff's bent position with his behind out while pulling at the snake's phallic tail. What is interesting is how Hurston's representation here of Jeff's rescue of his beloved has no simple explanation. Certainly once again male bonding while sharing danger depends on the woman's position on the side as passive spectator.[9] Since, moreover, it is not clear whether Jeff in this scene is the forced recipient of the master's power or the dominant agent, Jeff's need to rescue Jim divulges precisely the shameful gap within the performance of white male subjectivity: that white men might believe whiteness has the phallus, but in the end they have no such control and power. In this scene, Hurston invokes the recurrent fear that we saw even in the antebellum South about a reverse acculturation. This is a scene of humiliation for Jim, who had wanted to show off to Arvay but found, with injurious results, a disparity between the idea and the reality of his manly performance, of literally his control of the phallus. In this scene, white masculinity does not come out on the top, or really on the bottom, but only with its phallic signification wrested away from him.

Deliberately ambiguous and indeterminate, Hurston's novel avoids having to "out" Jim or Jeff as internal enemies during this era of McCarthy to their respective black and white communities. Instead, *Seraph on the Suwanee* leaves in play this fluid homoeroticism as subversive of the very identity closures that would force discriminations or exclusions along color or gender lines. As if worried about the eruption of same-sex desire into the script of his own masculine performance, Jim, after his rescue from the snake, tries to divert the possible conclusions Arvay and others might draw from this climatic scene. In the ensuing lovers' quarrel in which Arvay compares Jim's love for her to his affection for Jeff, she chides, "all I could ever see was that the only holt I ever had on you was the way you craved after my body." In response, Jim attempts to restore the text to heterosexual normality by accusing Arvay of still being Puritanically repressed. Jim remarks that "what the hell would I marry a woman for if I don't want her like that? If it wasn't for that, I could just as well couple up with another man for a buddy" (262). In his anger, Jim unintentionally exposes the homosexual who was seen as the enemy in the New South, a man who would betray not only his wife but the racial and gender boundaries that are linked with southern nationalism. To deny that he is someone who would engage in such a transgressive coupling, Jim marks a clear-cut distinction between the relations of men and women and men and men as a matter of the morphological determinacy of sex acts. But Jim's defense significantly leaves in place the "higher love between men," an intimacy that by definition the relations between husband and wife, based only on sex and property rights, does not have. Despite Jim's accusations that Arvay is sexually inhibited with her "old missionary foolishness" (263), it is unclear in this scene whose sexuality is most repressed. Jim's sudden accusations of Arvay's "frigidity" and her jealousy "of the time I had to spend with Joe" seems to protest too much, to project blame in order to cover up the contradictions within his performance of white manhood.

The novel's intervention into the stability of white male identity helps explain Hurston's depiction of Arvay and female identity. It is precisely a masculine panic about his own "effeminizing" loss of the phallus to the other that causes his oppression of women. Jim's rapes of Arvay are as much about his need to assert his control over her and to prove, as brutally and desperately as possible, the authenticity of his own manly performance. As he validates the fiction of his own strength in her cries, Jim does not just need Arvay for the assurance of his individual masculine heterosexual "normality" but for the legitimation of the larger "racialized" white performance of masculinity in the New South. Everything he has done, Jim reiterates, was done for the protection and glorification of the southern white woman: "I could see that your glory would be added to, but you haven't give me one bit of credit for love" (265). When Jim leaves to force Arvay to prove her love for him, he needs this submission in order to uphold "his story," the story of his control intrinsic to his identity as a white male pushing the development of the New South.

Throughout *Seraph on the Suwanee*, the possibilities of a different kind of sexuality are continually raised, particularly between Jim and Jeff and between Jim and Joe, but these interracial possibilities are never directly named, remaining only as the "ghostly figure" in the love and intimacy between men. In the narrative irregularities of the last third of the novel, in particular, Hurston contrasts the oddly paired loves of Arvay and Jim and Jim and Jeff. After Jim's separation from Arvay and absence from the citrus farm, it is Jeff who takes care of the groves and the house. In Jeff's steadfastness to the "old master," the novel seems to chart a disturbingly familiar plantation adventure in its use of the oft-told tale of the loyal "darkie" who has stayed true even after the master was gone. Yet if Hurston recruits the familiar plantation myth, it is finally only to subvert it. Although Arvay believes that the "faithful Jeff was carrying out an order" (315) and that "he seemed never to forget the slightest thing around the place, and never neglected to take care of it" (317), Jeff himself views his relation with Jim differently. Ignoring Arvay's residual ideas about dependent racial relations, Jeff announces that whites and blacks are part of the same family: when Arvay arrives back in Citronbelle after her mother's funeral, Jeff declares "you sure is folks" (314) and downplays her prior offenses against him "because us Meserves don't mistrust one another" (313). Now on the one hand Jeff's arrogation of the white "master's" name repeats all too closely the slave's compulsory naming and loss of cultural identity in the Old South, but Jeff's assertion of being part of the family calls into question, in the context of this novel, Arvay's possessive investment in whiteness organized through the active management of social differences.

As seen in Wright's *Savage Holiday*, antihomosexual discourse during the Cold War was linked to an "interpretive anxiety" about the inability to read and determine the lesbian and gay male bodies. The public fear of the gay male as the enemy within expressed an epistemological uncertainty about "the invisibility of homosexual difference" (160). *Seraph on the Suwanee* attempts to destabilize sexual and racial borders from within the New South's nationalism by confronting the reader with a similar anxiety about the legibility of the homosexual. As often as the novel scripts the story of Jim and Jeff in terms of southern plantation myths, it as frequently displaces this commonplace view with oppositional forms of white and black homo-masculinity. Neither Jeff nor Jim becomes clearly discernible as stereotypical servant and master, employer and employee, or as a pair of lovers. If Cold War rhetoric taught U.S. society to see the homosexual as a security risk, Hurston teases the reader with the idea that the New South may have been built on these very relations. That Hurston never really homosexualizes the white or black male body as we saw in the fiction of Wright and Demby demonstrates the novel's desire to complicate normative definitions of identity. It is just this ambiguity that, finally, undermines what may seem at first as a validation of the patriarchal subjectivization of women. In the novel's concluding sequence, Arvay replaces Jeff as the lover and the faithful servant "darkie" of the plantation myth. With irony, Hurston's novel links racial servitude and gender roles within middle-class marriage: as Arvay remarks at the end, "it was her privilege to serve him" (351). Although Arvay seems to agree to this masochism in her final meditation, we should not fail to note how Hurston winks at the knowing reader by suggesting that Arvay has agreed to become not a wife but a newly engendered Uncle Tom.

In "Reading the Blackboard: Youth, Masculinity, and Racial Cross-Identification," Leerom Medovoi has argued that all oppositional readings that refuse the meaning preferred by the dominant ideology are "premised on the denial of other oppositional readings" (164). In looking at Zora Neale Hurston's white life novel *Seraph on the Suwanee* in light of Cold War black and white representations of homosexuality, I have tried to argue that alternative readings of Hurston's novel that simply see her as a trickster pulling one over on white folks, directing laughter and anger back across the color line, may themselves silence other alternative readings. *Seraph on the Suwanee* is a queer text in which an ambivalent homosexual desire threatens both the dominant and subaltern, white and black, decodings of the texts. Not simply double-voiced, *Seraph on the Suwanee* is a text that tries to find possibilities both within and outside the white and black, heterosexual and homosexual social orders. In *Seraph on the Suwanee*, Hurston allowed herself in part to be exploited, to be led by the white publishing impresarios who demanded a pulp fiction sensation about white folks who make good. But in the end, she creates within this performance moments of narrative crises when the audience, both black and white, hears and sees too much, making visible the complex sexuality that has remained invisible behind stereotypical representations of patriarchal cultures.

7. QUEER AZTLAN, MESTIZING "WHITE" QUEER THEORY

Arturo Islas's The Rain God

The sacred landscape of *las playas, los llanos, y las montanas* of Aztlan have been central to the cultural nationalism of the Chicano movement, but in *The Rain God*, Arturo Islas indicates that this romanticized recollection of the lost homeland of the occupied U.S. Southwest has been a complicit figuration in the forging of the compulsory heterosexuality of the Chicano identity (Yarbro-Bejarano 17). To articulate a new conception of Chicano identity, Islas in his first novel thus embraces the geographical trope of Teotihuacan, the pre-Columbian city dedicated to the rain god Tlaloc. In the opening chapter, "Judgment Day," Islas's novel announces a significant relocation of the originary place of emergence for Chicano identity by tying together the private history of the Angel family and the mythic history of the rain god Tlaloc:

How silent she [Mama Chona] had been even when she talked—silent like those pyramids he had finally seen in Teotihuacan built in tribute to the sun and moon. He had felt the presence of the civilizations that had constructed them and, as he climbed the steep, stone steps so conceived as to give him the impression that he was indeed walking into the sky, he had seen why those people, his ancestors, thought themselves gods, and had been willing to tear out the hearts of others to maintain that belief. The feeling horrified him still. (27)

Islas's *The Rain God* begins with a remembrance of things past, and particularly the burden of a family past and its repressive legacy on the narrator

Miguel Chico (Marquez 5–6), but Islas links this personal recollection of Mama Chona with his journey back to the pre-Columbian indigenous city of Teotihuacan that flourished between A.D. 200 and 1521. Crossing over national, racial, and class borders to excavate the Meso-American capital city of Teotihuacan rather than the U.S. territory of Aztlan, Islas undertakes a revisionary project similar to that of his Chicana sisters, seeking to modify and transform a patriarchal culture that takes control of gay men's bodies, sexualities, and psyches. In the ceremonies to the rain god Tlaloc, Islas found a figure of heterogeneity and hybridity and even divergent sexual and gender practices excluded from Chicano racial masculinities. Yet as the sacrifice described at the end of this passage signals, Miguel's relation to this indigenous culture will be one of disavowal as well as identification ("the feeling horrified him still"). Although returning to the rain god's sacred city, Miguel will remain a migrant who is both at home in and alien to multiple residents: San Francisco and the recovered city of Teotihuacan, the queer community and the lost familia, Utopia and Dystopia.

In his introduction to Arturo Islas's works, David Raman has remarked that "for many readers of contemporary gay literature, Islas's depiction of same-sex desire may seem understated, if not down right dismal" (221). This regret, if not outright condemnation, of Islas for the silences in his novel and the gaps that address the narrator Miguel's homosexuality only in various disguises and displacements (Saldivar 170), however, assumes and even imposes on Islas's *The Rain God* white Western narratives of visibility. While Islas critiques exclusionary Chicano racial masculinities in *The Rain God*, his novel refuses to cooperate with hegemonic Western models of an "out" queer politics that takes a white Eurocentric standpoint as the norm for people of color. This tendency to draw upon Anglo-European paradigms in evaluating lesbian and gay fiction has caused, as Martin Manalansan argues, an ethnic "gay" identity to be seen as primitive or premodern in relation to the evolutionary or developmental end of a Western queer or gay sexuality (485–505). Anglo-European narratives of same-sex liberation that overlap with Western histories of modernization figure liberation as an embrace of a postmodern sexuality assumed to be synonymous with a repudiation of an oppressive traditional culture. Behind the Anglo-European stories of coming out lies a narrative contrast between before and after, between the past and the present, in which the former terms (frequently associated with the ethnic self) are always devalued. But such a contrast obscures the way Islas tries to take control of his sexuality in his own cultural context and in relation to other axes of difference—of nation, race, and class—obscured in white Western paradigms.

Behind queer readings of "migrant" writers such as Islas often lies the demand for an "outness" that translates into an implied "relocation" to an Anglo-European space, a space that is seen as a site of nonnormative sexual freedom but that indirectly globalizes a Western paradigm of sexual identity while trivializing particular conceptionalizations of gayness within "Chicano culture" as somehow "unenlightened" or "primitive." In his 1990 lecture "On the Bridge at the Border: Migrants and Immigrants," Islas argued for the substitution of the "migrant song" for the immigrant experience in an understanding of life in the U.S. borderland (qtd. in McKenna 9–10). By using the trope of the migrant to signify the Chicana/o experience as a fluid condition moving between the worlds of America and Mexico, of indigenous and European, of self and alien others, Islas counteracts, as did Chicana writers such as Gloria Anzaldua, the yearning for contained boundaries among the Chicano nationalists and among a neocolonial queer theory.[1] A border crosser, the migrant always dwells within a certain in-betweenness. Unlike other hyphenated Americans who might maintain residence in more than one country, Islas's migrant is a member of the working class and not a world citizen of transglobal capitalism with his/her financial and social privileges. The migrant is both a resident and an alien in the multiple places she/he calls "home."[2] An understanding of "homosexual" identity in Islas's *The Rain God* needs to take as its starting assumption Islas's understanding of migrant identity as being located in two different places, being both at home and an exile here and over there, in San Francisco and Teotihuacan. Through such a reconceptualization of identity, the familiar framing of Miguel's story as involving a choice between an ethnic identity or a visible and oppositional queer identity is no longer completely applicable. Instead, *The Rain God* sets up Miguel's choice as a question of adopting a "state-generated" identity, whether white or Mexican, or a "border-crossing" transnational identity. By grounding Miguel's history in the mythic/real indigenous city of Teotihuacan, Islas locates a sex and gender nonconformity that will repatriate the repressed of Chicano discourse.[3] As Miguel muses in the opening pages of Islas's novel, he "longed to return to the desert of his childhood, not to the family, but to the place" (5).

To give voice to a revisionary iconoclasm, Islas's *The Rain God* draws upon an alternative meaning for the archetypal myth of the rain god Tlaloc and the idyll place of Tlalocan. Through his invocation of pre-Columbian "Indianness" and the Meso-American deity of Tlaloc, Islas struggles to find a radical alternative site to Chicano and white queer masculinity, a place that has been in the past problematically joined to other putative narratives of race, class, and nation. Islas's *The Rain God* suggests the need to "brown" or "mestize" a queer theory that starts from the position of a universal white middle-class subject and brings together queer theory and border thinking in a new, productive crossing that opens up new spaces for the examination of "minority" texts. *The Rain God* exemplifies what Ellen McCracken has called a "doubly counterhegemonic practice" resisting both a patriarchal Chicano society and a white male–dominated subcultural language of queerness (152). As a gay Chicano who felt silenced within Chicano patriarchal culture as well as within the queer community, Islas had to find a new third space in which to invent himself, a space that could only be that of a migrant who refused the oppositional visibility demanded in each of his residences— whether California or Aztlan. He found that reparative site of transfiguration in the temples to Tlaloc and in the recovery of the richness of a queer tradition that could speak back to white gayness held up as "true" and "universal" for all people of color.

Mestizing Queer Theory

In her essay "Queer Aztlan," Cherrie Moraga criticizes a gay male Chicano movement for asking for inclusion around a shared masculinity with straight men rather than calling for a radical rethinking of masculinity that challenges the macho's fear of and desire to dominate the feminine (160–61). "In a queer Aztlan," Moraga goes on to imagine, "there would be no freaks, no 'others' to point one's finger at" because the nation would be open to a full range of gender and sexual practices. As a model of what this nation could be, Moraga suggests that the period of the pre-Columbian indigenous tribes may have represented a golden age of sexual freedom and gender tolerance before Chicana/os internalized and reinforced the colonizing Anglo's patriarchal laws, norms, and machismo: "My Native American friends tell me that in some Native American tribes, gay men and lesbians were traditionally regarded as 'two-spirited' people. Displaying both masculine and feminine aspects, they were highly respected members of their community, and were thought to possess a higher spiritual development" (164). By drawing upon the traditions of the pre-Columbian native peoples, Islas attempts to recoup a similar "two-spiritedness" and specifically to reconfigure the cultural signifier of Tlaloc as a way to rebel against a masculinist, heterosexist colonized culture. At the time that Islas was revising his novel in the late 1970s and early 1980s, changing its title from *Day of the Dead* to *The Rain God* before its publication in 1984, archaeologists were excavating the Templo Mayor dedicated to Tlaloc in the Aztec capital of Tenochtitlan. Among the findings at the Templo Mayor was the fragment of a monolith that showed the rain god Tlaloc joined in a single body with Chalchiuhlicue, the goddess of springs, rivers, and lakes who was often said to be the first or second wife of Tlaloc or the older sister of the *tlaloque*. Within the pre-Columbian pantheon, as Alfredo Lopez Austin notes, different deities frequently fused into one another, so that there was often a blurring of discrete divine identities. In the Templo Mayor monolith, the two bodies of Tlaloc and Chalchiuhlicue were thus paired and placed over one another, with the upper one female and the lower one male (210). As a consequence, there was no contradiction within Tlaloc's dual gender, for as Lord of the Earth, he/she was said to be both the mother and father of creation. As part of the uniting of divine energy, Tlaloc was also associated with the mother goddesses (as Islas associates the rain god with Mama Chona), and it was believed that when the gods performed different functions they often changed their nature and even gender to accommodate the new role (Arnold 49).

Reshaping the myth of Tlaloc, and specifically the rituals devoted to him, in *The Rain God*, Islas foregrounds the question of how to give voice to what has been hidden, repressed, and concealed within Chicano history.[4] Yet while Islas turns to the indigenous past as does Moraga and other Chicana feminists, he significantly modifies Moraga's own imagining of a "Queer Aztlan." While Moraga attempts to find the "queer"—the "two-spirited" one—within the nation-state or within the imaginary sovereignty of Aztlan, Islas locates a "queer space" in the pre-Columbian city of Teotihuacan and its rituals to Tlaloc, thus attempting to cross over national boundaries and across the very masculinist paradigms of nationhood (that Moraga often leaves unquestioned). In contrast to Moraga, Islas offers us a different dynamics of reterritorialization that transgresses nationalist terms by crossing into the migrant's transnational, multiculturally linked pathways. In doing so, Islas's fiction raises questions not only about how one should queer but also how one should diasporicize Aztlan.

By attempting to historicize a queerness in pre-Columbian Meso-American history with the figure of Tlaloc, Islas avoids the conceptual trap of "discovering/writing back in" the classical past a Western model of gay identity. In her celebration of a Native American "two-spirited-ness," Moraga replaces a model of sexual object choice with a gender-based model as characteristic of gay identity. Through such a substitution, Moraga attempts to address the marginalization of "femmes" within the gay male community and the remasculinization of gayness that would cooperate with the oppression of women. As sympathetic as Islas is to such a transvaluation, he wants more clearly to "unground" in his transnational migration any one monolithic construction of gay maleness, whether one tied to gender deviance, to sexual object choice, or some other "queer" performance. By embracing the shape-shifting Tlaloc—dual gendered but equally multivocal—Islas tries to form a community that allows for all kinds of homosexuality. His is a syncretic move, one embodied in the Templo Mayor figure of Tlaloc himself/herself, that works toward a multiplying of subject positions so as to allow for a heterogeneity of same-sex practices.

In choosing as his figure the fluid Tlaloc, Islas attempts to avoid the romanticization that can be part of the "queer" Chicana/o's recovery work. The danger, as Jasbir Puar has argued, is that one imports back onto the past a clearly definable and universal Western construct of sexual or gender identity that would erase the different configuration of earlier periods (412). While certainly the rain god had seized hold of Islas's imagination because this mythic figure could have a clearly definable dual gender, the rain god was not for Islas an icon of an assumed androgynous unity but of amorphous identity, simultaneously an anthropomorphized projection of the Rain King and Mother Earth, of life and death, of renewal and destruction. Because Tlaloc was a figure that belonged to a number of different "tribes," from the Aztecs to the Nahuatls to various other pre-Columbian peoples, he was also an inclusive deity that represented no single race, class, or gender constituency within the larger Chicano/a cultural group. In his reappropriation of Tlaloc in *The Rain God*, Islas attempts not to bring the gay body into visibility but to foreground the body's, and particularly same-sex desire's, denial of identity.

If Islas's bildungsroman is not the expected coming-out story or a conversion to "outness," as critics have lamented, it is because the writing into visibility of nonnormative same-sex desire involves the destruction of identity and identity categories.

In "Chicano Men: A Cartography of Homosexual Identity and Behavior," an essay that has been reprinted in key studies of queer identity (such as the 1993 *Lesbian and Gay Studies Reader*), Tomas Almaguer argues that the narrative of gay male Chicanos is structured by "the cultural dissonance that Chicano homosexual men confront in reconciling their primary socialization into Chicano family life with the sexual norms of the dominant culture" (75–100). Like much of the scholarship on gay minorities, Almaguer assumes that "there is no modern gay man" in the "Mexican/Latin-American sexual system," and therefore the struggle for Chicanos is whether they consider themselves to be "Chicano gay men" or to be "gay Chicano men" or whether their primary identification is as a gay male or as an ethnic subject (incompatible choices). Behind Almaguer's framing of the "issues" in Chicano gay writing is an assumption (as Homi Bhabha has noted in a different context) that one can expect the same critical strategies of resistance within all marginalized groups despite often incompatible systems of signification (175). While Almaguer attempts to take into consideration the multiples axes of difference that are often ignored in queer theory's centering of sexuality as the single divisive issue, he still preserves the whiteness of queer identity. The Chicano gay male must choose between a white queer identity or his ethnic identity, for there is no modern gay identity within the Chicano culture. In an inverted way, Almaguer recapitulates homophobic nationalist discourse by seeing the "homosexual" or the "queer" as somehow an inauthentic hybrid (if not a phantasmic danger) who would "reenter" the community after having been "radicalized" and "modernized" through an Anglo socialization. In his additive notion of identities, Almaguer catalogs discrete identity categories of race and sex along unacknowledged nationalistic, developmental lines. In focusing on which the Chicano prioritizes over the other, race or sexuality, he thus erases the dynamic and constitutive queerness within Chicano history. Almaguer's colored queer theory, even as it claims to move beyond exclusionary and normalizing identity politics models, is still based on a particular style of Anglo-American "outness," and any other political strategy is always already read as politically regressive, or not read as all, in the case of Islas's *The Rain God*.

In his attempt to recoup and to reshape the myth of Tlaloc, Islas moves beyond the idea (among both nationalists and queer theorists) that homosexuality is either an Anglo-European "disease" or its inverse, an "enlightenment," an advanced developmental stage that somehow belongs to Western culture. Instead of Almaguer's dissonance model of mandatory queer politics, where ethnicity and sexuality clash as premodern and postmodern configurations, Islas offers what might be called a reparative model of queerness. In using the word "reparative," I am in part borrowing from the work of Eve Kofsofsky Sedgwick in her introduction to the collection *Novel Gazing: Queer Reading in Fiction*. Finding at times within various postmodern approaches to literature a paranoid stance, Sedgwick questions the singular efficacy of exposing, demystifying, and denaturalizing a normative heterosexism. Instead, she calls for a corresponding emphasis on the "reparative," on a critical perspective that she describes as "additive" and "accretive" because it seeks to "assemble and confer plenitude on an object" by studying the "rich" and "dense" "communal practices" out of which the work arises (27). Such a reparative model best suits a writer like Arturo Islas, who in his first novel struggles less to come out as queer than to "return home" and, in doing so, to "queer *la familia*."[5] The assumption within queer theory is that one gains visibility through a simple opposition to a compulsory mainstream heteronormativity, or more largely the repressive norms of a "straight society." But this may only be true when the white European middle class is cast as the subject. As Norma Alarcon has argued in her essay "The Theoretical Subject(s) of *This Bridge Called My Back* and Anglo American Feminism," within the asymmetrical relations of race and class in U.S. society, the Chicana often comes out in opposition to other queers, for an opposition to heteronormativity cannot be so easily separated from an opposition to racial oppression or to class hierarchies (356–69).

In *American Homo: Community and Perversity*, Jeffrey Escoffier suggests that queer theory runs the danger of reducing the work of lesbian, gay, and transgendered politics to the individual's resistance to mainstream norms and therefore of acting as a substitute for a more elaborate social theory, especially one that acknowledges fully the collective struggles and multiple allegiances of minority lesbian, gay, bisexual, and transgendered individuals (22). In its centering of individual sexual freedom as a separate category from gender or racial freedom, queer theory can valorize the private solutions of a heroic Anglo-European individualism that stand in conflict with the rites of passage within Chicana/o bildungsromans such as *The Rain God*, narratives that do not privilege one character's voice over the collective voice of the community. By its suspicion of any communal norms, queer theory can disallow a struggle that can be affiliative. Any sense of community voiced by queer writers is seen as a tendency to civilize the "perverse" or "the transgressive" and therefore inherently normalizing.[6] As Islas's *The Rain God* takes great pains to recall, the oppositional model of a white queerness does not take into full account the Chicano's different social realities. Just as Chicano/a culture is described as being more collectivist than an individualistic Anglo-European culture, with the family being emphasized over the group, sociologists such as Bernardo Ferdman and Angelica Cortes have identified what they call a power-distance value system (qtd. in Kafka xiv–xv). In a power distance model, individuals are acculturated to show respect and deference to those in power and to conform to authority, especially the patriarchal authority of the family. As a consequence, "deviant" sexual identities are suppressed less because they transgress "norms" than because they "dishonor" and "disgrace" the family. As a consequence, a "queer" identity may involve defining oneself less against the heterosexual, or more generally the "normal," than against the family.[7] Thus although Islas has often been faulted for his "repression of history" to focus on the private "psychology" or "family" resentment of Miguel (Marquez 9), such a declaration of the novel's false consciousness ignores the way that Islas links the production of heteronormative masculine bodies to the patriarchal practices of the family. *The Rain God* emphasizes that Miguel's fight to gain a voice as a gay Chicano involves a dread of bringing "dishonor" to the family. When Miguel is caught playing with dolls and dressing in a homemade skirt as a child, his shame is connected with having disgraced the father, Miguel Grande. As a punishment he must, as his mother says, "apologize to [his] father" and "promise that he would never do it again" (17). Later, the adult Miguel recalls, too, that his macho father remained indifferent to Uncle Felix's sexual activities with the young soldiers and boys, as long as Felix did not bring dishonor to the family. Even when Miguel Grande is called to the police station presumably to bail out Felix for public indecency, his only reproach to his brother concerns the dishonor he has brought to his family, not his "perversity": "Goddammit Felix, you've got a wife and four kids" (80). For queer theory to travel into the borderland, Islas's *The Rain God* indicates, it would need to ensure

that a same-sex positivity is not purchased at the expense of cultural specificity. Islas's *The Rain God* discloses that gender deviance and homoeroticism within Chicano culture pose more of a threat to the patriarchal
authority of the father than to the power/knowledge system (in Foucaul-
tian terms) of norms.

In *The Rain God*, Islas's goal is not to create a new marginal queer identity for gay Chicanos on the order of the white narratives of liberation
that themselves assimilated nationalistic models of modernization.
Instead the novel retrieves from the past a culturally specific model of
"queer identity" that is already within *la familia*, or at least the cultural
family whose ancestors include the "multispirited" Tlaloc. In Islas's
reparative politics of queerness, a politics often unread by his critics, he
works to move beyond a simple macho obsession with transgressive rup-
ture. As the first step toward renarrating *la familia*, he recuperates powerful symbols of alternative masculinity that will disrupt a normative
bodily identity and sexuality. At the end of chapter 1, when Miguel enters
his garden, a foreshadowing of his final entrance into the garden of Tlalocan sacred to those suffering from internal ailments, Islas's protagonist
muses that "he felt he was still the child of these women, an extension of
them, the way a seed continues to be a part of a plant after it has assumed
its own form which does not at all resemble its origin . . . [he] wondered
if human beings, unlike plants, can water themselves" (26). Like the rain
god whom he seeks to restore to Chicano culture, Miguel attempts to
point toward an ever-inclusive model of Chicana/o-ness that crosses over
the borders of traditional categories of identity—and of identity itself. He
is both self and other, a self-determined male yet still connected (as was
Tlaloc) to the mother-sister goddesses, both different and same, both a
queer form of the future yet an origin unearthed from the past. As Miguel
imagines, he can water himself and claim his full rich plenitude when he
models himself on such a rain god.

Rituals of the Child

In the dream that Miguel has in the concluding chapter of *The
Rain God*, he grapples with a monster, the same "monster" he informs us
that had "killed her [Mama Chona]" (159). To most critics, as Marta Sanchez has argued, the monster represents the "repressed sexual pleasures"
that Mama Chona has denied herself and which in turn she would sup-

press in her children in accordance with a religious system of values that "embodies the tyranny of the spirit and mind over the psyche's instincts for pleasure" (M. Sanchez 289). But Islas's description of the monster is more ambiguous, or more allusive than its reduction to an external system of repression, even in the form of heteronormativity, would allow. As Islas's language makes clear, the monster is also an image of Tlaloc:

[The] monster . . . said to him softly, almost kindly, "I am a nice monster. Come into my cave." The two of them were standing on a bridge facing the incoming fog. The monster held Miguel Chico closely from behind and whispered into his ear in a relentless singsong way, "I am the manipulator and the manipulated." It put its velvet paw in Miguel Chico's hand and forced him to hold it tightly against his gut right below the appliance to his side. "I am the victim and the slayer." . . .

"Jump!" the monster said with exhilaration, "jump!"

Miguel Chico felt loathing and disgust for the beast. He turned to face it. Its eyes were swollen with tenderness. "All right," he said, "but I'm taking you with me." (159–60)

Although Tlaloc is the god of water and rain, most scholars of Meso-American culture have attributed the etymology of the word "Tlaloc" to "*tlalli*," or "earth," and sixteenth-century missionaries translated the name as meaning "Path Under the Earth" or "Long Cave" (Arnold 37). In addition, since Tlaloc was less a discrete anthropomorphized deity than an embodiment of the Valley of Mexico, there is general agreement that Tlaloc was associated with the sacred places of the hills, mountains, and caves from whence the rains came. When the monster whispers to Miguel to "come into my cave," Islas is invoking the iconography of the rain god. But the resonances are even more apropos here, for the paradise of Tlaloc, Tlalocan, was also the place of death where those who died under the hand or agency of Tlaloc—by drowning, by being struck by lightning, or by a mysterious internal ailment associated with water—were taken instead of going to the pre-Columbian Hades (Pasztory 19). As part of his dual personality, Tlaloc is Lord of the Earth and giver of life but also Lord of Death and the deity associated with the mythic afterlife. In his description of the "monster" in terms of contradictions—cruel yet kind, both victim and slayer—Islas conjures up a pre-Columbian deity who represents an intricate epistemology outside a Western European binary system of thinking where opposites are connected rather than divided. Since Miguel is dying by an unidentified internal disease associated with the rain god, it is appropriate, too, that Tlaloc would come to kill him and free him to jump into a sacred paradise.

It is also significant that Mama Chona would be associated with this "monster" of the rain god. In the classification of the gods associated with water and earth, Tlaloc was frequently connected with the Mother Goddess, so Miguel's dreamscape follows an archetypal chain of association. But Mama Chona's full name is Encarnacion Olmeca, tying her to one of the original tribes of the North, a people called the Olmec, who were said to have migrated to the Valley of Mexico in search of the earthly location of the mythic paradise of Tamoanchan (Austin 55–57). In contrast to the ancestors from whom the female figure takes her name, however, Mama Chona has emigrated from the land of Tlaloc north to the U.S. Southwest, and thus in her death the monster of a rain god comes to take her back to her place of origins and back to the past that she has lost and that she has repressed in her disavowal of an "Indian" heritage. The monster, as a consequence, that "kills" Mama Chona is both a lost sexuality and a lost "racial" and "class" consciousness. This god is, to put it another way, what would rip apart and tear out the heart of a symbolic identification with a compulsory heterosexuality and a privileged whiteness within Mama Chona's neocolonial identity formations.[8] Against the naive assumptions of a diasporic queerness that would assume some pre-existing, self-identified "queerness" throughout the world according to a "white" "Anglo-European" paradigm, in this monster, Miguel "clasps" to himself an "impure" "shape-changing" queer identity, one that is an oddly both utopian and dystopian. It is a "monstrous" or queer identity that refuses to take on a clear bodily or sexual form even to satisfy those who demand a culminating act of coming out.

The focus of Islas's novel, as in the work of many Chicana writers such as Gloria Anzaldua, Ana Castillo, and Cherrie Moraga, is to reappropriate and resignify upon an archetypal figure from Chicano cultural history. For Islas, it is Tlaloc or the rain god, instead of La Malinche or Llarona, who witnesses that the *joto* is no disgrace or dishonor to *la familia* but a figure who embodies the alternative model of masculinity associated with the ancestors. In his fiction, Islas figures a queer Teotihuacan that preceded Aztlan and that is the lost supplement that would overturn nationalist, heterosexist, and gendered boundaries. The myths of Tlaloc are central to Islas's text, particularly some of the ceremonies of devotion and sacrifice to him. As an anthropomorphic deity, Tlaloc had three principal visual characteristics that anthropologists have used to identify various pre-Columbian sculptures and drawings as depicting the rain god. These visual markers include two intertwined serpents forming an eyebrow but also converging to suggest a nose, features that again connect the rain god to the Mother Goddess who was associated with the two-headed serpent; large, gogglelike eyes, which underscored his association with fountains, springs, and caves (as Miguel's monster has swollen eyes); and finally prominent predacious teeth and wide mouth, which suggested that Tlaloc was the "eating" god, a deity who demanded restitution in kind before the rain would come (Arnold 34–38). Most accounts of the pre-Columbian devotions to Tlaloc and the interpretations of his meaning have been framed by or directly come from the works of sixteenth-century missionaries, particularly Fray Bernardino de Sahagun's account of the ritual sacrifices to Tlaloc, *The Florentine Codex*. Written to justify American Indian conversions to Christianity, Sahagun's accounts are less important for their accuracy than for their prominence as the inherited legends Islas's imaginative retelling are set against.

Of the monthly sacrifices the Meso-American people held in honor of the deities, according to Sahagun in his *Florentine Codex*, four were directly related to Tlaloc and nine more generally to the rain deities. Within the pre-Columbian calendar at Teotihuacan, a month lasted twenty days, and there were eighteen months, each of which had its own seasonal ritual, and five extra days. Two of these rituals are particularly important in a recontextualization of Islas's *The Rain God*. The first is the ritual that addressed the drought during the dry season, called I-ATL-Cahualo, a name that refers to the "raising up of poles" or paper banners during the festivities (Sahagun 72–74). The relevance of this ceremony as an mythopoetic resonance in Islas's novel appears in the recurring allusions to the desert, to dryness, and to thirst in the novel, with an attendant symbolic invocation of desiccations of all kinds, spiritual, emotional, and physical. In the opening chapter, for example, Miguel specifically ties his body's "dis-ease" to the parchment of the desert, suggesting that the rain god is necessary for his body's wholeness as well as a general renewal of life: "He could not move his lips to ask for water, and from neck to crotch his body felt like dry ice, the desert on a cold, clear day after snowfall" (8). Throughout the novel, Islas continues to equate both emotional need and sexual yearning with a dryness of the heart. Thus, when Lola comes to desire Miguel Grande after her husband's death, Islas writes that "he [Miguel Grande] stopped up the cracks in the roof and the desert shifted from the kitchen into her heart. She was

always thirsty" (69). By twinning together sexual repression and the arid-
ity of the desert throughout the novel, Islas underscores that the arrival
of the rain god Tlaloc will be about a reembodiment of sexual desire for
women and for gay men.

The ceremony of I-ATL-Cahualo is also central to Islas's *The Rain God*
because it is the one most closely tied to the sacrifice of children, for in
order for the proper amount of water to fall, the Meso-American peoples
believed that the tears and blood of children must be offered as "debt
payment."⁹ While there was an elaborate semiotic system detailing the
proper costume for the children from the precious green stones, or *chal-
chihuitl*, that were said to attract moisture and the quetzal feathers and
rubber garments, Islas does not use obscure icons from the ceremony in
his novel; rather, he reshapes the larger myths. As part of the "drought
ceremony," children who were of noble birth were forced to keep an all-
night vigil in the company of the priests at the mist house, or *ayauhcalli*.
If during this vigil the children cried, this release of tears was taken as a
sign—indeed, a direct sympathetic correspondence—to the amount of
water that Tlaloc would rain down. As part of the drought ceremony, or
I-ATL-Cahualo, the more the children cried, the more content the people
became as they accepted that such violence was necessary for the reformation of the landscape and the survival of the people.

Islas's *The Rain God* is a novel, bluntly put, about the sacrifice of children (Leonardo, Tony, JoEl, Felix, and even Miguel himself), about a sacrifice of children that must occur before the arrival of the rain god in the
vision of Mama Chona upon her death. Islas underscores the mythopoetic resonance of the novel with the Tlaloc rituals through his emphasis
upon the necessity of the children's tears as debt payment before the
rains' descent. In relating his own inner dryness at the novel's beginning,
Miguel recounts his inability to cry as a child when his eight-year-old
friend Leonardo committed suicide by hanging himself with a belt: "He
wanted to cry too, but was able to make only funny faces. His heart was
not in it" (10). After the death of Tony, Miguel again highlights the inability of Tony's father, Ernesto, to weep, as an angel even appears to him
and demands "why he did not weep" (50). The first stories that Miguel
relates are marked by the absence of the proper lachrymose offering to
the rain god. In the mythopoetic structure of the novel, if the rain god is
the lost object, the full presence that ought to be there but is missing,
Islas suggests that this lack stems from an insufficiency of suffering, the

inadequacy of sacrifice that would fulfill the demands of a rain god who seems to require for his/her gift-giving the child's victimization.

By bringing together Mama Chona and the Angel family's treatment of their "rebellious" children with the sacrifices to Tlaloc, Islas offers a critique of an authoritarian familism in Chicano culture and specifically implicates the collusion of the *abuela* and other women with this patriarchal family that disseminates and perpetuates oppressive constructions of gender and sexuality. Islas's ambivalence toward the practice of familism is not hard to find in the novel and is expressed in a two-fold strategy of denouncing the Chicana's economic, political, and cultural suppression and blaming her for her participation in a rigid patriarchal rule. Becoming detached and self-absorbed in her pursuit of the family's economic betterment, Miguel's aunt Nina sacrifices her son, Tony, who drowns himself to be restored to the paradise of the rain god. Although she herself had rebelled against her own authoritarian father who demanded, even in his dying breath, that his daughters "behave themselves," Aunt Nina repeats the same words as the family "gatekeeper" to her son, repressing his individuality and sexual independence. After investing in some property in the desert and forcing Tony to be uprooted from his school and his friendships, Aunt Nina furthers her control over Tony by forbidding him to drive his car or to smoke his cigarettes, actions signaling an autonomous manhood. Although Juanita warns her sister about what she is doing to her son, Nina declares that "it's for his own good" and tells him to "behave himself" (47). Through his drowning, Tony chooses a ritual form to literalize the sacrifice that the family has already demanded of him, but this time seeking entrance into the sacred landscape of Tlalocan.

In Islas's description of the "Tlaloc" monster within Miguel's dream, both women and men play the role of collaborators as well as victims in the repressive structures of patriarchal familism. Nevertheless, it is too straightforward a reading of Islas's invocations of the rain god to see Islas as simply condemning or opposing familism for exploiting women and gay men and repressing their self-fulfillment and sexuality. Although showing the violence of the family against the child, Islas's fiction also refuses to hold up some private, individualistic solution, as many Anglo-European queer theorists do. In laying claim to his sexual freedom and defying the norms of Chicano masculinity, Miguel does not isolate himself from his Chicana sisters and the extended *familia*. While Islas's *The*

Rain God invokes the rituals of child sacrifice to Tlaloc to speak out against familism, it also hopes to usher in a different kind of *familia*, one that recognizes the queerness and the racial otherness that was once a constitutive part of its "divine" history. Placed within the ceremonial history of the sacrifices to Tlaloc, Tony's and the other children's deaths do not just become tragic testimony to a life-denying authoritarianism. These deaths become sacrifices that will assure the emergence of a different kind of family that will allow multiple and diverse gender and sexual identifications. In making their deaths sacrifices for and not just to the family, Islas's novel does not try to redeem the children's suffering within a traditional Christian or psychoanalytic context as necessary for knowledge or resurrection. Instead, the children are both the sacrificed and "sacrificers" because they submit to their individual "deaths," to the death of individuality, for the transformation and renewal of the community. These children die in anticipation of the advent of a different kind of family and culture. To oversimplify for a moment, it might be argued that the sacrificed children—Tony, JoEl, Miguel—are the Chicano sons who remain among multiple spaces seeking not just to be "out" or "free" in the Anglo-European world but also to be disruptive at home to usher in a different *familia* that will work collectively to transform all family members.

JoEl's self-sacrifice must be read as both a visible failure of patriarchal authority and heterosexuality and as a supplication to an abjected or "monstrous" gender and sexual fluidity signified in the rain god Tlaloc. In the penultimate chapter, "Ants," JoEl undergoes a modern-day mist-house ritual that provokes the tears that announce the coming of Tlaloc. Reconceiving this ritual to the rain god, Islas's novel divorces it from its heterosexist purposes and reassesses the meaning of this inherited knowledge. In "Ants," Miguel relates the descent of his cousin JoEl into "lunacy" after JoEl's father's brutal murder in a desert canyon by a homophobic soldier from Tennessee. As a child, JoEl had had nightmares that ants were crawling all over his body, but here the ants that would devour him are his aunts, Eduviges and Jesus Maria, who would insist that the Angel family members replicate the normative behavior of the patriarchal family. Prior to JoEl's institutionalization in a halfway house for "addicts," we are told he held all-night vigils with his aunts, arriving full of "alcohol and sexual indulgence" and "weeping all the while" in his aunt's lap (151). During these presacrificial mist-house rituals, JoEl cries because he regrets not being able to tell his murdered father, Felix, "that I understand and that I love him" (155). If JoEl's tears are what finally bring the appearance of the rain god in the last chapter, it is significant that this boy's tears are a plea less for his individual forgiveness than for a reconstitution of the *familia* to include the sexual other. While the Angel family and particularly Miguel Grande have refused to demand justice for the murder of Felix for fear that it would shame them and ruin Miguel Grande's chances to be elected sheriff, JoEl's tears plead for the return of a Tlaloc, a higher authority embodied in the fluidity of a nonnormative gendered and sexual in-betweenness. In the third space of Tlalocan, the *joto* is not just accepted, but such a "disgraceful" identity is deeply and inextricably intertwined with cultural identity. Through JoEl's tears that cry out, "I love my mother. I love my father" (156), Islas portrays more than a tragedy that might provoke the Angel family to rethink their class and gender prejudices or might prompt Chicano nationalists to denounce their homophobia. Since JoEl's tears over his father's brutal murder are part of a larger ("timeless") ritual sacrifice to Tlaloc, they plead for a recognition of the "queer" *already inside* an indigenous Chicano culture. Not simply begging for the inclusion of the *joto* in an already "naturalized" and "centered" Chicano racial masculinity, Islas draws upon the ceremonies to Tlaloc to suggest gender trouble and identitarian ambiguity are a constitutive ancestral legacy within Chicano cultural history.

Islas's reshaping of the rituals to Tlaloc during the dry season can also be clearly seen in the confrontation between Miguel Grande and his son when the father comes to Los Angeles to discuss his conflicted love for both his wife, Juanita, and his mistress, Lola. In the narrative reversal of the I-ATL-Cahualo ceremony in this scene, it is the child who sacrifices the father to assure the coming of the rain god. Unlike his "contact" with his father in the past, when Miguel Grande visits Los Angeles to discuss his affair with Lola and to demand that the child identify with the father, Miguel is in control, "interrogating" his father. Islas's language in this scene calls attention to the ceremonial overlay of Miguel's defiance of his father. After Miguel challenges his father's patriarchal faith in the obedience of the women, especially Lola, to him, asking, "Are you sure of that? She doesn't look a meek woman to me," Islas writes,

> The tears began anew. Miguel Chico began to taste his father' blood.
> "Women are shit, you know that? Why do you live alone?"

Miguel Chico remained silent. He felt his own manliness in choosing not to answer his father; it was his turn to question.

"She doesn't want you to leave Mother, does she?"

"She doesn't know what she wants. She wants me to tell her. She's forcing me to tell her."

"How?" The son used the knife as if had been in his hands forever.

"I keep finding her with other men and it's tearing my guts out." (96–97)

In this scene, Islas brings together the different discursive threads that are part of his reshaping of the Tlaloc myth. Miguel comes into his manhood when he refuses to identify with his father and his machismo, one that would depend on the domination of women, or as the father says more directly, "Women are shit." In this scene, the father for the first time confronts his son about his sexual identity as a recrimination to defend himself against the son's own tough questioning: his father demands, "why do you live alone?" Yet unlike the boy in childhood, Miguel refuses to apologize for playing with dolls, for siding with women, or for performing a different role that would "disgrace" the family. His silence affirms an acceptance of his same-sex desire, if not an Anglo-American validation of "queer" identity. This acceptance of his homosexuality and defiance of machismo is seen metaphorically as wielding a knife and sacrificing the father on the altar stone of Tlaloc, as Miguel begins to taste his father's blood. In the final part of this brief passage, Islas suggests that this sacrifice of the father ("the tearing out of his guts") is a collusion between self-authorizing Chicana women and gay men. Unlike his uncle Felix, Miguel refuses to accept the sexism and the misogyny of a patriarchal culture and tries to define an alternative masculinity in alliance with his Chicana sisters.

Yet Islas finally leaves the passage indeterminate. In the opening line of the conversation, "The tears began anew" (the tears that are a sign of Tlaloc's release of the renewing rains), it is unclear whose tears they are. While Miguel in an Oedipal move enjoys a verbal act framed in the language of ritual sacrifice, in the absence of a clear referent his tears are joined to his father's tears. The tears finally belong to the community and are part of a collective identity, and while Miguel can kill the father and his machismo image, he does not want to assume an autonomous identity that would use the knife to cut him apart from his *familia*. As in the Tlaloc myth, the sacrifice of the child may still be necessary for his survival, and if such a contradiction makes no sense in Anglo-European or even queer identity politics, this ambiguity represents Islas's attempt to speak a gay male subjectivity as part of a mestiza consciousness that goes beyond the dualism of traditional Western thinking. Although in this scene one might argue that Islas tries to reconcile occidental and indigenous cultures, as well as tradition and modernity, in the retention of both filial love and individual freedom, his novel, by holding these two opposites in suspension, seeks to exceed any simple resolution of binary oppositions. In his invocation of Tlaloc, Islas seeks to point toward an alterity that is outside Anglo-European rites of passage or even a sense of a visible ending.

Refusing the Whiteness of the Middleman

In the scene in which Miguel refuses to reconcile with his father, Miguel not only rejects an affiliation with patriarchy, but he also chooses to reject a gay male sexual freedom that would come at the expense of women. In sacrificing the father to Tlaloc (indeed, he substitutes Tlaloc for the father), Miguel also surrenders the Chicano's common interest in the ownership of women that would deny them their own "voice": after all, the father, Miguel Grande, believes that women want men to tell them what to do. Significantly, Islas's reparative model of pre-Columbian queerness raises questions about the sometimes problematic antagonism between antiphobic (or queer) discourse and feminism. While commentators such as Cherríe Moraga have argued that Islas disguises a "bold gayness" behind vague stories of sinners or oppressed women, Islas does not reroute the issue of same-sex desire behind "feminine" displacements; rather, he tries to reconcile what are often viewed as competing liberations, gender liberation for women and sexual liberation for queers who are mostly figured as male. In response to the editors of the *Lesbian and Gay Studies Reader*'s definition of queer studies in terms of a defining break from feminism (or gender studies) by identifying sex as a separate site of oppression, Judith Butler has argued that gender and sexuality must be seen as convergent challenges to a normative patriarchy ("More Gender Trouble" 1–26). Extending Butler's caution, Biddy Martin has argued that the "antifoundationalist celebrations of queerness [should not] rely on their own projections of fixity, constraint, or subjection onto a fixed ground, often onto feminism or the female body" (104). Indeed, Islas, in his reshaping of the Tlaloc sacrifices to include the father, seeks to locate a queer positivity that "ungrounds" the female body by denying the father's understanding of a dependent "femininity" and makes the father the victim of what this patriarch sees as an inappropriate female sexual freedom. But Islas's text also raises questions about the way that white Western narratives of "queerness" can recycle (often unproblematically) the fixed ground of a male body and its subjection to whiteness.

The canonization of Islas's *The Rain God* as the queer Chicano text (more Chicano than John Rechy's novels, more uncloseted and queer than Richard Rodriguez's work) depends on the novel's representation of Felix, Miguel's uncle, who confers on him his name "Mickie" to "distinguish him from his father Miguel Grande" (4). But if Felix is such a problematic signifier of queerness—he, after all, is a closeted married man who reinscribes domestic patriarchy in his family relations—part of the problem lies in our desire to find in Felix the "modern out gay or queer man," a desire that forces *The Rain God* into the very narratives of visibility that Felix's migrant song subverts. To open a space for "queers" in a homophobic Chicano culture, Islas offers us not the role model of Felix but the restoration of the "pre-Columbian queerness" of Tlaloc. In such a juxtaposition of character, Felix stands in for the co-optation of gay males in the reconstruction of a Chicano patriarchy, an alliance between straight and gay males that would "tolerate" a sexual visibility in exchange for a shared involvement in the active suppression of other axes of difference, of race, of class, and of the female body. By connecting Felix with another of the ritual ceremonies to Tlaloc, Islas offers us a different nonpatriarchal, nonwhite narrative of visibility.

Another of the rituals to Tlaloc as recorded by Sahagun in *The Florentine Codex* was the Festival of the Mountains (or Tepeilhuitl) held during the thirteenth month of the pre-Columbian calendar. Since Felix, especially in terms of his queer identity, is known for his special hideaway in the mountain canyons where he takes the young fair "gods" and soldiers that he meets in the bar, Islas provides a direct mythopoetic link between his character and this pre-Columbian ceremony. As Sahagun writes, the Aztecs would frequently make mountains for people who had died, especially those who were said to be close to Tlaloc. During the festival, a ceremonial meal was placed before the mountain, and music, dancing, and drunkenness were offered to the mountain images. It is important that Felix is labeled the rain dancer because as a child he "would run outside and dance when the storm clouds passed over," unafraid that he would be struck by the lightning of Tlaloc (114). In addition to the dance to the mountain dead during the Festival of the Mountains, these ceremonies also included sacrifice, but this time a sacrifice of adults, five women and one man, a numerology that could suggest the sacrifices of the women in the novel and the one uncle. As part of the ceremony, the priests led the victims to the top of the temple of Tlaloc, where they were stretched across the sacrificial stones and their hearts cut out. Afterward, their bodies were rolled down the temple stairs, but only after their heads had been cut off and placed on pikes at the head row place. As a final act of ritual violence as part of the mountain ceremony to Tlaloc, the bodies of these adult victims were often said to be cooked into a stew of maize and beans in order to be eaten by the community as a whole (Sahagun 120–22; Arnold 110–11).

There are clear parallels between the story of Uncle Felix and the Festival of the Mountains. In addition to the association of Felix with his secret place in the mountains, Islas in describing Felix's beaten body emphasizes that his head had been almost severed from his torso. Upon seeing his brother's body, Miguel Grande remarks that "it was unrecognizable. There was no face, . . . and the back of the head was mushy" (81). Similarly, as if to invoke the cutting out of the sacrificial male's "heart," Islas tells us that when the soldier kicks Felix to death, Felix felt a pain in his groin and "near his heart" (137). As Felix is lapsing into unconsciousness, his blood, in the manner of the Tlaloc rituals, is transformed into or calls up water, offering a syncretic blending of Christian myths of Christ's martyrdom and indigenous beliefs. As the narrator says in the concluding line of "The Rain Dancer," "The desert exhaled as he sank into the water" (158), a water that in this arid land could only be his blood. To extend the parallels between the Tlaloc ceremony and Felix's death figuratively, if not literally, arguably it is from the communion that Miguel takes from Felix's sacrificial body, his eating of the uncle, that the nephew comes to his own awakening into consciousness.

While Islas sets up a homology between pre-Columbian martyrdoms and modern hate crimes, Felix is not simply a "victim" who died before self-realizing himself as "gay." Such an interpretation still assumes that the reading of "queer" minority texts should be a reading for a universal white queer subject. Significantly, rather than being a failed figure of liberation, Felix is what must be sacrificed for a queerness that does not pattern itself after Anglo-European norms of masculinity, with their consent to asymmetrical relations of race and class. In *The Rain God*, Islas makes Felix into a representative of what Moraga identified as a queer identity that seeks only to challenge norms of sexuality but fails to offer a radical rethinking of masculinity. Felix asks for the *joto*'s acceptance into the Chicano family by insisting on his shared racial and masculine identity with the macho, specifically, with his brother, Miguel Grande.

In telling the history of his uncle, Miguel calls him a "middleman" because as the foreman in a U.S. manufacturing plant he has been "put in charge of hiring cheap Mexican workers" (115). But what does it mean for Islas to make the only "visible" queer in the novel a "middleman." From the point of view of Chicano/Mexicano nationalist, Felix as the homosexual would be seen as a "race traitor" or a "hybrid" who is inauthentically ethnic because he has accepted the alien practices of the white world. Although some of the Mexican immigrants view him as the "loathsome coyote," Felix worked hard to win their affection and only consented to cooperate with his Anglo bosses on the condition that "these men immediately be considered candidates for American citizenship" (115). While Islas's novel might seem to repeat nationalist homophobia, *The Rain God* instead warns against a gay male Chicano discourse that puts on a white face. Despite Felix's own evasion of norms of heterosexuality, his freedom to act on his sexuality depends upon the subordination of women and an exploitation of labor, and his gay affirmation opposes only heteronormativity, remaining unconcerned about other repressive codes of class, race, or even gender. The story of Uncle Felix is an allegory about the reconciliation of fathers and sons, gay men and patriarchy. This reconciliation is marketed through a common consent to a transnational capitalism that would dominate workers (especially undocumented workers) and would resubordinate women in traditional feminine roles. As Gail Bederman has argued about turn-of-the-century Anglo-European feminists who appealed to a common whiteness and its fear of immigrant others who might dilute the Anglo-European vote (100), Uncle Felix promotes his own acceptance by allying himself with an oppressive ideology of Chicano masculinity and whiteness.

It would be easy to document the ways in which Felix is the false middleman, the mediator who would try to bring out a "queer Chicano sexuality" that is in solidarity with whiteness and patriarchy rather than a figure who helps to create a true border consciousness. Abusing the power of his job, Felix lies to the workers he brings into the States by making them submit to unnecessary *examinaciones* so that he can "take pleasure in touching them so intimately" (116). Although the narrator insists that only "the most insecure harbored ill will toward him" (116), Felix's actions are an extension of the "well-meaning" and "civilizing" opportunities that are supposed to be a part of the common interests the laborer can share with global capitalism. Only in a white reading of queerness that privileges individual sexual freedom above other such oppressions of race or class can Felix's handling of the bodies of others be so easily dismissed. In his own family, Felix insists upon his right to a male dominance that would repress his wife, son, and daughters. In one of his quarrels with JoEl, Felix confronts his wife, Angie, who has defended her son: "What freedom? . . . Freedom to turn into a delinquent or to turn into a selfish little brat? He belongs to a family and he must learn to share" (124). While Felix can transgress norms of sexuality, he cannot escape fully a value system that would grant men the privilege of family authority.

While Felix does defy Mama Chona to marry the dark-skinned Angie, his action stems more from a resentment against the family than an insubordination to racial hierarchies. As a father, Felix retains greater affection for his light-skinned second son JoEl over the older, dark-skinned brother. But Felix's love of racial norms, even as he defies norms of sexuality, and his love of conventional white heterosexuality are most clearly seen in his search in the border bar "around the corner from the courthouse" for the "shy and fair gods" (115). In these scenes of Felix's cruising, Islas's reference to the "white soldiers" as "fair gods" is more than figurative, as a sign of Felix's passion. In referring to the white, mostly "straight," in the sense of not identified as gay, soldiers whom Felix worships as "gods," Islas once again calls attention to the mythopoetic resonance of Felix's story with the ceremonies to Tlaloc. Indeed, it would seem as if Felix is seeking a false god, the false god of white masculinity, the fair-complexioned men for whom he wants to be a middleman, even if it comes at the expense of women and Mexican laborers who occupy a position he once held. Felix's tragedy, although Islas's novel does not blame the hate-crime "victim," arises from his failure to love the "rain god" for whom he has been recognized to be a dancer. Instead of embracing an indigenous Chicano queerness that exceeds the frames of a modern white gayness and a Chicano masculinity, Felix seeks to find inclusion in the very racialized and gendered structures that oppress him.

Like the monster who both kills and is Mama Chona, Felix is both "manipulator and manipulated."

Rather than trying to bring a singular gay male body into representation according to the white narrative of "coming out," Islas's novel reconfigures the epistemology of the closet. If the epistemology of the closet, as Sedgwick has argued, depends on a binary opposition of hetero/homo, public/private, normal/abnormal, outer/inner (*Epistemologies* 91–130), such oppositions no longer make "sense" when one thinks about "coming out" simultaneously in defiance of other racial and class demarcations. In contrast to Miguel's (dis)identification with his uncle Felix and his uncle's assimilation of class prejudices and gender norms is the son's emergence into "gay visibility" as a writer and as a character through his identification with his nursemaid, the "other" Maria. Islas makes the queerness of Miguel visible in the novel through his cross-dressing play with his nursemaid Maria, a play that provokes his mother's stern reprimand that he "apologize" to the father for "disgracing" the patriarchal family. Here Islas links Miguel's illegibility as a gay male in the Chicano family to the analogous invisibility of Maria within Chicano patriarchy as the lower-class, dark-skinned laborer from across the border. When he disciplines his son for "cutting out dolls and dressing them" with the consent of his nursemaid, Miguel Grande consciously does not scold directly the family servant but harangues his wife, Juanita, in Maria's presence: "He [Miguel Grande] did not like to speak directly to the Mexican women Juanita and his sisters took on to help them with the household chores" (15). Even Miguel's aunts, Eduviges and Jesus Maria, attempt to avoid speaking as much as possible to their domestics by leaving notes regarding what chores ought to be done. Since Miguel Grande's chastisement of his son involves the silencing of Maria's public voice—the nursemaid is not allowed to "appear," let alone speak, during the quarrel to defend her self and her "child"—Miguel Grande's (the Chicano's) naturalization of heterosexuality comes through a joined oppression of those who embody race and class differences. Through his gender transgression of playing with paper dolls with his nursemaid, Miguel has crossed over the many borders that would render the Mexican dark-skinned domestic invisible.

Although Miguel ends up betraying Maria by confessing to his father that his nursemaid had taken him to a Seventh Day Adventist Church, Maria represents the subversion within the household, the cultural and sexual seductions of an other. In contrast to Felix, Maria would lead Miguel to transgress the race and class oppressions that are inextricably tied to sexual normativity. Beginning with Miguel's love for the servant and not simply his mother, Islas's *The Rain God* rewrites the Freudian Oedipal narrative, revealing that the child's repressed unconscious desire may be directed toward the hired help as much as the mother. But if the story of Miguel's relation to Maria returns to the Chicano family romance the connection between bourgeois identity and racial and class hierarchies, Islas's novel also places Maria's story in relation to the ceremonies to Tlaloc. In the scenes describing Miguel's sensual/erotic play with his nursemaid, Islas emphasizes that it is her (and not the "white queer" Felix's) sacrificed body that will be eaten to bring in the renewal and transformation of the community as part of the mountain rituals:

> When he was very young, Maria made him laugh by putting her eyes very close to his face and saying in her uneducated Spanish, "Do you want to eat my raisin eyes?" He pretended to take bites out of her eyelids. She drew back and said, "Now it's my turn. I like your chocolate eyes. They look very tasty and I'm going to eat them!" She licked the lashes of his deeply set eyes and Miguel Chico screamed with pleasure. (13)

Before Miguel learned to identify with the racialized bourgeois masculinity of his father, the boy had seen himself reflected in the mirror of this other mother. The clearly erotic language of the scene points to a fluid and polymorphous sexuality unstructured by the father's phallocentric law. But if Miguel eats of the dark raisin eyes of the racial other as a way to come to know and experience the open and extravagant, even monstrously excessive, subjectivity of the rain god, he also allows himself to be eaten and places himself in the "feminine" position. In this scene, we see a foreshadowing of the monster who inhabits the adult Miguel's dream, a monster who is both aggressor and recipient, slayer and victim, sacrificer and object of sacrifice. In relating the lost innocence of Miguel's childhood with Maria, *The Rain God* connects this "pre-Oedipal" lack before the break into the patriarchal world of the father to the lost paradise of Tlalocan. This lost sacred landscape of Tlaloc is mapped across exclusionary race, gender, class, and national boundaries, marking the fact that Miguel had earlier known an intimation of a queerness not tied to whiteness or to Chicano patriarchal masculinity, or indeed to identity at all.

A Final Vision

Revising the sentimental tableau of the deathbed conversion of Mama Chona at its end, *The Rain God* finally offers a vision of the resurrected rain god. Yet if the children's sacrifices and the sacrifices of the children have finally served as the necessary restitution for the return of Tlaloc, the rain giver is a god who is both there and not there, both a divine visitor and an earthly family member. In its closing figuration of Tlaloc, Islas's novel once again fuses (recalling the monolith found in the Templo Mayor) Tlaloc with the Mother Goddess, Tlaloc with Uncle Felix, and both Uncle Felix and Tlaloc with Miguel, as ones who cross over borders of gender, race and sexual subjectivities. Islas's language in this final scene (as we saw in the early confrontation between Miguel and his father) is particularly indeterminate. As Islas's novel describes the descent of the rain god, it is often hard to keep the separate identities of the characters apart:

> Miguel Chico felt the Rain God come into the Room.
> —Let go of my hand, Mama Chona. I don't want to die.
> "*La familia*," she said.
> Felix walked toward her out of the shadows. "Mama," he called in a child's voice that startled her.
> "All right," she said to the living in the room, "If you want to, you can cry a little bit."
> To Felix, she said, "Where have you been *malcriado*? He took her in his arms. He smelled like the desert after a rainstorm. (180).

In his blend of Spanish and English styles of punctuating dialogue, Islas relocates the domestic scene in a borderland. But amid the crossing of linguistic and cultural borders, Islas also blurs discrete identities, as Miguel blends into Felix, who blends into the rain god, who blends into Mama Chona. It is finally impossible to pin down who "takes" Mama Chona into his arms, whether Miguel or Felix or the rain god, or perhaps Mama Chona in some hallucination only embraces herself. As in the earlier scene between Miguel and his father, Miguel's acceptance into the family is once again linked with his death, for he pleads with Mama Chona to let him go, not to make him die with her. In this last scene, Islas's fiction works by knotting paradoxes together, tying self-sacrifice and particularly the sacrifice of children with self-authorization: Miguel can be reborn into the multispirited rain god only by dying in relationship to the family. Islas's protagonist is both free and still clutched; he is both transformed into a higher state and yet still earthbound; he is both queer and invisible. He is no one identity. He is the rain god.

In important ways Islas uses his novel to reshape the myth of the rain god, a fluid body that recovers the queerness missing from Chicano history. But, as important, Islas's fiction offers a useable past to bring queer studies into a new "mestized" border space to map out the pitfalls of universalizing white theory without adapting it to the specific historical and cultural experiences of ethnic groups. In its final textual moves, *The Rain God* offers us a reparative queer identity that valorizes the migrant movement of the borderland consciousness itself, one that crosses over Anglo-European dichotomies of self and community, male and female, dying and rebirth, inside and outside, freedom and the responsibilities of *la familia*. In such a reparative queer identity, healing cannot come through a macho individualist rebellion against norms but only through a return to origins, to the queerness that was already within *la familia*. As Mama Chona announces, the rain god has always been the lost son, the radical alternative to heteronormative masculinity.

CODA

Anti-Racist Apartheid

In the *New York Times's* coverage of the Whiteness Studies movement, November 30, 1997, "Getting Credit for Being White," Michael Eric Dyson expressed the uneasiness and distrust among some African Americans that such an anti-racist politics might re-privilege whiteness by making it the center of attention: "There's a suspicion among African Americans that whiteness studies is a sneaky form of narcissism. At the very moment when African-American studies and Asian-American studies and so on are really coming into their own, you have whiteness studies shifting the focus and maybe the resources back to white people and their perspective" (qtd. in Talbot 118). Throughout this study I too have tried to express doubts about an anti-racist project that seems too much focused on what individual whites can do to unlearn the advantages accrued from their possessive investment in whiteness. But at the same time I find troubling Dyson's all-too-familiar stealing-the-agenda argument that assumes whiteness studies has emerged as a recent academic backlash—and one that can be defined through its difference from critical race and ethnic studies. If I have succeeded at little else through the writing of this project, I hope to have complicated the erroneous binary between not only whiteness studies and African American studies, but also the fictive binary that depicts racial communities as distinct, isolated, and segregated groups confronting a pure normative white center. One of whiteness's key narcissistic fiction, I have claimed, is its avowed "centeredness" and "purity" dependent on the absence of color and on the fantasy that its formation has not been relational. White identities, although white people might deny such a recognition, have always been heterogeneous and hybrid, constituted within a dialogical relation with a supposed racial "other." Rather than writing a whiteness studies project that might cooperate with the white flight into narratives of a separate ethnic history and community that can be lost in a new multi-racial, multi-cultural world, as Dyson warns, I have tried to recover whiteness studies's roots. More than the latest, postmodern trend of anti-racist work, whiteness studies continues a long history of co-racial interventions into the shifting and variously deployed formations of whiteness as both an ideology and identity. This history of co-racial interventions into the fugitive race of whiteness has always linked the deconstruction and denaturalization of whiteness with a radical social re-organization and commitment to justice.

But in citing Dyson's warning at the end of this project, I am not just trying to make one last defense of the relevance of whiteness studies, or more baldly, of my own work. Dyson's suspicion raise questions about the outcome, if not the intent, of whiteness studies, and his suspicion reflects a growing apartheid among anti-racist scholars in the academy. His is a suspicion, in the end, I sometimes share. In writing this project on the "black (and for want of better language, brown and yellow) looks" back at whiteness, I have been increasingly struck by the way as scholars we continue to talk past each other on matters of race. In a recent article on the emerging practices of anti-racist organizations, Michael Omi contends that people of color and people of non-color (whites) tend to understand what constitutes anti-racist work differently. In contrast to whites who have traditionally located racism in "color consciousness and find its absence in color-blindness," peoples of color have emphasized more how racism involves "institutionalized systems of power" and racialized practices that are part of everyday experiences (267–68). While certainly there are few critical race scholars of whiteness, or of any other racial or ethnic identity, that would not connect "race" to economic, social, and political practices, the "white" perspective that racism can end with the elimination of color consciousness, or in postmodern jargon, the exposing of the fictive construction of racial consciousness, has led to an increasing impatience with those intellectuals who just do not seem to appreciate these simple aesthetic solutions to racism and who do perceive the goal of an anti-racist project as a "race-blind" integrated Utopia. We need to be careful as scholars to avoid an increasing linguistic slippage from the fiction of race into the fiction of racism. I started this project as an attempt to map the shifting character of whiteness over time and within different gendered, regional, and class locations. I end this project heeding Dyson's suspicion that we also need as complex and rigorous a mapping of the multifarious formations of *"racism"* as of "race."

In an essay for the January 2001 issue of *PMLA*, Stephen Greenblatt recalls his encounter with the South African actress/director Janet Suzman after a lecture discussing her staging of *Othello* for the Market Theatre in Johannesburg in the mid-1970s. I want to examine Greenblatt's comments not to single out or denigrate his work—which I admire and which has influenced my own interest in cultural studies—but because it expresses the current academic revenge of the aesthetics against an intransigent race studies. As Greenblatt notes, he felt compelled to challenge "with some annoyance" (55) Suzman's explanation that she could "access racial memories" in her staging of *Othello* to protest South African Apartheid. Against what he sees as Suzman's uncritical and romantic essentializing of "memory," Greenblatt asserts that "racial memory [is] simply and entirely a theatrical performance, a fictive construction," and announces that "when I hear words like racial memory or *volk*, my blood runs cold" (55–56). By invoking the word *"volk,"* Greenblatt calls up the specter of the Holocaust as an incontrovertible witness to the horror of a fascist or nationalist race consciousness (a parallel Paul Gilroy makes in his own work *Against Race*). While I do not have space here in this epilogue to dispute the easy equivalency between all kinds of "racial performance," as if the different historical contexts behind Nazi-ism and a diasporic Pan-Africanism were "immaterial," and while I do not want to repudiate Greenblatt's point that collective racial memories are scripted, rehearsed, and thus learned, I am saddened by the implications of Greenblatt's remark. Greenblatt's remarks hint at the way the liberal white faith in colorblindness now masquerades as hip post-identity politics. From this white perspective, those intellectuals, most often people of color (but not exclusively so) who will not, or can not, get with the program are somehow "backwards," or more politely suggested here, "naïve," because they fail to accept the tactical superiority of post-race consciousness. They fail to see, so we can only infer from Greenblatt's remarks, that a fight against the textuality of racial identities, rather than a building of solidarity through narrative memory, would have been a more effective answer to Apartheid or to the Holocaust—a dubious point. They fail to

see that racism has ended, except for supposedly enforced identity performances. In starting with these buried assumptions, however, Greenblatt denies the residual script of whiteness and white privilege in his own
memory of anti-racism. In naming insular group/race/national consciousness as the problem holding back the evolution of the new "world
citizen," he elides the denaturalization of contingent racial categories
with the eradication of racism. My point is not, as other critics have
argued more deftly, that racial identities may still be strategically needed
to mobilize political activism. I concede Greenblatt's point that it might
be a more effective tactic to organize people around cross-ethnic, racial
issues of fairness and justice. What lies unexamined is the white developmental, teleological narratives of Greenblatt's anti-racism, narratives pri-
oritizing the solution of color-blind consciousness and individual
freedom from any supposed collective performance of race and identity
(57).

In my introduction I began with a critique of the misleading trope of
"abolitionism" that has organized whiteness studies, indicting its sugges-
tions of a white-directed and voluntaristic anti-racist movement, its
denial of whiteness's inherent hybridity and dialogic formation, and its
naivete that whiteness, as if it were a single monolithic racism, could be
simply "abolished" by exposing its unnaturalness and unmarked racial
privileges. Yet in highlighting whiteness's history of morphing, I want to
end by suggesting we need to be hypervigiliant about the future shape
the contingent fluid property of whiteness takes, as it tries to remain
structurally privileged. We need a mobilization against whiteness (and
not an imagined revolutionary abolition) that does not displace attention
from racism to race. We need a whiteness studies that does not tap into
(as I argued in my introduction) a white fantasy of returning to an adolescent free play at identities, especially when the persistence of racism
means there is no play for many. And we need a whiteness, as I have tried
to argue in this brief conclusion, that has its roots in a co-racial counterhegemonic tradition and not in a white liberal or radical tradition of "colorblindness." Whiteness is not an empty signifier, but is tied up with
socio-economic status, ideologies of individualism, and nationalistic formations, to name only a few intersections. As a fugitive race, whiteness,
or the ideologies associated with it, may still be embedded in the very
academic discourse that seeks its demise. To end racism we need to do
more than point out race's fictive construction. We must listen to the

"black look" back at it, and not dismiss such a return gaze as complaint or pre-modern. It is pre-modern, as I hope my book has shown. And it is part of a dialogue we need to keep in the foreground, lest whiteness persist as the unacknowledged foundation of a supposedly cosmopolitan, post-race society.

NOTES

Introduction

1. Many readings of Douglass's slave narratives have focused on his struggle for self-representation. See, for example, Priscilla Wald's *Constituting Americans: Cultural Anxiety and Narrative Form*, 76, for a thoughtful analysis of Douglass's attempt to find a black self against American narratives of the slave as a nonperson. In her reading of the "color line" in nineteenth-century U.S. literature, Samira Kawash uses the trope of the "fugitive" to signify Douglass's in-betweenness, that is to say, his standpoint outside the constraining representations of slave as property or free white male American subject. See Kawash, *Dislocating the Color Line: Identity, Hybridity, and Singularity in African-American Narrative*, 50. In my study, I want to turn the focus to Douglass's attempt to make the white self a "fugitive," one who can no longer remain secure within his/her own exclusionary boundaries. It is just this "fugitiveness," this state of being outside a unifying self-authorizing representation, that the free white citizen denies.

2. As Jane Tompkins has most notably argued, antebellum women, such as Harriet Beecher Stowe in *Uncle Tom's Cabin*, often sought to initiate through their writing a matriarchal revolution. For the controversy surrounding this empowerment through domestic influence and its relation to the sphere of true womanhood, see Lora Romero, *Home Fronts: Domesticity and Its Critics in the Antebellum United States*, chapter 1. Since Tompkins's study was published, critics of antebellum sentimental fiction have tended to complicate the question of female agency by examining its participation in contemporary national formations and imperialist projects. See Amy Kaplan, "Manifest Domesticity," and also P. Gabrielle Foreman's discussion of Douglass's recrafting of the sentimental tradition associated with Harriet Beecher Stowe in "Sentimental Abolition in Douglass' Decade."

3. Throughout this study, I am indebted to the pioneering work in investigating the historical formations of "whiteness" that has been done by Theodore Allen, *The Invention of the White Race*; Alexander Saxton, *The Rise and Fall of the White Republic: Class Politics and Mass Culture in Nineteenth-Century America*; Richard Dyer, "White"; Ruth Frankenberg, *White Women, Race Matters: The Social Construction of Whiteness*; bell hooks, "Representations of Whiteness"; Toni Morrison, *Playing in the Dark: Whiteness*

and the Literary Imagination; Vron Ware, *Beyond the Pale: White Women, Racism, and History*; Eric Lott, *Love and Theft: Blackface Minstrelsy and the American Working Class*; and David Roediger, *The Wages of Whiteness: Race and the Making of the American Working Class*.

4. Throughout this study, I will use the word "coracial" rather than "minority" or "marginalized" to avoid reintroducing into my critique of whiteness the center/margin, major/minor oppositions that leave "whiteness" in place as the norm against which "difference" is defined.

5. I take the term "possessive investment" from George Lipsitz's important study of whiteness, "The Possessive Investment in Whiteness: Racialized Social Democracy and the 'White' Problem in American Studies."

6. We can see this starting assumption at work in a special 1998 issue of *Transitions* 78 in which whiteness is defined by its "transparency" or "freedom from having to think about race" (5). For an extended discussion of this foundational belief within whiteness studies, see most notably Richard Dyer's *White*, in which whiteness is defined in terms of its suspension of meaning, its nothingness.

7. For a discussion of Anglo-Saxon racism in nineteenth-century U.S. culture, see Reginald Horsman, *Race and Manifest Destiny: The Origins of American Racial Anglo-Saxonism*; Ronald Takaki, *Iron Cages: Race and Culture in Nineteenth-Century America*; and Thomas Gossett, *Race: The History of an Idea in America*. I am also indebted to Kenneth Warren's and Dana Nelson's studies of race as a "discursive building block" within early U.S. culture; see Warren's *Black and White Strangers: Race and American Literary Realism* and Nelson's *The Word in Black and White: Reading "Race" in American Literature, 1638–1867*.

8. For a discussion of the how the black look forces white people into a self-alienating moment of awareness of the discrepancy between their own internalized image and the view from the other, see E. Ann Kaplan, "The 'Look' Returned: Knowledge Production and Constructions of 'Whiteness' in Humanities Scholarship and Independent Film."

9. I am particularly indebted in this study to Homi Bhabha's notions of "disjunctive temporality" in his chapter "The Postcolonial and the Postmodern: The Question of Agency" in *The Location of Culture* and to Judith Butler's reading of Derrida's citationality in *Bodies that Matter: The Discursive Limits of "Sex."* Several other studies have influenced my thinking of performativity in this study, especially Anne Pellegrini, *Performance Anxieties: Staging Psychoanalysis, Staging Race*; Diana Fuss, *Identification Papers*; and Kobena Mercer, *Welcome to the Jungle: New Positions in Black Cultural Studies*.

10. In the past few years there has been a growing list of important contributions to the field of whiteness studies. In the field of law I want to single out the work of Ian F. Haney Lopez, *White by Law: The Legal Construction of Race*; Barbara Flagg, *Was Blind but Now I See: White Race Consciousness and the Law*; and Cheryl Harris's 1993 *Harvard Law Review* essay, "Whiteness as Property," reprinted in *Black on White*, ed. David Roediger. In the field of communication, see Thomas Nakayama and Judith Martin's edited volume, *Whiteness: The Communication of Social Identity*, and Ann Louise Keating for the particular application of whiteness studies to classroom pedagogy. I have previously listed major early works in the whiteness studies movement in history and sociology, but see also the study of whiteness within southern culture by Grace Elizabeth Hale,

Making Whiteness: The Culture of Segregation in the South, 1890–1940, and, in relation to questions of class, see Matt Wray and Annalee Newitz, *White Trash: Race and Class in America*. For what is still the best overview of the early major works in whiteness studies, see Shelley Fisher Fishkin, "Interrogating 'Whiteness,' Complicating 'Blackness': Remapping American Culture."

11. For a discussion of boundary moments, see Francis Winddance Twine, "Brown-Skinned White Girls: Class, Culture, and the Construction of White Identity in Suburban Communities," 231.

Chapter 1. Narrative Interruptions of Panic

1. Critics such as Karen Sanchez-Eppler, Ann McClintock, Carroll Smith-Rosenberg, and Amy Kaplan have begun to dispute the notion of separate male and female spheres of influence that grounded earlier evaluations of the function of sentimental fiction to argue for the "shared racial underpinnings of domestic and imperialist discourse" (A. Kaplan 583) Over the past decade, the scholarly debate over the "cultural work" (to use Jane Tompkins's groundbreaking term from *Sensational Designs*) of sentimental "women's" fiction has grown increasingly divided. To some, the sentimental genre represented a capitulation to a woman's economy of exclusion and a retreat from public discourse, while to other feminist revisionists such as the contributors to the recent *Stowe Debate*, it permitted a relocating of the center of human life and moral suasion from the pulpit or podium to the kitchen as part of a matriarchal revolution. For an introduction to the debate over sentimentalism, see *The Stowe Debate: Rhetorical Strategies in* Uncle Tom's Cabin, ed. Mason I. Lowance Jr., Ellen E. Westbrook, and R. C. DeProspo, and see also Shirley Samuels's introduction to *The Culture of Sentiment: Race, Gender and Sentimentality in Nineteenth-Century America*.

2. Increasingly, literary historians have become interested in questions of affectivity, especially in terms of readers' response. See, for example, the recent collection *Sentimental Men: Masculinity and the Politics of Affect in American Culture*, ed. Mary Chapman and Glenn Hendler, and *An Emotional History of the United States*, ed. Peter N. Stearns and Jan Lewis. But too often affect in nineteenth-century literature is rendered synonymous with sympathy or sentimentality rather than an emotional culture that includes fears, anxieties, and unconscious traumas as well as feelings constructed as part of society's invention of the psychological.

3. William Pierson, *Black Legacy: America's Hidden Legacy*, 72, also discusses this passage.

4. See also Winthrop Jordan's analysis of the "black plot" in *White over Black: American Attitudes toward the Negro, 1550– 1812*, 117.

5. For another interpretation of the question of whiteness in Brown's plays, see John Ernest, "The Reconstruction of Whiteness: William Wells Brown's *The Escape; or A Leap for Freedom*."

6. Brown's imputation of "begging" invoked more than the obvious worries about condescension, for as J. Noel Heermance has pointed out, Brown personally prided himself on being self-supporting, so much so that at the beginning of his *Travel Sketches* he invented himself in public forums as an independent artist by differentiating himself from other importuning antislavery speakers: "Most of the fugitive slaves . . . come

upon begging missions, either for some society or for themselves. Mr. Brown has been almost the only exception. He maintained himself and his family by his own exertions" (159).

Chapter 2. Miscegenated Whiteness

1. These are all familiar readings of the metaphorical power of the tragic mulatto to a white audience. See, for example, Judith Berzon, *Neither White nor Black: The Mulatto Character in American Fiction*, which still offers one of the best overviews of the meanings placed onto the tragic mulatto in the "white" imagination. For a poststructuralist interpretation of the mulatto as the imaginative embodiment of the instability of cultural categories, see Elaine Ginsberg's introduction to *Passing and the Fictions of Identity*, 1–13.

2. Central to my argument is the assumption that literature functions to mediate narratives of national identity and thereby to interpellate national subjects. See, for example, Lauren Berlant's *The Anatomy of National Fantasy: Hawthorne, Utopia and Everyday Life* and Dana Nelson's reading of the connection between national identity and heterosexual white male subject formation in *National Manhood: Capitalist Citizenship and the Imagined Fraternity of White Men*.

3. In speaking of a "border" consciousness, I am applying Gloria Anzaldua's ideas about a new mestiza consciousness among those who live in the borderland to Davis's ambiguous crossing of gender, regional, and racial borders. See Anzaldua, *Borderlands: The New Mestiza* = La Frontera.

4. Albert Von Frank makes a similar point about some civic and religious leaders' response to the Anthony Burns's fugitive slave trial. See Von Frank, *The Trials of Anthony Burns: Freedom and Slavery in Emerson's Boston*, especially 252.

5. While I do not have space in this chapter to discuss Davis's response to the antebellum debate comparing slavery to wage labor, Davis several times invokes this controversy in her novel—for example, when Otley remarks that "the Negro" will be kept down because "there is not an Irish hodman, or Dutch mechanic who does not know the Negro is his inferior, and will not join to put him down if he tries to compete with him in free labor" (13).

6. I borrow the term "migratory subjectivity" from Carol Boyce Davies's study of black women in the diaspora, *Black Women, Writing, and Identity: Migrations of the Subject*.

7. As Elizabeth Young has argued in relation to Louis May Alcott's short stories during the Civil War, women writers "feminized" the war by their "self-conscious use of the theme of feminization within their fictional plots," but in such a narrative trajectory in which the masculine protagonists must undergo, as does Garrick Randolph, "feminization" is balanced by his connected "racialization." See Young, "A Wound of One's Own: Louisa May Alcott's Civil War Fiction," 440.

Chapter 3. "Corporeal Suspicion"

1. Among the common assumptions implied within post-Reconstruction race theory, as Thomas Gossett notes, was a belief that social advantages and status were a sign of racial character. In his *Hereditary Genius*, for example, the British-born Francis Gal-

ton, a cousin of Charles Darwin who helped to start the eugenics movement in England, posited that those who achieved eminence in society or showed signs of superior intelligence tended to come from a "common stock." In turn, many of society's ills, from poverty to crime to feeblemindedness, were the result of hereditary influences rather than environment. Extrapolating from Galton's premises, American social scientists felt confident that "blood would always tell." It is just this repression of indeterminacy and doubt or suspicion about the legibility of the white character that Hopkins would disrupt in her counterdiscursive history. See Gossett, *The History of an Idea in America*.

2. While reevaluations of Hopkins's novels have frequently begun with an examination of the racial discourse in turn-of-the-century America in order to demonstrate how Hopkins resignified the language of blood and hereditary that "scientifically proved" the inferiority of blacks (see Kassanoff 158–82), we have overlooked the counterhegemonic discourse within the *Colored American Magazine* that saw the national crimes during this nadir of African American history as a "white problem."

3. The *Colored American Magazine* was certainly not alone in positing that there was no permanency in constituent elements of racial character and hence no inherent superiority or inferiority of the races. In 1907 the French anthropologist Jean Finot would publish his *Race Prejudice*, which called into question the essentialism of racial distinctions. In an earlier essay, I have argued that Charles Chesnutt, in essays such as "What is a White Man?" and "The Future American," also worked to denaturalize and hybridize "white" identities. See Knadler, "The Untragic Mulatto: Charles Chesnutt and the Discourse of Whiteness," 426–48.

4. This same class-based analysis of southern whiteness can be founded in the article entitled "The Negro North and South" by S. C. Cross in the November 1902 edition of the *Colored American Magazine*. Again trying to explain the "immorality, depravity and deviltry" of white folks, Cross ties them to an hereditary racial habit, the origin of which lies in the history of slavery: "This bloated and brutal persecution perpetrated by irresponsible depravity and perpetrated by the social attitude of the aristocratic class, became so deeply planted in the unprincipled citizenship that it is almost hereditary instinct to murder malign, ravage, rob and brutalize the blacks today" (73). Although Cross qualifies his racial analysis here with "almost"—as if hereditary were only to be read metaphorically—he later asserts the literalness of this biologism: the criminality "became hereditary." In another essay from earlier in the same year, S. A. Hamilton writes about "The New Race Question in the South," the race war between different "classes" or "types" of whites—the crackers and the aristocrats. This cracker white—"a race as hardy and virile as the heart of an oak"—will need to intermarry with the white "aristocratic" race to prevent both the reversion of the upper- and the further degeneration of the lower-class white citizens (378).

5. As Joel Black has argued in *The Aesthetics of Murder: A Study of Romantic Literature and Contemporary Culture*, 62, detective fiction often depends on a psychological doubling or a resemblance between the criminal and the detective. If the detective can solve the mystery (based on his/her intuitions and sympathetic identifications with the mind of the criminal), it is because he/she is often a barely transformed criminal. Such a doubling has frequently led to psychoanalytic analysis of crime fiction in which the detective's own unconscious fantasies are implicated in his/her capture of the criminal

"other." It is thus not uncommon for the hero to discover that he/she is the criminal whom he/she has been seeking all along. In the unfolding of the plot, readers as well are often confronted with their own unconscious "dark side" in the criminal's machinations. This is the starting premise of Hopkins's detection history in *Hagar's Daughter*.

6. In her study of Hopkins's reworking of the nineteenth-century discourse of "Hagar," *Dreaming Black/Writing White: The Hagar Myth in American Cultural History*, Janet Gabler-Hover also points out how Hopkins develops a black female perspective (and subjectivity) in her novel through moments of narrative focalization and free indirect discourse.

7. In using the term "serial racist killer," I want to play upon some of Mark Seltzer's comments in *Serial Killer: Death and Life in America's Wound Culture* that the postmodern serial killer is one who experiences the traumatic loss of clear boundaries between self/other, inside/outside, depth/simulation.

8. I am, of course, here suggesting that Hopkins anticipates some of the comments that Toni Morrison makes in *Playing in the Dark* about the "serviceability" of the black presence.

Chapter 4. Unacquiring Negrophobia

1. Drawing upon postcolonial and critical race theory, recent Asian American studies has undergone a paradigm shift, moving away from a concern for an appropriate Asian American race-based identity and toward the forming of a "diasporic sensibility." Yet I want to raise the question whether this diasporic model does not still depend on a buried or reified foundation of race. Despite the desire to transcend national boundaries as part of a larger cultural movement toward post-Americanist narratives in a world of transnational organizations and global capitalism, the leading question in these "postmodern reimaginings" is still the formation of an "Asian" subjectivity (now in quotation marks)—a term that by its very framing excludes or renders secondary the individual's connection to other minority groups. When speaking of a "diasporic" Asian sensibility, for example, David Leiwei Li still raises the questions: how do "Asians" represent themselves as a people with a "unique experience," and how do they claim a non-Western cultural specificity? (17). This interrogative mode demands that one not ask how one might form an identity in relations of affiliation and reciprocity with other groups and thus reinscribes, as I will try to show in what follows, the "Negrophobic" structure of twentieth-century U.S. whiteness's biracial consciousness. Fearful of the threat of "derealization" and of "political disempowerment," we critics of ethnicity can not imagine a politics not mobilized around "identities"—even as we "de-essentialize" and "diasporize" them. One still wants to think in terms of transterritorialized communities in which the common link is the "racial body" rather than a coalitional or cosmopolitan consciousness inspired by a desire for justice. In the absence of "nation," people find their ethnic identity even more clearly in "race"—now abstracted as "Asian" (in quotes)—and thus capitulate to a reinscribed essentialist logic.

2. Particularly during the period after the Japanese invasion of Korea, first-generation Korean Americans turned to political organizations such as the Korean Nationalist Association (1909) and its support for the independence struggle at home as a source of ethnic identity and community. Suffering acutely as a people without a

"home" to return to, brutally separated from wives and families, the numerous *chong gak* (bachelors) in America developed a strong sense of ethnic nationalism (Takaki, *Strangers* 277).

3. In using the term "transpositional," I am indebted to Cheryl Walker's study of nineteenth-century Native American autobiographies, *Indian Nation: Native American Literature and Nineteenth-Century Nationalisms*, see especially 46.

4. In my reading of the *Ozawa* case, I am drawing upon Walter Benn Michaels's investigation into the shifting meaning of "race" during the modernist era from supremacy to difference, from biological character to a "spirit" legitimating a distinctive cultural consciousness. See Michaels, *Our America: Nativism, Modernism, and Pluralism*, particularly 122, 140–41.

5. Although I do not have space to discuss other prerequisite cases, the same logic of naturalization circulated within other Supreme Court rulings. In 1927, five years after the *Ozawa* case, Gong Lum, a Chinese American from Mississippi, sued to be admitted to the white public schools. In its decision against Lum, the Supreme Court cited the landmark *Plessy v. Ferguson* case to uphold the constitutionality of the legal segregation of Chinese in the Jim Crow South. By determining the separate but equal clause applied to Asian Americans as well as to African Americans, the Court placed all "nonwhites" in the same social and economic class (see Loewen). Throughout the nineteenth century, as Alexander Saxton has argued, it was common for Asian immigrants to be assigned an economic position similar to freed blacks and marked as "near Negro" (*Indispensable Enemy* 8). Although Lum was suing for equal access and not naturalization, the courts, as in the Ozawa case, declared Asians and blacks kindred peoples in relation to a history of oppression and exploitation. As a consequence of legal decisions such as that in the Lum case, the courts further disseminated the logic of naturalization: that in struggling against oppression, it was in the Asian American's best interest to struggle to be nearer white than black and that black culture ought to be as alien to Asian immigrants as it was to "hard-working" middle-class white Americans.

6. Mr. Lively's promotion of Chungpa as the "genuine article" resonates with Kang's own career. As a writer who made his name, like Lafcadio Hearn, as a retailer/reteller of Asian images in his first autobiography, *The Grass Roof*, he knew that his middle-class white readers saw him as a safe, feminized object of their patriarchal gaze. Like the audience at Rev. Bonheure's revival, they saw him not as an individual but as the "genuine" native insider who could speak about the mysteries and manners of the Orient. Kang, moreover, was able to make his literary debut as a reviewer for the *New York Times* and the *New Republic* only by serving as a spokesperson for the "authenticity" of books on China. In an incendiary review of Pearl S. Buck's *The Good Earth* for the *New Republic* (July 1, 1931), however, Kang incited the furor of a number of letter writers because he questioned her "genuine" understanding of Chinese civilization. Kang's message in his critique of Pearl S. Buck has relevance for our consideration here. While he faults Buck for not fully understanding the more than ornamental details of Chinese culture, he inveighs as well against the universalizing of a "white" American/Western experience (here romantic love) and applying it to the inner life of people from another culture. This assumption of the normativity of their own experience, as Kang implies, is a common trait of "white" Westerners, and both in his review and his later fictional autobiography he would resort to the strategic practice of challenging whiteness's naturalized normativity.

7. In many ways, Kang's *East Goes West* seems to appeal to a "romance of likeness" between Asians and Americans to argue for the "Yankee Oriental's" naturalization because he/she is nearer white. Like other Asian writers, such as Dr. No Yong Park in an *Oriental View of American Civilization*, who noted cultural similarities to promote harmony between East and West (K. Lee 65), Kang emphasizes the parallels between traditional Korean society and New England's (the originary America's) Puritan legacy. Although such a rhetorical strategy would allow Kang to repudiate the stereotypes of Asians as almond-eyed brutes, insidious Fu Manchus, or unemotional Spartans, to insist on this common civilized "whiteness" would replicate the Negrophobia that isolates Asians from other minority groups. But throughout *East Goes West*, Kang tends to invoke, so as only to satirize and resignify, the meaning of this logic of naturalization that legitimates white supremacism. Thus when Chungpa Han goes to work for the New England farmer, Mr. Higgens, he ponders the commonality between the lives of the simple rustic New England farmer and the hard-working rural Koreans. On the one hand, he denies Anglo-Americans their identitarian difference: "Life here for me was simple, sound, wholesome, and primitive. The typical Oriental is all of these—the view the West has yet to form of him, it seems, since as a stock character he is either [a] cruel and brutish heathen with horrid outlandish customs, or a subtle and crafty gentleman of inscrutable sophistication" (209). Yet in countering pernicious representations of Koreans, Kang does not just offer more positive images: he implies an originary spiritual affinity that would reconfigure the Korean as not alien but kinsperson. While, as Walter Benn Michaels has argued, many of the great modernist texts were committed to the "nativist project of racializing the American" (*Our America* 13), Kang likens the Korean and New Englander to imply that the admittance of Asians would provide an atavistic renewal of the nation's premodern soul.

8. As the *New York Times* wrote in its opening paragraph: "While the American woman is considered emancipated and on an equal basis with men, economically this equality does not hold true, Dr. Younghill Kang, Professor of Oriental Culture at New York University declared yesterday" (1).

Chapter 5. Dis-integrating Third Spaces

1. For a discussion of Wirth's conceptualization of the Jewish Ghetto in terms of his own identity struggles, see Roger A. Salerno, *Louis Wirth: A Bio-Bibliography*, 9–10. Salerno, in his brief biography, suggests that Wirth tended to see the city as both a place of freedom and of impersonality with the loss of older communal values. This tension is one that structures other Jewish writers' erasure of "third multi-cultural spaces" in their ghetto fiction. We also see familiar binaries structure Worth's paradigmatic 1938 essay, "Urbanism as a Way of Life": *gemeinschaft/gesellschaft*, rural/urban, past/present, tradition/modernism.

2. The phrase "polyglot boarding house" is from Edward Corsi's 1925 essay for *Outlook* (September 16, 1925) entitled "My Neighborhood," 92. Also cited in Mario Maffi, *Gateway to the Promised Land: Ethnic Cultures on New York's Lower East Side*, 97.

3. In using the term "dis-integration" I want to draw upon theories of embodiment developed within the writing of Michel Foucault, Julia Kristeva, and Judith Butler. In his studies from *Discipline and Punish* to *Care of the Self*, Foucault has sought to recover

the social and historical malleability of the body, particularly to look at how its social construction often "de-forms" it. Through an analysis of what he called "disciplinary regimes," Foucault maintained that hegemonic social forces continue to shape our subjectivity. Although basing her work on the psychoanalytic theories of Jacques Lacan, Kristeva has argued that this sense of self or subjectivity depends on generative processes of exclusion as well as incorporation. Calling what fails to be subsumed within the dominant social image of the body as the abject, Kristeva asserts that this abject marks the boundaries between normal and abnormal. In her work, Butler attempts to restore a sense of the performative to the process of subjectification. The exclusion of the abject does not take place at any one totalizing moment but continually must be performed again and again through a process of "dis-identification." In her work, Gail Weiss has referred to the "excessive coherence" of embodiments that require a repudiation of multiple body images—domination depends on the lack of fluidity and multiplicity.

4. In posing these questions about the relation between the Jewish immigrant writer's representation of the "ghetto" and the struggle over a hybrid space, I am drawing upon some of the insights of Christopher Mele's work in *Selling the Lower East Side: Culture, Real Estate, and Resistance in New York City*, especially 13–15.

5. In his discussion of the "walker" as one susceptible to the signatures of many others, Certeau modifies in important ways the usual figuration of the flaneur, or urban dandy, as represented in turn-of-the-century discourse. As Rhonda Garelick argues in *Rising Star: Dandyism, Gender and Performance in the Fin de Siecle*, 9, the flaneur engaged in a highly stylized and constructed performance that was designed to provoke reactions in others. As a spectator to the urban scene, moreover, he was depicted as gazing on all the city's commodified spectacle, but his own "subjectivity" (even in the criticisms of his detachment) is viewed as safely protected behind a privileged voyeuristic distancing.

Chapter 6. White Dissolution

1. For an overview of African American fiction during the era of integration, see, for example, Bernard Bell, *The Afro-American Novel and Its Tradition*, especially 150, 188; W. Lawrence Hogue, *Discourse and the Other: The Production of the Afro-American Text*, 8–9; and Arthur Davis's early study, *From the Dark Tower: Afro-American Writers, 1900–1960*, 139.

2. While the title of Jarrett's essay taps into the postwar turn to psychology, his invocation of Van Wyck Brooks's 1915 *America's Coming of Age*, which mapped out a distinctive racialized national "American" literary tradition is thus also a call for African American inclusiveness (or integration) into U.S. literary exceptionalism. See Jarrett, "Toward Unfettered Creativity: A Note on the Negro Novelist's Coming of Age."

3. In "Tearing the Goat's Flesh: Homosexuality, Abjection, and the Production of a Late Twentieth-Century Black Masculinity," Robert F. Reid Pharr investigates how the black gay male functioned as the scapegoat to a feared "Black boundarylessness" (373). Building on Reid Pharr's insights, I would argue that in white life novels it was the white male homosexual who, as "external menace," reassured the black community that there was no enemy within its racial borders despite nationalism's intense same-sex male bonds.

4. I have borrowed the term "homosexualization" from Robert Corber's cinematic study of 1950s' Cold War America in *Homosexuality in Cold War America: Resistance and the Crisis of Masculinity*, in which he explores the linking of homosexuality to Communism as a way of containing competing political ideologies as well as (as is more typically argued) enforcing gender and sex norms.

5. I am greatly indebted in my reading to Kaja Silverman's psychoanalytic studies of masculinity, *Male Subjectivity at the Margins*.

6. Certainly I do not want to suggest that the entire scientific community helped to feed such hysteria. In his *The Folklore of Sex*, published in 1951, Albert Ellis accused the media of "cater[ing] to this public fear of sex crimes" and insisted that the true "sex law breakers are sex-law makers" who restrict and distort "normal sex conduct." But in his denial of criminality and nonnormative sexuality, Ellis attests to the postwar era's climate of exaggerated sex crimes that made every child vulnerable to assault from the twinned pedophilic/homosexual pervert.

7. For this traditional reading of Demby's *Beetlecreek*, see Jay Berry, "The Achievement of William Demby," especially 434–40. Most critics have tended to ignore Demby's first novel in evaluating his career, seeing it as an imitative 1950s' existentialist experiment with only an indirect sociopolitical "race" theme. In *Native Sons: A Critical Study of 20th-Century Black American Authors*, for example, Edward Margolies writes, "Although *Beetlecreek* is by no means a 'Negro novel' in any provincial sense, its existential themes are particularly applicable to the Negro experience" (179).

8. Specifically, Hurston exposes the black soul within the white male identity. Although Jim Meserve may be accredited with having pulled himself up by his bootstraps, it is "black" knowledge that allows his business achievements and only his white privilege (and investment in it) that permits this expertise to enrich him. When Jim first arrives in Citrabelle and wants to learn the trade of the citrus growers, he expropriates the accumulated wisdom of the black community: "How he had finally decided that since the colored men did all of the manual work, they were the ones who actually knew how things were done, and how he had taken up around the jooks and gathering places in Colored Town, and swapped stories, and stood treats, and eased in questions in desperate hope, wondering if his money would hold out until he could get a footing, and how he had finally gotten information which landed him his job" (74). In giving this list of Jim's borrowings from Colored Town, Hurston writes that she is telling us what Arvay does not know, but here we might substitute as well white readers who in their similar love for the myth of the southern maverick do not know the masquerade of autonomy and originality that the maverick likes to suppress. Like his father, the "artist" son, Kenny, rises as a celebrity musician by making over the sounds of black ragtime and jazz. When Arvay and Jim attend the homecoming in which their son's band is featured, Jim tells Arvay, "Looks like Kenny knows what he's talking about. Those white boys are playing that rag-time down to the bricks, . . . you could almost think those were colored folks playing that music" (212). Several critics have argued that Hurston, in writing her white novel, failed to distinguish the voices of her white characters from her black citizens of Eatonville. But the common accent fitted, even if not consciously so, in with the larger project of the novel to suggest that white male identity has its own formative black component. The story of Jim Meserve's white male triumphalism is unveiled as a denial of a mixing and hybridity. In Hurston's story,

such a cross-fertilization becomes dangerously close to theft, a synergistic borrowing possible only because of the magnanimity of black folks willing to teach both father and son.

9. In his discussion of the interracial bonds between men in "buddy cop" films, Ed Guerrero notes that these bonds depend on the exclusion of women. See "The Black Image in Protective Custody: Hollywood's Biracial Buddy Films of the Eighties," in *Black American Cinema*, ed. Manthia Diawara, 239.

Chapter 7. Queer Aztlan, Mestizing "White" Queer Theory

1. Behind my reading is the idea that Aztlan, as a siteless locale with no territorial sovereignty, suggests a yearning for the security of contained boundaries and for the fixity of a nation-state enjoyed by some other diasporic people. See, for example, Rafael Perez-Torres's reconceptualizing of the nationalist model of Aztlan in "Refiguring Aztlan."

2. I am drawing upon Mark Chiang's comments about a transnational capitalist class in his discussion of diasporic queers in "Coming Out into the Global System: Postmodern Patriarchies and Transnational Sexualities in *The Wedding Banquet*," 376.

3. In trying to think through the problems of a transnational Chicana/o-ness with links to multiple communities, I am particularly indebted to Angie Chabram-Dernersesian's "'Chicana! Rican? Chicana Riquena!' Refashioning the Trans-national Connection."

4. For a discussion of the issue of gay visibility in Chicano visual arts, see Antonio Viego, "The Place of Gay Male Chicano Literature in Queer Chicana/o Cultural Work." In contrast to Viego, I would argue that Islas finds a common ground with Chicana feminism, whereas Viego argues male sexuality must develop its own separate system of signification.

5. In using the term "coming home" versus "coming out," I am quoting from Essex Hemphill's introduction to *Brother to Brother: New Writings by Black Gay Men*, xxix.

6. In my review of Leo Bersani's *Homo*, "Leo Bersani and the Nostalgia for White Male Radicalism," I have questioned the suspicion of community (implicated with a feminization of the male body) in Bersani's work.

7. In "Who Is That Queer Queer? Exploring Norms around Sexuality, Race, and Class in Queer Theory," 172, Ruth Goldman contends that queer theories' focus on antinormative identities can obscure the experience of queers of color.

8. Siobhan Somerville in *Queering the Color Line*, 16, makes a similar point about the intersection of race and sexuality.

9. As Alfredo Lopez Austin, *Tamoanchan, Tlalocan: Places of Mist*, 244, explains, Meso-Americans in their worship of Tlaloc believed that a sacrifice had to be made of the same nature as that which was returned. Since as a deity Tlaloc had "died" in order to be "born," that is to say, his transcendent spirit had been pulled down by being filled with earth so that he could become a "human god," a similar payment of "death" was needed to acquit humanity's debt.

WORKS CITED

Abel, Elizabeth. "Black Writing, White Reading: Race and the Politics of Feminist Interpretation." *Critical Inquiry* 19 (spring 1993): 470–98.

Abelove, Henry, Michele Aina Barale, and David M. Halperin. *The Lesbian and Gay Studies Reader*. New York: Routledge, 1993.

Abraham, Roger. *Singing the Master: The Emergence of African-American Culture in the Plantation South*. New York: Pantheon Books, 1992.

Abu-Lugod, Janet L., ed. *From Urban Village to East Village: The Battle for New York's Lower East Side*. Oxford: Blackwell, 1994.

Agassiz, Louis. "The Diversity of Origin of the Human Races." *Christian Examiner* 49 (July 1850): 110–45.

———. *Essay on Classification*. Ed. Edward Lurie. Cambridge: Belknap Press of Harvard University Press, 1962.

Alarcon, Norma. "The Theoretical Subject(s) of This Bridge Called My Back and Anglo-American Feminism." In *Criticism in the Borderlands: Studies in Chicano Literature, Culture and Ideology*, ed. Hector Calderon and Jose David Saldivar, 28–39. Durham, N.C.: Duke University Press, 1991.

Alexander, Elizabeth. "Can You Be Black and Look at This?: Reading the Rodney King Video(s)." In *Black Male: Representations of Masculinity in Contemporary American Art*, ed. Thelma Golden, 98–110. New York: Whitney Museum of Art, 1994.

Allen, Theodore W. *The Invention of the White Race*, vol. 1, *Racial Oppression and Social Control*. London: Verso, 1994.

Almaguer, Tomas. "Chicano Men: A Cartography of Homosexual Identity and Behavior." *differences: A Journal of Feminist Cultural Studies* 3 (1991): 75–100.

Althusser, Louis. "Ideology and Ideological State Apparatus." In *Lenin and Philosophy*. Trans. B. Brewster. New York: New Left Books, 1971.

Ammons, Elizabeth. "Afterward: Winona, Bakhtin, and Hopkins in the Twenty-First Century." In *The Unruly Voice: Rediscovering Pauline Elizabeth Hopkins*, ed. John Cullen Gruesser, 211–19. Urbana: University of Illinois Press, 1996.

Ammons, Elizabeth, and Annette White-Parks. *Tricksterism in Turn-of-the-Century American Literature*. Hanover, N.H.: University Press of New England, 1994.

Andrews, William. Introduction to *The Oxford Frederick Douglass Reader*. Ed. William Andrews, 3–19. New York: Oxford University Press, 1996.

221

———. *To Tell a Free Story: The First Century of Afro-American Autobiography, 1760–1865*. Urbana: University of Illinois Press, 1986.

Antin, Mary. *The Promised Land*. Boston: Houghton Mifflin, 1912.

Anzaldua, Gloria. *Borderlands: The New Mestiza* = La Frontera. San Francisco: Spinsters/ Aunt Lute, 1987.

Armstrong, Nancy. *Desire and Domestic Fiction: A Political History of the Novel*. New York: Oxford University Press, 1987.

Arnold, Philip P. *Eating Landscape: Aztec and European Occupation of Tlalocan*. Niwot: University Press of Colorado, 1999.

Austin, Alfredo Lopez. *Tamoanchan, Tlalocan: Places of Mist*. Trans. Bernard R. Ortiz de Montellano and Thelma Ortiz de Montellano. Niwot: University Press of Colorado, 1997.

Babb, Valerie. *Whiteness Visible: The Meaning of Whiteness in American Literature and Culture*. New York: New York University Press, 1998.

Baker, Ray Stannard. *Following the Color Line: American Negro Citizenship in the Progressive Era*. 1908. Reprint, New York: Harper and Row, 1964.

Bakhtin, Mikhail. *Dialogic Imagination*. Ed. Michael Holquist. Trans. Caryl Emerson and Michael Holquist. Austin: University of Texas Press, 1981.

Baldwin, James. "The Black Boy Looks at the White Boy." In *Nobody Knows My Name*, 216–41. New York: Dial Press, 1961.

———. "On Being White and Other Lies." *Essence* (April 1984): 80–84.

Bancroft, George. *History of the United States, from the Discovery of the American Continent*, vol. 7. Boston: Charles C. Little and James Brown, 1875.

Banks, Marva. "Uncle Tom's Cabin and the Antebellum Black Response." In *Readers in History: Nineteenth-Century American Literature and the Contexts of Response*, ed. James Machor, 209–27. Baltimore: Johns Hopkins University Press, 1993.

Bantha, Martha. *Imagining American Women: Ideas and Ideals in Cultural History*. New York: Columbia University Press, 1987.

"Barbarism and Civilization." *Atlantic Monthly* 7 (January 1861): 51–61.

Bayn, Nina. *Woman's Fiction: A Guide to Novels by and about Women in America, 1820–70*. Ithaca, N.Y.: Cornell University Press, 1978.

Bederman, Gail. *Manliness and Civilization: A Cultural History of Gender and Race in the United States, 1880–1917*. Chicago: University of Chicago Press, 1995.

Bell, Bernard. *The Afro-American Novel and Its Tradition*. Amherst: University of Massachusetts Press, 1987.

Bell, David, and Gill Valentine. *Mapping Desire: Geographies of Sexualities*. London: Routledge, 1995.

Bentley, Nancy. *The Ethnography of Manners: Hawthorne, James, Wharton*. Cambridge: Cambridge University Press, 1995.

Bercovitch, Sacvan. *The Rites of Assent: Transformations in the Symbolic Construction of America*. New York: Routledge, 1993.

Berlant, Lauren. *The Anatomy of National Fantasy: Hawthorne, Utopia and Everyday Life*. Chicago: University of Chicago Press, 1991.

Bernardi, Daniel. *The Birth of Whiteness: Race and the Emergence of U.S. Cinema*. New Brunswick, N.J.: Rutgers University Press, 1996.

Berry, Jay. "The Achievement of William Demby." *College Language Association* 26, no. 4 (June 1983): 434–40.

Berzon, Judith R. *Neither White nor Black: The Mulatto Character in American Fiction.* New York: New York University Press, 1978.

Bhabha, Homi. *The Location of Culture.* London: Routledge, 1994.

———. "The Other Question." In *Literature, Politics and Theory,* 158. London: Methuen, 1986.

———. "The Third Space." In *Identity, Community, Culture, and Difference,* ed. J. Rutherford, 207–22. London: Lawrence and Wishart, 1991.

———. "The World and the Home." In *Dangerous Liaisons: Gender, Nation, and Postcolonial Perspectives,* ed. Anne McClintock, Aamir Mufti, and Ella Shohut, 445–55. Minneapolis: University of Minnesota Press, 1998.

Binder, Frederick M., and David M. Reimers. *All the Nations Under Heaven: An Ethnic and Racial History of New York City.* New York: Columbia University Press, 1995.

Black, Joel. *The Aesthetics of Murder: A Study of Romantic Literature and Contemporary Culture.* Baltimore: Johns Hopkins University Press, 1991.

Black, Phil. "I Live in Two Worlds." *Our World* (October 1953): 19.

Blair, Sarah. *Henry James and the Writing of Race and Nation.* Cambridge: Cambridge University Press, 1996.

Bloom, James. *Left Letters: The Culture Wars of Mike Gold and Joseph Freeman.* New York: Columbia University Press, 1992.

Blumin, Stuart. *The Emergence of the Middle Class: Social Experience in the American City, 1760–1900.* Cambridge: Cambridge University Press, 1989.

Bone, Robert. *The Negro Novel in America.* New Haven, Conn.: Yale University Press, 1958.

Boone, Joseph Allen. *Libidinal Currents: Sexuality and the Shaping of Modernism.* Chicago: University of Chicago Press, 1998.

Bremen, Brian. "Du Bois, Emerson, and the Fate of Black Folks." *American Literary Realism* 24, no. 3 (spring 1992): 80–88.

Brennen, Timothy. *At Home in the World: Cosmopolitanism Now.* Cambridge: Harvard University Press, 1997.

Bristow, Edward J. *Prostitution and Prejudice: The Jewish Fight against White Slavery, 1870–1939.* New York: Schocken Books, 1983.

Brodhead, Richard. *Cultures of Letters: Scenes of Reading and Writing in Nineteenth-Century America.* Chicago: University of Chicago Press, 1993.

Brooks, Kristina. "Mammies, Bucks, and Wenches: Minstrelsy, Racial Pornography, and Racial Politics in Pauline Hopkins's *Hagar's Daughter.*" In *The Unruly Voice: Rediscovering Pauline Elizabeth Hopkins,* ed. John Cullen Gruesser, 119–57. Urbana: University of Illinois Press, 1996.

Brown, Josephine. *Biography of an American Bondman: Two Biographies by African-American Women.* Ed. William Andrews. New York: Oxford University Press, 1991.

Brown, William Wells. *The Black Man, His Antecedents, His Genius, and His Achievements.* New York: Thomas Hamilton, 1863.

———. *Clotel; or, The President's Daughter.* Intro. William Edward Farrison. 1853. Reprint, New York: Arno Press, 1969.

———. *Clotelle: A Tale of the Southern State.* In *Violence in the Black Imagination.* Ed. Ronald Takaki. New York: Oxford University Press, 1993.

———. *The Rising Son; or, The Antecedents and Advancements of the Colored Race.* 1874. Reprint, Miami: Mnemosyne Publishers, 1969.

————. *Sketches of Places and People Abroad; The American Fugitive in Europe.* 1855. Reprint, Freeport, N.Y.: Books for Libraries Press, 1970.

Bruce, Dickins D., Jr. *Black American Writing from the Nadir: The Evolution of a Literary Tradition, 1877–1915.* Baton Rouge: Louisiana State University Press, 1989.

Bullock, Penelope. *The Afro-American Periodical Press, 1838–1909.* Baton Rouge: Louisiana State University Press, 1981.

Burstein, Janet. *Writing Mother/Writing Daughter: Tracing the Maternal in Stories by American Jewish Women.* Urbana: University of Illinois Press, 1996.

Butler, Judith. *Bodies that Matter: On the Discursive Limits of "Sex."* New York: Routledge, 1993.

————. *Excitable Speech: A Politics of the Performative.* New York: Routledge, 1997.

————. *Gender Trouble.* New York: Routledge, 1989.

————. "More Gender Trouble: Feminism Meets Queer Theory." *differences: A Journal of Feminist Cultural Studies* 6 (summer/fall 1994): 27–61.

Cahan, Abraham. *The Education of Abraham Cahan.* Trans. Leon Stein, Abraham P. Conan, and Lynn Davison. Philadelphia: Jewish Publication Society of America, 1969.

————. *The Rise of David Levinsky.* 1917. Reprint, New York: Harper and Row, 1960.

————. *Yekl, and The Imported Bridegroom and Other Stories of Yiddish New York.* Intro. Bernard G. Richards. New York: Dover. 1970.

Carby, Hazel. *Race Men.* Cambridge: Harvard University Press, 1998.

————. *Reconstructing Womanhood: The Emergence of the Afro-American Woman Novelist.* New York: Oxford University Press, 1987.

Carter, Robert. "Queen Victoria—The Friend of the Negro." *Colored American Magazine* (March 1901): 354–56.

Caruth, Cathy. *Trauma: Explorations in Memory.* Baltimore: Johns Hopkins University Press, 1995.

————. *Unclaimed Experience: Trauma, Narrative, and History.* Baltimore: Johns Hopkins University Press, 1996.

Cawelti, John. *Adventure, Mystery, and Romance: Formula Stories as Art and Popular Culture.* Chicago: University of Chicago Press, 1976.

Certeau, Michel de. *The Practice of Everyday Life.* Trans. Steven Randall. Berkeley: University of California Press, 1984.

Chabram-Dernersesian, Angie. " 'Chicana! Rican? Chicana Riquena!' Refashioning the Trans-national Connection." In *Between Woman and Nation: Nationalisms, Transnational Feminisms, and the State,* 264–94. Durham, N.C.: Duke University Press, 1999.

Chambers, Ross. "The Unexamined." *Minnesota Review* 47 (May 1997): 141–56.

Chametzky, Jules. *From the Ghetto: The Fiction of Abraham Cahan.* Amherst: University of Massachusetts Press, 1977.

Chan, Sucheng. *Asian American: An Interpretive History.* Boston: Twayne, 1991.

Chapman, Mary, and Glenn Hendler. *Sentimental Men: Masculinity and the Politics of Affect in American Culture.* Berkeley: University of California Press, 1999.

Chauncey, George. *Gay New York: Gender, Urban Culture, and the Making of the Gay Male World, 1890–1940.* New York: Basic Books, 1994.

Cheah, Pheng, and Bruce Robbins. *Cosmopolitics: Thinking and Feeling beyond the Nation.* Minneapolis: University of Minnesota Press, 1998.

Cheung, King-Kok. *Articulate Silences: Hisaye Yamamoto, Maxine Hong Kingston, Joy Kogawa.* Ithaca, N.Y.: Cornell University Press, 1993.

Chiang, Mark. "Coming Out into the Global System: Postmodern Patriarchies and Trans-national Sexualities in *The Wedding Banquet*." In *Q & A: Queer in Asian American*, ed. David Eng and Alice Y. Hom, 374–97. Philadelphia: Temple University Press, 1998.

Child, Lydia Maria. *A Romance of the Republic*. Intro. Dana Nelson. Lexington: University of Kentucky Press, 1997.

Chin, Frank. *Chickencoop Chinaman and the Year of the Dragon*. Seattle: University of Washington Press, 1981.

Conboy, Katie, Nadia Medina, and Sarah Stanbury. *Writing on the Body: Female Embodiment and Feminist Theory*. New York: Columbia University Press, 1997.

Coontz, Stephanie. *The Way We Never Were: American Families and the Nostalgia Trip*. New York: Basic Books, 1992.

Corber, Robert. *Homosexuality in Cold War America: Resistance and the Crisis of Masculinity*. Durham, N.C.: Duke University Press, 1997.

———. *In the Name of National Security: Hitchcock, Homophobia and the Political Construction of Gender*. Durham, N.C.: Duke University Press, 1993.

Corsi, Edward. "My Neighborhood." *Outlook* 16 (September 1925): 92.

Cory, Donald Webster (Edward Sagarin). *The Homosexual in America: A Subjective Approach*. New York: Greenbergs Publishing, 1951.

Craft, William. *Running a Thousand Miles for Freedom, or the Escape of William and Ellen Craft from Slavery*. In *Great Slave Narratives*, ed. Arna Bontemps, 269–331. Boston: Beacon Press, 1969.

Cronin, Gloria. Introduction to *Critical Essays on Zora Neale Hurston*, ed. Gloria Cronin, 1–32. New York: G. K. Hall, 1998.

Crosby, Ernest. *Garrison, the Nonresistant*. Chicago: Public Publishing Company, 1905.

Cross, S. C. "The Negro North and South." *Colored American Magazine* (November 1902): 62–73.

Davies, Carol Boyce. *Black Women, Writing and Identity: Migrations of the Subject*. London: Routledge, 1994.

Davis, Arthur. *From the Dark Tower: Afro-American Writers, 1900–1960*. Washington, D.C.: Howard University Press, 1974.

Davis, Rebecca Harding. *Bits of Gossip*. Cambridge: Riverside, 1905.

———. "Out of the Sea." In *A Rebecca Harding Davis Reader*, ed. Jean Pfaelzer, 139–65. Pittsburgh: University of Pittsburgh Press, 1995.

———. *Waiting for the Verdict*. New York: Sheldon and Company, 1868.

Demby, William. *Beetlecreek*. Chatham, N.J.: Chatham Bookseller, 1950.

D'Emilio, John. *Sexual Politics, Sexual Communities: The Making of a Homosexual Minority in the United States, 1940–1970*. Chicago: University of Chicago Press, 1983.

Devere Brody, Jennifer. "Memory Movement, Minstrelsy, Miscegenation, and American Race Studies." *American Literary History* 11, no. 4 (winter 1999): 736–45.

Diawara, Manthia. *Black American Cinema*. New York: Routledge, 1993.

Diner, Hasia. *Lower East Side Memories: A Jewish Place in America*. Princeton, N.J.: Princeton University Press, 2000.

Douglas, Ann. *The Feminization of American Culture*. New York: Alfred A. Knopf, 1977.

Douglass, Frederick. "The Heroic Slave." In *The Oxford Frederick Douglass*, ed. William Andrews, 132–63. New York: Oxford University Press, 1996.

DuCille, Ann. *The Coupling Convention: Sex, Text, and Tradition in Black Women's Fiction.* New York: Oxford University Press, 1993.

Dyer, Richard. *White.* New York: Routledge, 1997.

———. "White." *Screen* 29, no. 4 (1988): 44–64.

Edel, Leon. *Henry James, the Master, 1901–1916.* Philadelphia: J. B. Lippincott, 1972.

Edelman, Lee. *Homographesis: Essays in Gay Literary and Cultural Theory.* New York: Routledge, 1994.

Ellis, Albert. *The Folklore of Sex.* New York: C. Boni, 1951.

Emerson, Ralph Waldo. "American Civilization." *Atlantic Monthly* 9 (April 1862): 502–11.

Eng, David. "Out Here and Over There: Queerness and Diaspora in Asian American Studies." *Social Text* 52/53 (fall/winter 1997): 31–52.

Epstein, Jacob. *Epstein: An Autobiography.* New York: Dutton, 1955.

Ernest, John. "The Reconstruction of Whiteness: William Wells Brown's *The Escape; or, A Leap for Freedom.*" *MLA* 113, no. 5 (September 1998): 1108–21.

Escoffier, Jeffrey. *American Homo: Community and Perversity.* Berkeley: University of California Press, 1998.

Fabre, Michel. *The Unfinished Quest of Richard Wright.* Trans. Isabel Barzon. New York: William Morris, 1973.

Fanon, Frantz. *Black Skin, White Masks.* Trans. Charles Lam Markmann. New York: Grove Press, 1967.

Farrison, William. *William Wells Brown: Author and Reformer.* Chicago: University of Chicago Press, 1969.

"Female Impersonators." *Ebony,* March 1952, 91.

Fessenden, Tracy. "The Soul of America: Whiteness and the Disappearing of Bodies in the Progressive Era." In *Perspectives on Embodiment: The Intersection of Nature and Culture,* ed. Gail Weiss and Honi Fern Haber, 23–41. New York: Routledge, 1999.

Fishkin, Shelley Fisher. "Interrogating 'Whiteness,' Complicating 'Blackness': Remapping American Culture." *American Quarterly* 47 (September 1995): 428–66.

Fitzhugh, George. *Cannibals All; or, Slaves without Masters.* Cambridge: Belknap Press of Harvard University Press, 1960.

Flagg, Barbara. *Was Blind but Now I See: White Race Consciousness and the Law.* New York: New York University Press, 1998.

Folsom, Michael Brewster. "The Education of Michael Gold." In *Proletarian Writers of the Thirties,* ed. David Madden, 222–51. Carbondale: Southern Illinois University Press, 1968.

Foreman, P. Gabrielle. "Sentimental Abolition in Douglass' Decade: Revision, Erotic Conversion, and the Politics of Witnessing in *The Heroic Slave* and *My Bondage and My Freedom.*" In *Sentimental Men: Masculinity and the Politics of Affect in American Culture,* 149–62. Berkeley: University of California Press, 1999.

Foucault, Michel. *The History of Sexuality.* Trans. Robert Hurley. New York: Pantheon Books, 1978.

Frankenberg, Ruth. *White Women, Race Matters: The Social Construction of Whiteness.* Minneapolis: University of Minnesota Press, 1993.

———., ed. *Displacing Whiteness: Essays in Social and Cultural Criticism.* Durham, N.C.: Duke University Press, 1997.

Frazier, E. Franklin. *Black Bourgeoisie: The Rise of a New Middle Class.* New York: Free Press, 1957.

Fredrickson, George M. *The Arrogance of Race: Historical Perspectives on Slavery, Racism, and Social Inequality.* Middletown, Conn.: Wesleyan University Press, 1988.

———. *The Black Image in the White Mind: The Debate on Afro-American Character and Destiny, 1817–1914.* New York: Harper and Row, 1971.

Freeman, Estelle. "'Uncontrolled Desires': The Response to the Sexual Psychopath, 1920–1960." *Journal of American History* 74 (July 1987): 83–106.

Friedman-Kasaba, Kathie. *Memoirs of Migration: Gender, Ethnicity, and Work in the Lives of Jewish and Italian Women in New York, 1870–1924.* Albany: State University of New York Press, 1996.

Fuss, Diana. *Identification Papers.* New York: Routledge, 1995.

Gabler-Hover, Janet. *Dreaming Black/Writing White: The Hagar Myth in American Cultural History.* Lexington: University of Kentucky Press, 2000.

Gandal, Keith. *The Virtues of the Vicious: Jacob Riis, Stephen Crane, and the Spectacle of the Slum.* New York: Oxford University Press, 1997.

Garelick, Rhonda. *Rising Star: Dandyism, Gender, and Performance in the Fin de Siecle.* Princeton, N.J.: Princeton University Press, 1998.

Garnet, Henry Highland. "Speech in Boston." In *Henry Highland Garnet: A Voice of Black Radicalism in the Nineteenth Century*, ed. Joel Schor, 89–92. Westport, Conn.: Greenwood Press, 1977.

Gatens, Moira. "Spinoza, Law and Responsibility." In *Thinking through the Body of the Law*, ed. P. Cheah, D. Fraser, and J. Grobrich, 40–42. New York: New York University Press, 1996.

Gates, Henry Louis, Jr. Introduction to *Our Nig; Or, Sketches from the Life of a Free Black*, by Harriet Wilson, xi–lv. New York: Vintage Books, 1983.

———. *The Signifying Monkey: A Theory of Afro-American Literary Criticism.* New York: Oxford University Press, 1988.

Geismar, Maxwell. "Gentle Arapesh." *Nation*, October 30, 1937, 482.

Gilroy, Paul. *Against Race: Imagining Political Culture Beyond the Color Line.* Cambridge: Belknap Press of Harvard University Press, 2000.

Ginsberg, Elaine. *Passing and the Fictions of Identity.* Durham, N.C.: Duke University Press, 1996.

Glazener, Nancy. *Reading for Realism: The History of a U.S. Literary Institution, 1850–1910.* Durham, N.C.: Duke University Press, 1997.

Gold, Michael. *Jews without Money.* Intro. Alfred Kazin. 1930. Reprint, New York: Carroll and Graf, 1946.

———. "Toward a Proletarian Art." In *Mike Gold: A Literary Anthology*, ed. Michael Folsom, 62–70. New York: International Publishers, 1972.

Goldberg, David Theo. *Racist Culture: Philosophy and the Politics of Meaning.* Oxford: Blackwell, 1993.

Golden, Thelma. *Black Male: Representations of Masculinity in Contemporary American Art.* New York: Whitney Museum of Art, 1994.

Goldman, Ruth. "Who Is That Queer Queer? Exploring Norms around Sexuality, Race, and Class in Queer Theory." In *Queer Studies: A Lesbian, Gay, Bisexual and Transgender Anthology*, ed. Brett Beemyn and Mickey Eliason, 169–82. New York: New York University Press, 1996.

Gordon, Linda. *Heroes of Their Own Lives: The Politics and History of Family Violence, Boston 1880–1960.* New York: Viking Press, 1988.

Gossett, Thomas. *Race: The History of an Idea in America*. Dallas: Southern Methodist Press, 1963.

Gounard, J. F., and Beverly Roberts Gounard. "Richard Wright's *Savage Holiday*: Use or Abuse of Psychoanalysis." *CLA Journal* 22, no. 4 (June 1974): 344–49.

Graves, A. J. *Woman in America, being an Examination into the Moral, Intellectual Condition of American Female Society*. New York: Harper and Brothers, 1843.

Greenblatt, Stephen. "Racial Memory and Literary History." *Publications of the Modern Language Association*. 116 1 (January 2001): 48–63.

Gubar, Susan. *Racechanges: White Skin, Black Face in American Culture*. New York: Oxford University Press, 1997.

Guerrero, Ed. *Framing Blackness: The African American Image in Film*. Philadelphia: Temple University Press, 1993.

Halberstam, Judith. *Skin Shows: Gothic Horror and the Technology of Monsters*. Durham, N.C.: Duke University Press, 1995.

Hale, E. E. "Northern Invasions." *Atlantic Monthly* 13 (February 1864): 245–50.

Hale, Grace Elizabeth. *Making Whiteness: The Culture of Segregation in the South, 1890–1940*. New York: Pantheon Books, 1998.

Hall, Charles Winslow. "Racial Hatred." *Colored American Magazine* (September 1900): 249–52.

Hall, Stuart. "Cultural Identity and Diaspora." In *Contemporary Postcolonial Theory: A Reader*, ed. Padmini Mongia, 110–21. London: Arnold, 1996.

———. *Representations: Cultural Representations and Signifying Practices*. London: Sage Publications, 1998.

Halttunen, Karen. *Confidence Men and Painted Women: A Study of Middle-Class Culture in America, 1830–1870*. New Haven, Conn.: Yale University Press, 1982.

Hamilton, S. A. "The New Race Question in the South." *Colored American Magazine* (April 1902): 376–80.

Hapgood, Hutchins. *The Spirit of the Ghetto*. 1902. Reprint, Cambridge: Belknap Press of Harvard University Press, 1967.

Harper, Philip Brian. "Walk-on Parts and Speaking Subjects: Screen Representations of Black Gay Men." In *Black Male: Representations of Masculinity in Contemporary American Art*, ed. Thelma Golden, 141–48. New York: New York University Press, 1996.

Harris, Cheryl. "Whiteness as Property." In *Black on White: Black Writers on What It Means to Be White*, ed. David Roediger, 103–8. New York: Schocken Books, 1998.

Harris, Sharon. *Rebecca Harding Davis and American Realism*. Philadelphia: University of Pennsylvania Press, 1991.

Hartman, Geoffrey. "Literature High and Low." In *The Fate of Reading and Other Essays*, 203–23. Chicago: University of Chicago Press, 1975.

Hawes, Joel. *Lectures to Young Men, On the Formation of the Character*. Hartford, Conn.: Cooke, 1832.

Heermance, J. Noel. *William Wells Brown and* Clotelle: *A Portrait of the Artist in the First Negro Novel*. Hamden, Conn.: Archon Books, 1969.

Hellwig, David. "Afro-American Reactions to the Japanese and the Anti-Japanese Movement, 1906–1924." *Phylon* 38, no. 1 (1977): 93–104.

Hemenway, Robert. *Zora Neale Hurston: A Literary Biography*. Urbana: University of Illinois Press, 1977.

Hemphill, Essex. *Brother to Brother: New Writings by Black Gay Men*. Boston: Alyson Publications, 1991.

Herman, Judith. *Trauma and Recovery*. New York: HarperCollins/Basic Books, 1992.

Hill, Mike, ed. *Whiteness: A Critical Reader*. New York: New York University Press, 1997.

Hodes, Martha. *Sex, Love, Race: Crossing Boundaries in North American History*. New York: New York University Press, 1999.

Hogue, W. Lawrence. *Discourse and the Other: The Production of the Afro-American Text*. Durham, N.C.: Duke University Press, 1986.

hooks, bell. *Black Looks: Race and Representation*. Boston: South End Press, 1992.

Hopkins, Pauline. *Hagar's Daughter*. In *The Magazine Novels of Pauline Hopkins*, 1–284. Intro. Hazel Carby. New York: Oxford University Press, 1988.

———. "Munroe Rogers." *Colored American Magazine* (November 1902): 20–26.

———. "Whittier, the Friend of the Negro." *Colored American Magazine* (September 1901): 326–30.

Horsman, Reginald. *Race and Manifest Destiny: The Origins of American Racial Anglo-Saxonism*. Cambridge: Harvard University Press, 1981.

Hughes, Langston. "The Negro Artist and the Racial Mountain." *Nation*, June 23, 1926, 692–94.

Hurston, Zora Neale. *Dust Tracks on a Road: An Autobiography*. Ed. Robert Hemenway. 1942. Reprint, Urbana: University of Illinois Press, 1984.

Ichioka, Yuji. "The Early Japanese Immigrant Quest for Citizenship: The Background of the 1922 *Ozawa* Case." In *Japanese Immigrants and American Law; The Alien Land Laws and Other Issues*, ed. Charles McClain, 397–418. New York: Garland, 1994.

Ignatiev, Noel. *How the Irish Became White*. New York: Routledge, 1995.

Ignatiev, Noel, and John Garvey. *Race Traitor*. New York: Routledge, 1996.

Islas, Arturo. *The Rain God: A Desert Tale*. New York: Avon Books, 1984.

Jacobson, Matthew Frye. *Whiteness of a Different Color: European Immigrants and the Alchemy of Race*. Cambridge: Harvard University Press, 1998.

James, Henry. *The American Scene*. Ed. Leon Edel. 1905. Reprint, London: Hart Davis, 1968.

———. "Waiting for the Verdict." *Nation*, November 21, 1867, 410–11.

Jameson, Frederic. *The Political Unconsciousness: Narrative as Symbolic Act*. Ithaca, N.Y.: Cornell University Press, 1981.

———. "Third-World Literature in the Era of Multinational Capitalism." *Social Text* 15 (fall 1986): 65–88.

Jarrett, Thomas D. "Toward Unfettered Creativity: A Note on the Negro Novelist's Coming of Age." *Phylon* 11, no. 4 (1950): 313–18.

Johnson, Barbara. "Threshold of Difference: Structures of Address in Zora Neale Hurston." *Critical Inquiry* 12 (autumn 1985): 278–89.

Johnson, Ronna. "Said but Not Spoken: Elision and the Representation of Rape, Race, and Gender in Harriet E. Wilson's *Our Nig*." In *Speaking the Other Self: American Women Writers*, ed. Jeanne Campbell Reesman, 96–116. Athens: University of Georgia Press, 1997.

Jordan, Winthrop. *White over Black: American Attitudes toward the Negro, 1550–1812*. Chapel Hill: University of North Carolina Press, 1968.

Kafka, Phillipa. *(Out)Classed Women: Contemporary Chicana Writers on Inequitable Gendered Power Relations*. Westport, Conn.: Greenwood Press, 2000.

Kang, Younghill. "The Amateur Spirit and Korean Letters." *New York Times Book Review* 26 (July 1931): 8, 19.

———. "China Is Different: Review of *The Good Earth*." *New Republic*, July 1, 1931, 185–86.

———. *East Goes West: The Making of an Oriental Yankee*. New York: Charles Scribner's Sons, 1937.

———. *The Grass Roof*. New York: Charles Scribner's Sons, 1931.

———. "Our Culture Likened to China's in 800 B.C., or Kang Sees Economic State as Only Difference." *New York Times*, October 11, 1931.

Kaplan, Amy. "Manifest Domesticity." *American Literature* 70, no. 3 (September 1998): 581–606.

Kaplan, Amy, and Donald Pease. *Culture of United States Imperialism*. Durham, N.C.: Duke University Press, 1993.

Kaplan, E. Ann. "The 'Look' Returned: Knowledge Production and Constructions of 'Whiteness' in Humanities Scholarship and Independent Film." In *Whiteness: A Critical Reader*, ed. Mike Hill, 316–28. New York: New York University Press, 1997.

Karcher, Carolyn. *The First Woman of the Republic: A Cultural Biography of Lydia Maria Child*. Durham, N.C.: Duke University Press, 1994.

Kassanoff, Jennie A. " 'Fate Has Linked Us Together': Blood, Gender, and the Politics of Representation in Pauline Hopkins's *Of One Blood*." In *The Unruly Voice: "Rediscovering Pauline Elizabeth Hopkins*, ed. John Cullen Gruesser, 158–81. Urbana: University of Illinois Press, 1996.

Kawash, Samira. *Dislocating the Color Line: Identity, Hybridity, and Singularity in African-American Narrative*. Stanford, Calif.: Stanford University Press, 1997.

Keating, Ana Louise. "Investigating 'Whiteness,' Eavesdropping on 'Race.' " *JAC: A Journal on Composition Theory* 20, no. 2 (spring 2000): 426–33.

Kelley, Mary. "Negotiating a Self: The Autobiography and Journals of Catharine Maria Sedgwick." *New England Quarterly* 66, no. 3 (September 1993): 366–98.

Kelley, Robin. *Race Rebels: Culture, Politics and the Black Working Class*. New York: Free Press, 1994.

Kemble, Francis Anne. *Journal of a Residence on a Georgian Plantation in 1838–1839*. Ed. John Scott. New York: Alfred A. Knopf, 1961.

Kerber, Linda. *Women of the Republic: Intellect and Ideology in Revolutionary America*. New York: W. W. Norton, 1980.

Kim, Elaine. *Asian-American Literature: An Introduction to the Writing and Their Social Context*. Philadelphia: Temple University Press, 1982.

Knadler, Stephen P., "Leo Bersani and the Nostalgia for White Male Radicalism." *Minnesota Review* 47 (spring 1997): 169–76.

———. "The Untragic Mulatto: Charles Chesnutt and the Discourse of Whiteness." *American Literary History*, 8, no. 3: 426–48.

Kramer, Michael. "Assimilation in the Promised Land: Mary Antin and the Jewish Origins of the American Self." *Prooftexts* 18 (1998): 130–31.

Kristeva, Julia. *Powers of Horror: An Essay on Abjection*. Trans. Leon S. Roudiez. New York: Columbia University Press, 1982.

LaCapra, Dominick. *Representing the Holocaust: History, Theory and Trauma*. Ithaca, N.Y.: Cornell University Press, 1994.

Lane, Christopher. *The Psychoanalysis of Race*. New York: Columbia University Press, 1998.

Langer, Lawrence. *Holocaust Testimonies: The Ruins of Memory*. New Haven, Conn.: Yale University Press, 1991.

Lapansky, Phillip. "Graphic Discord: Abolitionist and Anti-Abolitionist Images." In *The Abolitionist Sisterhood: Women's Political Culture in Antebellum America*, ed. Jean Fagan Yellin and John Van Home. Ithaca, N.Y.: Cornell University Press, 1994.

Lee, Kyhan. "Younghill Kang and the Genesis of Korean-American Literature." *Korea Journal* 31, no. 4 (winter 1991): 63–78.

Lee, Sunyoung. "The Unmaking of an Oriental Yankee." In *East Goes West: The Making of an Oriental Yankee*, ed. Sunyoung Lee, 375–99. New York: Kaya Production, 1997.

Li, David Leiwei. *Imaging the Nation: Asian American Literature and Cultural Consent*. Stanford, Calif.: Stanford University Press, 1998.

Ling, Jinqui. *Narrating Nationalisms: Ideology and Form in Asian American Literature*. New York: Oxford University Press, 1998.

Lipsitz, George. *The Possessive Investment in Whiteness: How White People Profit from Identity Politics*. Philadelphia: Temple University Press, 1998.

Locke, Alain. "Self-Criticism: The Third Dimension in Culture." *Phylon* 11, no. 4 (1950): 391–94.

Loewen, James W. *The Mississippi Chinese: Between Black and White*. Cambridge: Harvard University Press, 1971.

Lopez, Ian F. Haney. *White by Law: The Legal Construction of Race*. New York: New York University Press, 1996.

Lott, Eric. *Love and Theft: Blackface Minstrelsy and the American Working Class*. New York: Oxford University Press, 1993.

Lowance, Mason I., Jr., Ellen E. Westbrook, and R. C. DeProspo. *The Stowe Debate: Rhetorical Strategies in* Uncle Tom's Cabin. Amherst: University of Massachusetts Press, 1994.

Lowe, Lisa. *Immigrant Acts: On Asian American Cultural Politics*. Durham, N.C.: Duke University Press, 1996.

Lurie, Susan. *Unsettled Subjects: Restoring Feminist Politics to Poststructuralist Critique*. Durham, N.C.: Duke University Press, 1997.

Ma, Sheng-mei. *Immigrant Subjectivities in Asian American and Asian Diasporic Literatures*. Albany: State University of New York Press, 1998.

Maffi, Mario. *Gateway to the Promised Land: Ethnic Cultures on New York's Lower East Side*. New York: New York University Press, 1995.

Manalansan, Martin F., IV. "In the Shadows of Stonewall: Examining Gay Transnational Politics and the Diasporic Dilemma." In *The Politics of Culture in the Shadow of Capital*, ed. Lisa Lowe and David Lloyd, 485–505. Durham, N.C.: Duke University Press, 1997.

"The Man Who Lived 30 Years as a Woman: Georgia Black Married Twice, Even 'Mothered' Devoted Son." *Ebony*, October 1951, 93–96.

Marcus, Sharon. "Fighting Bodies, Fighting Words: A Theory and Politics of Rape Prevention." In *Feminists Theorize the Political*, ed. Judith Butler and Joan W. Scott, 385–404. New York: Routledge, 1992.

Margolies, Edward. *Native Sons: A Critical Study of Twentieth-Century Black American Authors*. Philadelphia: J. B. Lippincott, 1968.

Marovitz, Sanford. *Abraham Cahan*. New York: Twayne, 1996.

Marquez, Antonio. "The Historical Imagination in Arturo Islas's The Rain God and Migrant Souls." *MELUS* 19, no. 2 (summer 1994): 3–16.

Martin, Biddy. "Sexualities without Genders and Other Queer Utopias." *differences: A Journal of Feminist Cultural Studies* 6, nos. 2/3 (summer/fall 1994): 1–26.

Marty, Debian. "White Antiracist Rhetoric as Apologia: Wendell Berry's The Hidden Wound." In *Whiteness: The Communication of Social Identity*, ed. Thomas Nakayama and Judith Martin, 51–68. Thousand Oaks, Calif.: Sage Publications, 1999.

May, Elaine. *Homeward Bound: American Families in the Cold War Era*. New York: Basic Books, 1988.

McClintock, Ann. *Imperial Leather: Race, Gender, and Sexuality in the Colonial Contest*. New York: Routledge, 1995.

McCracken, Ellen. *New Latina Narrative: The Feminine Space of Postmodern Ethnicity*. Tucson: University of Arizona Press, 1999.

McKenna, Teresa. *Migrant Son: Politics and Poetics in Contemporary Chicano Literature*. Austin: University of Texas Press, 1997.

McPherson, James M. *The Abolitionist Legacy: From Reconstruction to NAACP*. Princeton, N.J.: Princeton University Press, 1975.

Medovoi, Leerom. "Reading the Blackboard: Youth, Masculinity, and Racial Cross-Identification." In *Race and the Subject of Masculinities*, ed. Harry Stecopolous and Michael Uebel, 139–69. Durham, N.C.: Duke University Press, 1997.

Meisenhelder, Susan Edwards. *Hitting a Straight Lick with a Crooked Stick: Race and Gender in the Work of Zora Neale Hurston*. Tuscaloosa: University of Alabama Press, 1999.

Mele, Christopher. *Selling the Lower East Side: Culture, Real Estate, and Resistance in New York City*. Minneapolis: University of Minnesota Press, 2000.

Mercer, Kobena. *Welcome to the Jungle: New Positions in Black Cultural Studies*. New York: Routledge, 1994.

Michaels, Walter Benn. *Our America, Nativism, Modernism, and Pluralism*. Durham, N.C.: Duke University Press, 1995.

———. "Race into Culture: A Critical Genealogy of Cultural Identity." *Critical Inquiry* 18 (summer 1992): 655–85.

Miller, D. A. *The Novel and the Police*. Berkeley: University of California Press, 1988.

Moraga, Cherrie. "Queer Atzlan: The Re-formation of Chicano Tribe." In *The Last Generation: Prose and Poetry*, 145–74. Boston: South End Press, 1993.

Morrison, Toni. *Playing in the Dark: Whiteness and the Literary Imagination*. Cambridge: Harvard University Press, 1992.

Mumford, Kevin. *Interzones: Black/White Sex Districts in Chicago and New York in the Early Twentieth Century*. New York: Columbia University Press, 1997.

Murray, Albert. *The Omni-Americans: Some Alternatives to the Folklore of White Supremacy*. 1970. Reprint, New York: Da Capo Press, 1990.

Nakayama, Thomas, and Judith Martin. *Whiteness: The Communication of Social Identity*. Thousand Oaks, Calif.: Sage Publications, 1999.

Nash, Gary. "Hidden History." In *Sex, Love, Race: Crossing Boundaries in North American History*, ed. Martha Hodes, 2–19. New York: New York University Press, 1999.

Nelson, Dana. *National Manhood: Capitalist Citizenship and the Imagined Fraternity of White Men*. Durham, N.C.: Duke University Press, 1998.

———. *The Word in Black and White: Reading "Race" in American Literature, 1638–1867.* New York: Oxford University Press, 1993.

Ofari, Earl. *"Let Your Motto Be Resistance": The Life and Thought of Henry Highland Garnet.* Boston: Beacon Press, 1972.

Okihiro, Gary. *Margins and Mainstreams.* Seattle: University of Washington Press, 1994.

Omi, Michael. "(E)racism: Emerging Practices of Antiracist Organizations." *The Making and Unmaking of Whiteness.* Ed. Birgit Brander Rasmussen, Eric Klinenberg, Irene J. Nexica, and Matt Wray. Durham: Duke University Press, 2001.

Omi, Michael, and Howard Winant. *Racial Formation in the United States from the 1960s to the 1980s.* New York: Routledge and Kegan Paul, 1986.

"The Ordeal by Battle." *Atlantic Monthly* 8 (July 1861): 88–94.

"Our Culture Likened to China's in 800 B.C.; Dr. Kang Sees Economic State Only Difference." *New York Times,* October 11, 1931.

Parsons, C. G. *An Inside View of Slavery: A Tour among the Planters.* Intro. Harriet Beecher Stowe. Boston: J. P. Jewett, 1855.

Pasztory, Esther. *Teotihuacan: An Experiment in Living.* Norman: University of Oklahoma Press, 1997.

Patterson, Anita Haya. *Emerson to King: Democracy, Race and the Politics of Protest.* New York: Oxford, 1997.

Peiss, Kathy. "Charity Girls and City Pleasures: Historical Notes on Working-Class Sexuality, 1880–1920." In *Powers of Desire: The Politics of Sexuality,* ed. A. Snitow, C. Stansell, and S. Thompson, 74–87. New York: Monthly Review Press, 1983.

Pellegrini, Ann. *Performance Anxieties: Staging Psychoanalysis, Staging Race.* New York: Routledge, 1997.

Perez-Torres, Rafael. "Chicano Ethnicity, Cultural Hybridity, and the Mestizo Voice." *American Literature* 70 (March 1998): 153–73.

———. "Refiguring Aztlan." In *Postcolonial Theory and the United States: Race, Ethnicity, and Literature,* ed. Amritjit Singh and Peter Schmidt, 103–21. Jackson: University of Mississippi Press, 2000.

Pfaelzer, Jean. *Parlor Radical: Rebecca Harding Davis and the Origins of American Social Realism.* Pittsburgh: University of Pittsburgh Press, 1996.

Pfeil, Fred. *White Guys: Studies in Postmodern Domination and Difference.* London: Verso, 1995.

Pierson, William. *Black Legacy: America's Hidden Legacy.* Amherst: University of Massachusetts Press, 1993.

Plant, Deborah. *Every Tub Must Sit on Its Own Bottom: The Philosophy and Politics of Zora Neale Hurston.* Urbana: University of Illinois Press, 1995.

Posnock, Ross. *Color and Culture: Black Writers and the Making of the Modern Intellectual.* Cambridge: Harvard University Press, 1998.

Pride, Armistead, and Clint C. Wilson. *A History of the Black Press.* Washington, D.C.: Howard University Press, 1997.

Puar, Jasbir K. "Transnational Sexualities: South Asian/(Trans)national(alism)s and Queer Diaspora." In *Q & A: Queer in Asian America,* ed. David Eng and Alice Y. Hom, 405–24. Philadelphia: Temple University Press, 1998.

Quarles, Benjamin. *Black Abolitionists.* New York: Oxford University Press, 1969.

"Queer People." *Newsweek,* October 10, 1949, 52–54.

Radhakrishnan, R. *Diasporic Meditation: Between Home and Location.* Minneapolis: University of Minnesota Press, 1996.

Ramon, David. "Arturo Islas (1938–1991)." In *Gay American Novelists: A Biobibliographical Critical Sourcebook,* ed. Emmanuel S. Nelson, 220–25. Westport, Conn.: Greenwood Press, 1993.

Reid Pharr, Robert F. *Conjugal Union: The Body, the House, and the Black American.* New York: Oxford University Press, 1999.

———. "Tearing the Goat's Flesh: Homosexuality, Abjection, and the Production of a Late Twentieth Century Black Masculinity." In *Novel Gazing: Queer Readings in Fiction,* ed. Eve Kofsofsky Sedgwick, 353–76. Durham, N.C.: Duke University Press, 1997.

Reilly, John. "Richard Wright's Curious Thriller, Savage Holiday." *CLA Journal* 21, no. 2 (December 1977): 218–23.

Reimers, David. *All the Nations under Heaven: An Ethnic and Racial History of New York City.* New York: Columbia University Press, 1995.

Riis, Jacob. A. *How the Other Half Lives: Studies among the Tenements of New York.* 1890. Reprint, New York: Hill and Wang, 1957.

Roediger, David R. *Black on White: Black Writers on What It Means to Be White.* New York: Schocken Books, 1998.

———. *Towards the Abolition of Whiteness: Essays on Race, Politics, and Working Class History.* London: Verso, 1994.

———. *The Wages of Whiteness: Race and the Making of the American Working Class.* London: Verso, 1991.

Rogers, J. A. "Jazz at Home." In *The New Negro,* ed. Alain Locke, 216–24. Intro. Arnold Rampersand. 1925. Reprint, New York: Atheneum, 1992.

Rogin, Michael. *Blackface, White Noise: Jewish Immigrants in the Hollywood Melting Pot.* Berkeley: University of California Press, 1996.

Romero, Lora. *Home Fronts: Domesticity and Its Critics in the Antebellum United States.* Durham, N.C.: Duke University Press, 1992.

Roosevelt, Theodore. "The Strenuous Life." In *The Strenuous Life: Essays and Addresses,* 1–24. New York: Century, 1900.

Rose, Jane Atteridge. *Rebecca Harding Davis.* New York: Twayne, 1993.

Rosenberg, Carroll Smith. "Subject Female: Authorizing American Identities." *American Literary History* 5 (1993): 481–511.

Ross, Dorothy. *The Origins of American Social Sciences.* Cambridge: Cambridge University Press, 1991.

Rossen, Ruth. *The Lost Sisterhood: Prostitution in America, 1900–1918.* Baltimore: Johns Hopkins University Press, 1982.

Roth, Marty. *Foul and Fair Play: Reading Genre in Classic Detective Fiction.* Athens: University of Georgia Press, 1995.

Rushdie, Salmon. "Imaginary Homeland." In *Imaginary Homeland: Essays and Criticism, 1981– 1991,* 19–29. London: Granta, 1991.

Rushmore, Robert. *Fanny Kemble.* London: Crowell-Collier Press, 1970.

Ryan, Mary. *The Empire of the Mother: American Writing about Domesticity, 1830–1860.* New York: Haworth Press, 1982.

Saab, William. "My Mother Was a Man." *Ebony,* June 1953, 75–76.

Sahagun, Fray Bernardino de. *A History of Ancient Mexico: Anthropological, Mythological, and Social.* Trans. Fanny R. Bandelier. Nashville, Tenn.: Fisk University Press, 1932.

Saldivar, Jose David. "The Hybridity of Culture in Arturo Islas's *The Rain God*." In *Cohesion and Dissent in America*, 1559–73. Albany: State University of New York Press, 1994.

Sale, Maggie Montesinos. *The Slumbering Volcano: American Slave Ship Revolts and the Production of Rebellious Masculinity*. Durham, N.C.: Duke University Press, 1997.

Salerno, Roger A. *Louis Wirth: A Bio-Bibliography*. New York: Greenwood Press, 1987.

Samuels, Shirley. *The Culture of Sentiment: Race, Gender, and Sentimentality in Nineteenth-Century America*. New York: Oxford University Press, 1992.

Sanchez, Marta. "Arturo Islas' *The Rain God*: An Alternative Tradition." *American Literature* 62, no. 2 (June 1990): 284–304.

Sanchez, Rosaura. "Ideological Discourses in Arturo Islas's *The Rain God*." In *Criticism in the Borderlands: Studies in Chicano Literature, Culture, and Ideology*, ed. Hector Calderon and Jose David Saldivar, 114–26. Durham, N.C.: Duke University Press, 1991.

Sanchez-Eppler, Karen. *Touching Liberty: Abolition, Feminism, and the Politics of the Body*. Berkeley: University of California Press, 1993.

Sandoval, Chela. "Theorizing White Consciousness for a Post-Empire World: Barthes, Fannon, and the Rhetoric of Love." In *White Women, Race Matters: The Social Construction of Whiteness*, ed. Ruth Frankenberg, 86–106. Durham, N.C.: Duke University Press, 1997.

Savran, David. *Communists, Cowboys, and Queers: The Politics of Masculinity in the Works of Arthur Miller and Tennessee Williams*. Minneapolis: University of Minnesota Press, 1992.

Saxton, Alexander. *The Indispensable Enemy: Labor and the Anti-Chinese Movement in California*. Berkeley: University Of California Press, 1971.

———. *The Rise and Fall of the White Republic: Class Politics and Mass Culture in Nineteenth-Century America*. London: Verso, 1990.

Schneider, Mark R. *Boston Confronts Jim Crow, 1890–1920*. Boston: Northeastern University Press, 1997.

Sedgwick, Catharine Maria. *The Linwoods; or "Sixty Years Since" in America*. New York: Harper and Brothers, 1835.

Sedgwick, Ellery. *The* Atlantic Monthly, *1857–1909: Yankee Humanism at High Tide and Ebb*. Amherst: University of Massachusetts Press, 1994.

Sedgwick, Eve Kofsofsky. *Epistemologies of the Closet*. Berkeley: University of California Press, 1990.

———. *Novel Gazing: Queer Readings in Fiction*. Durham, N.C.: Duke University Press, 1997.

Seltzer, Mark. *Serial Killer: Death and Life in America's Wound Culture*. New York: Routledge, 1998.

Sharpe, Jenny. *Allegories of Empire: The Figure of Woman in the Colonial Text*. Minneapolis: University of Minnesota Press, 1993.

Shavelson, Susanne. "Anxieties of Authorship in the Autobiographies of Mary Antin and Aliza Greenblatt." *Prooftexts* 18 (1998): 161–86

Shen, Fan. "The Classroom and the Wider Culture: Identity as a Key to Learning English Composition." In *Signs of Life in the U.S.A.*, ed. Sonia Maasik and Jack Solomon. Boston: Bedford/St. Martin's, 2000.

Sigourney, Lydia. *Letters to Mothers*. Hartford, Conn.: Hudson and Skinner, 1838.

Silverman, Kaja. *Male Subjectivity at the Margins*. New York: Routledge, 1992.

Smith, Lillian. *Killers of the Dream*. New York: W. W. Norton, 1949.

Soja, Edward. *Thirdspace: Journeys to Los Angeles and Other Read and Imagined Places*. Cambridge, Mass.: Blackwell Publishers, 1996.

Sollors, Werner. *Beyond Ethnicity: Consent and Descent in American Culture*. New York: Oxford University Press, 1986.

———. *The Invention of Ethnicity*. New York: Oxford University Press, 1989.

Somerville, Siobhan. *Queering the Color Line*. Durham, N.C.: Duke University Press, 2000.

Soyer, Daniel. *Jewish Immigrant Associations and American Identity in New York, 1880–1939*. Cambridge: Harvard University Press, 1997.

Spivak, Gayatri. *The Postcolonial Critic: Interviews, Strategies, Dialogues*. Ed. Sarah Harasyn. New York: Routledge, 1990.

Stearns, Peter N., and Jan Lewis. *An Emotional History of the United States*. New York: New York University Press, 1998.

Stern, Julia A. "Excavating Genre in *Our Nig*." *American Literature* 67, no. 3 (September 1995): 439–66.

Stoler, Ann Laurie. *Race and the Education of Desire: Foucault's History of Sexuality and the Colonial Order of Things*. Durham, N.C.: Duke University Press, 1995.

Strange, David. "Thomas Wolfe's Korean Connection." *Thomas Wolfe Review* 18, no. 2 (1984): 36–41.

Stuckey, Sterling. *The Ideological Origins of Black Nationalism*. Boston: Beacon Press, 1972.

Sundquist, Eric J. *To Wake the Nations: Race in the Making of American Literature*. Cambridge: Harvard University Press, 1993.

Takaki, Ronald. *Iron Cages: Race and Culture in Nineteenth-Century America*. New York: Alfred A. Knopf, 1979.

———. *Strangers from a Different Shore: A History of Asian Americans*. Boston: Little Brown, 1989.

Talbot, Margaret. "Getting Credit for Being White." *New York Times* 30 November 1997: 118.

Tate, Claudia. *Domestic Allegories of Political Desire: The Black Heroine's Text at the Turn of the Century*. New York: Oxford University Press, 1992.

———. *Psychoanalysis and Black Novels: Desire and the Protocols of Race*. New York: Oxford University Press, 1998.

Tilman, N. P. "The Threshold of Maturity." *Phylon* 11, no. 4 (1950): 388.

Tompkins, Jane. *Sensational Designs: The Cultural Work of American Fiction*. Oxford: Oxford University Press, 1985.

Trowbridge, J. T. "We Are a Nation." *Atlantic Monthly* 14 (November 1864): 771.

Turner, George Kibbe. "Daughters of the Poor: A Painful Story of the Development of New York City as a Leading Center of the White Slave Trade." *McClure's* 34 (November 1909): 45–61.

Twine, Francis Winddance. "Brown-Skinned White Girls: Class, Culture, and the Construction of White Identity in Suburban Communities." In *Displacing Whiteness: Essays in Social and Cultural Criticism*, ed. Ruth Frankenberg, 214–43. Durham, N.C.: Duke University Press, 1997.

Von Frank, Albert J. *The Trials of Anthony Burns: Freedom and Slavery in Emerson's Boston*. Cambridge: Harvard University Press, 1998.

Viego, Antonio. "The Place of Gay Male Chicano Literature in Queer Chicana/o Cultural Work." *Discourse* 21, no. 3 (fall 1999): 111–31.

Villard, Osward Garrison. *William Lloyd Garrison on Non-resistance, Together with a Personal Sketch.* New York: J. S. Ozer, 1924.

Wald, Priscilla. *Constituting Americans: Cultural Anxiety and Narrative Form.* Durham, N.C.: Duke University Press, 1995.

Walker, Cheryl. *Indian Nation: Native American Literature and Nineteenth-Century Nationalisms.* Durham, N.C.: Duke University Press, 1997.

Walker, David. *The Political Culture of the American Whigs.* Chicago: University of Chicago Press, 1979.

"War and Literature." *Atlantic Monthly* 10 (June 1862): 674–84.

Ware, Vron. *Beyond the Pale: White Women, Racism and History.* London: Verso, 1992.

———. "Island Racism: Gender, Place, and White Power." In *Displacing Whiteness: Essays in Social and Cultural Criticism,* ed. Ruth Frankenberg, 283–311. Durham, N.C.: Duke University Press, 1997.

Warner, Michael, ed. *Fear of a Queer Planet: Queer Politics and Social Theory.* Minneapolis: University of Minnesota Press, 1993.

Warren, Kenneth. *Black and White Strangers: Race and American Literary Realism.* Chicago: University of Chicago Press, 1993.

Weiss, Gail. "The Abject Bodies off the Body Images." In *Perspectives on Embodiment: The Intersection of Nature and Culture,* ed. Gail Weiss and Honi Fern. New York: Routledge, 1999.

Welchman, Kit. *Erik Erikson: His Life, Work and Significance.* Buckingham, England: Open University Press, 2000.

West, Cornel. *The American Evasion of Philosophy: A Genealogy of Pragmatism.* Madison: University of Wisconsin Press, 1989.

———. "I'm Ofay, You're Ofay." *Transitions* 73 (summer 1998): 176–203.

"What I Told Kinsey about My Sex Life." *Ebony,* December 1948, 47.

Whyte, William H., Jr. *The Organization Man.* New York: Simon and Schuster, 1956.

Wiegman, Robyn. *American Anatomies: Theorizing Race and Gender.* Durham, N.C.: Duke University Press, 1995.

Williams, C. Grant. "Reminiscences of the Life of Harriet Beecher Stowe and Her Family." *Colored American Magazine* (December 1902): 127–39.

Williams, Charleea H. "Recent Developments in the 'Land of the Free.'" *Colored American Magazine* (August 1902): 284–95.

Williams, Charles S. "The Rise and Fall of Peoples and Nations." *Colored American Magazine* (February 1904): 137–39.

Williamson, Joe. *New People: Miscegenation and Mulattoes in the United States.* Baton Rouge: Louisiana State University Press, 1995.

Wilson, Harriet. *Our Nig; Or, Sketches from the Life of a Free Black.* Intro. Henry Louis Gates Jr. New York: Vintage Books, 1983.

Wirth, Louis. *The Ghetto.* Chicago: University of Chicago Press, 1928.

———. "Urbanism as a Way of Life." In *Community Life and Social Policy: Selected Papers,* ed. Elizabeth Wirth Maverick and Albert J. Reiss Jr., 110–32. Chicago: University of Chicago Press, 1956.

Woman's Influence and Woman's Mission. Philadelphia: W. P. Hazard, 1854.

Woods, Katharine. "Making of an Oriental Yankee." *New York Times Book Review*, October 17, 1937, 11.

Wray, Matt, and Annalee Newitz. *White Trash: Race and Class in America*. New York: Routledge, 1997.

Wright, Richard. *Black Power: Reactions in a Land of Pathos*. New York: Harpers, 1954.

———. *Savage Holiday*. Ed. Gerald Early. 1954. Reprint, Jackson: University Press of Mississippi, 1994.

Yarbro-Bejarano, Yvonne. "Gloria Anzaldua's Borderlands/La Frontera: Cultural Studies, 'Difference,' and the Non-Unitary Subject." In *Contemporary American Women Writers: Gender, Class, Ethnicity*, ed. Lois Parkinson Zamora, 11–31. London: Longman, 1998.

Yellin, Jean Fagan. "The 'Feminization' of Rebecca Harding Davis." *American Literary History* 22 (summer 1990): 203–19.

Young, Elizabeth. *Disarming the Nation: Women's Writing and the American Civil War*. Chicago: University of Chicago Press, 1999.

———. "A Wound of One's Own: Louisa May Alcott's Civil War Fiction." *American Quarterly* 48 (September 1996): 439–74.

Young, Robert. *Colonial Desire: Hybridity in Theory, Culture, and Race*. London: Routledge, 1995.

———. *White Mythologies: Writing History and the West*. London: Routledge, 1990.

Yun, Chung-Hei. "Beyond City Walls: Korean American Literature." In *Reading the Literature of Asian America*, ed. Shirley Geok-in and Amy Ling, 79–96. Philadelphia: Temple University Press, 1992.

Zangwill, Israel. *Children of the Ghetto: A Study of a Peculiar People*. 1893. Reprint, Leicester, England: Leicester University Press, 1977.

INDEX

Aaron, Daniel, 32

Abject, theories of, 23, 216–17 n 3

Abolitionism: W. W. Brown's involvement in, 19–20; as historical movement, vii–ix, 19; New England heirs, response to, 65–69; in relation to whiteness studies, xxi–xxii, 206; views of black women, 25–26 (*see also* Parsons, C. G.); women in, 5, 7–10

Abraham, Roger, 8

Adams, Henry, 107

Affectivity, and discursive analysis, 6–7

Affiliation, in relation to cross-ethnic/racial coalition building, 88–92

Africa, images of, in Wright's writing, 147–49

Agency: antebellum black agency, 16–30; everyday practices of, 117–19; interventionist strategies, xiii–xiv

Alarcon, Norma, 183

Alexander, Elizabeth, 144

Alien: in New York City public spaces, 121–26; as threat to antebellum national identity, 11–12

Allen, Theodore, 209 n 3

Almaguer, Tomas, on queer Chicano identity, 182–83

Americanization: competing representations of, 114, 115, 126–29, 132–34; Kang's alteration of, 100–02; repression within, xx–xxi; in *Yekl*, 130–43

Ammons, Elizabeth, 60

Anderson, Sherwood, in relation to primitivism, 99, 159

Andrews, William: on Douglass, vii; on slave narratives, 17

Anglo-Saxonism: within antebellum culture, x, 34, 42–46; in Progressive Era, 64–70

Antin, Mary, xxvii, 115, 121; escape into whiteness, 128–29; interracial conflicts, 127–29; *Promised Land*, 125–29; unsaid of Americanization, 126–27

Anti-racist strategies: individualistic nature of, 83–84; problems in definitions of, 61

Anti-slavery. *See* Abolitionism

Anzaldua, Gloria, xxvii, 178, 187, 212 n 3

Arnold, Philip, on Tlaloc myths, 180, 186, 188, 195–96

Ashcan artists, 128

Asian American: ambiguous racial identification of, 93–94; history in relation to African Americans, 85–88

Atlantic Monthly, xxvi, 32; R. H. Davis's relation to, 32, 36–38, 40–41; masculine anxiety in, 45–46; publication of Antin, 125; racialized nationalism within, 42–46; and realism, 34; writings about the Civil War, 42–46

Austin, Alfredo Lopez, on Tlaloc myths, 180, 187, 219 n 9